Inside Ethnography

Inside Ethnography

RESEARCHERS REFLECT ON THE CHALLENGES
OF REACHING HIDDEN POPULATIONS

*Edited by Miriam Boeri
and Rashi K. Shukla*

UNIVERSITY OF CALIFORNIA PRESS

University of California Press
Oakland, California

© 2019 by The Regents of the University of California

Library of Congress Cataloging-in-Publication Data

ISBN 978-0-520-29823-1 (cloth: alk. paper) |
ISBN 978-0-520-29824-8 (pbk.: alk. paper) |
ISBN 978-0-520-97045-8 (ebook)

Manufactured in the United States of America

26 25 24 23 22 21 20 19
10 9 8 7 6 5 4 3 2 1

I dedicate this book to all the people I have met in the field who have shown me time and again how critical ethnographic work is for the betterment of society.
—*Miriam Boeri*

This book is dedicated to my mother Jaya Shukla and my late father Krishna Kumar Shukla, to those who contributed to my research over the decades, and to all who continue to help along the way.
—*Rashi Kumari Shukla*

[Ethnography] rests on the peculiar practice of representing the social reality of others through the analysis of one's own experience in the world of these others. Ethnography is therefore *highly particular* and *hauntingly personal,* yet it serves as the basis for grand comparison and understanding within and across a society.

—VAN MAANEN,
1988, ix (italics added)

CONTENTS

ACKNOWLEDGMENTS

Special thanks to our editor at the University of California Press, Maura Roessner, for believing in this project and for all of the support and encouragement along the way. We thank Madison Wetzell for taking the time to guide our steps as we moved toward production. We are awed by the support of the amazing team of contributors to this book. We thank them for believing in the goal of this book project and for the honest and authentic reflections about their ethnographic work. If they had not been willing to so deeply reflect on their ethnographic experiences, sharing their mistakes, lessons, and difficulties without reservations, this book would be considerably less impressive. Finally, we are thankful that John Van Maanen wrote a small book, *Tales of the Field,* which inspired us throughout our ethnographic journeys and was one of the inspirations for this book.

MIRIAM BOERI

I thank my mentor, Claire Sterk, for introducing me to ethnographic fieldwork among hidden populations and teaching me to trust my instincts. She is the main reason this book was written, as she facilitated situations where I could meet some of the exceptional ethnographers who were contacted to contribute to this book. Thank you, Claire, and thank you, Kirk Elifson, for introducing me to Claire.

I want to thank my husband, Mike Brooks, for not complaining when I spent most of our time together in the evenings, on weekends, or on vacation working on this book. He did the shopping, cooked the meals, cleaned up, and entertained himself many times when I was focused for hours at my desk, on my phone, or with a computer on my lap. Thank you, Mike, for being such a renaissance man.

Likewise, I thank my children, now adults, for allowing me to work on this book even when I was visiting them. Living around the world, from South Korea to Brazil, it is so rare that I see them . Yet, they did not complain (much) when I stole from our precious time together to work on writing. I also appreciate their partners and partners' families, who must have wondered why I came so far to sit at a table much of the day and night with my laptop. I hope to make it up to you next time!

Special thanks goes to my Chair, Gary David, and the faculty in the Sociology Department for supporting my work in different ways, but mainly by being good colleagues. And a heartfelt thank you to my coeditor, Rashi K. Shukla, who encouraged our collaboration on this edited volume at the beginning and throughout this journey. I appreciate your candor, inquisitiveness, flexibility, and discipline, each characteristic engaged when needed and never overbearing. I hope I was as supportive to you as you have been to me.

Finally, I thank all the people I have met in the field over the many years I have been doing ethnography. They have given me faith in humankind, which was sorely missing before I began going in the field. Above all, I thank the many ethnographers who capture the hopes and fears of individuals who are often ignored, doubted, or forgotten. Without their rigorous dedication to truth, the story of human life would be incomplete.

RASHI K. SHUKLA

I am humbled by the endless love, encouragement, support, and patience of my mother, Jaya Shukla, and late father, Krishna Kumar Shukla. Thank you for always being on the front lines cheering me on and providing essential advice along the way. You are always in my heart. Thank you to my family, including Kanchana, Tulsi, and Dev Ranjan Saha and Neel, Patty, Emma Anjali, Sage Prasad, and Xavier Neel Shukla. Thank you to C.G. for believing in me and supporting the seemingly never-ending queue of projects always heading my way. I am grateful to my colleagues and friends at the University of Central Oklahoma (UCO) and beyond, including John Barthell, Kathy Bell, Sid and Mary Ann Brown, Jaime Burns, Sharon Chamard, Shawna Cleary, Kendra Crouch, Joyce Crawley, Mathew Daniel, Julie Dearing, Carl Dement, John Duncan, Steven Dunn, David Ford, Phyllis Fry, Elsa Gonzalez,

Kathryn Grooms, Shona Hardwick, Nona Harris, Saba Holloway, Willis Holloway Jr., Rachel Waldrop Holzhauser, Miranda Houck, Michael Jenkins, Trace Johnson, Fred Matt Jones, Gary Jones, Karel Kalaw, James Lofton, Pam Lumen, Elizabeth Maier, Alina Mizell, Don Mizell, Nina Michalikova, Sue and Steve Marom, Niki Morgan, Cindy Mueller, Deepa Narayanan, Aneesh Nireshwalia, Melissa Powers, Austin and Kelly Ralstin, Cassie Redig, Kelly Ross, Aundre and Jerry Rookstool, Torrey Rowe, Judi Ryder, Phyllis Schultz, Christy Lucas Sheppard, Brenda Simpson, Burle Steeleman, Angela Taylor, Anje Vela, K. Dean Walker, Nicole Warehime, Catherine Webster, Greg Wilson, R. J. Woods, and David Wright. Thank you to Gisela Bichler for providing insights on producing an edited book and to my mentors, Ronald V. Clarke, Marcus Felson, Mary Eckhart Felson, Marti Smith, and Derek Cornish. I thank Mercer Sullivan for teaching me about qualitative methodology; without you, I might never have had an opportunity to engage in ethnographic research. I am grateful to DeWade Langley for helping me conceptualize and craft my wording regarding the concept of authenticity in the final days before the manuscript was due. Special thanks to Cora M. Bradley and Danielle Stoneberg, for their endless support and assistance reviewing drafts and brainstorming ideas at critical junctures along the way. Funding for my research projects over the years was provided through grants from the Office of Research and Sponsored Programs at UCO.

Thank you to Kody Kinder and Chief Jon Shepard (Ret.), Fletcher, OK Police Department, for enticing me to visit rural Oklahoma in the early days, and to Emelia Chrisco and Jordan Crump for accompanying me on some of my first ethnographic field visits. I am indebted to Agent Dub Turner (Ret.) for his invaluable insights over the years and for taking the chance to teach, and then collaborate with, an academic. I am grateful for the advice and assistance provided by Melissa Inglis and Jennifer Brown and am appreciative to Kenzi Lockwood, Mandy Dorman, and Paige Copple for helping during the early stages of this book. I express gratitude to all of my research and teaching assistants, past and present, for their time, dedication, and commitment; you are the backbone of all that I do. Thank you to Carley Dancer, Lorin Glover, Bethany Holley-Griffith, Meredith Ille, Kristina Kave, Chance McCollum, Amanda Raper, Sheridan Self, and Abigail Smart. I will forever be beholden to all of the law enforcement officials including chiefs, sheriffs, undersheriffs, special agents, drug agents, deputies, narcotics investigators, and medical professionals, and others who have taken the time to educate me over the years. Special thanks to Chief Agent Jerry Flowers (Ret.) and the

Oklahoma Department of Agriculture, Food, and Forestry. I am appreciative to Special Agents Patrick Blake, Paul Cornett, Eddie Davenport, Dusty Goforth, Michael Hooper, Ryan Hensley, Ricky Rushing, and Jason Smith. I am appreciative to all of the individuals who have entrusted me with their life stories, be it formally or informally, so that we could better understand things we didn't know. Thank you to those who have taken the time to listen and to the countless others who play a part in this story. Named here or not, you matter. I could never have dreamed of a life like this and am humbled to be part of any project focused on advancing what is known. It is time to reignite critical dialogues about social ills such as drugs and crime and think through what is needed to develop effective responses and strategies moving ahead.

I am honored to have had this opportunity to work with and learn from Miriam Boeri. Your willingness to meet me in 2013 when I was on sabbatical writing my first book changed my life. I have learned through the struggles and will always look back at this experience as a highlight. I am forever appreciative of the journey we have taken together. It has been incredible materializing our ideas. Thank you for the collaboration. You inspire me.

PREFACE

This is a collection of behind-the-scenes stories of ethnographic studies among hidden populations by twenty-one contributors writing with uncensored candor to reveal how ethnography is practiced, particularly when faced with logistical obstacles and unexpected personal tolls. Our intention is not to add to the literature on how to conduct ethnographic studies or write ethnography. Instead, our purpose is to reveal true-to-life challenges encountered during fieldwork that are rarely discussed or published.

The editors of this book, a sociologist and a criminologist, have a combined thirty-five years of experience conducting ethnography. We have encountered many challenges to our efforts to better understand the hidden populations we study. Over the years we have heard similar stories, sometimes harrowing accounts, of incidents faced by ethnographers that are never written about in books or articles. We saw a gap in the teaching of ethnography and, perhaps more importantly, a hesitancy to write about obstacles encountered before, during, and after conducting fieldwork.

Monographs of ethnographic studies have an enduring appeal (e.g., Bourgois, 1996; Goffman, 2015; Sheper-Hughes, 1989; Sterk, 2011; Whyte, 1943), but in contemporary writing, the reality of day-to-day fieldwork often gets cut in the editing stage. While conducting ethnography can be exciting and sometimes dangerous, there is a lot of work that is just plain boring: hours of "hanging out" in the field, waiting for interview respondents who never show up, and seemingly endless reading, writing, and editing. Failures in recruitment efforts, Institutional Review Board delays to the study, modifications or abrupt changes in the research from the original plan, and the emotional drain of energy and motivation when noble goals crumble against the wall of political realism are rarely discussed, or only fleetingly mentioned, in ethnographies and textbooks. To fill this gap, we invited ethnographers who work among hidden and hard-to-reach populations to write about the challenges they faced and lessons they learned.

The contributing authors are drawn from a variety of disciplines that use ethnography, including anthropology, criminology, criminal justice, sociology, social work, nursing, medicine, business, political science, and public health. Their topics of investigation are diverse, and their research fields were located in different continents. The authors discuss cutting-edge techniques such as rapid assessment, public/activist ethnography, applied ethnography, and mixed-methods, along with the more traditional ethnography of oral history, photo-ethnography, long-term participant observation, and in-depth interviewing. They provide illustrative accounts representing one view or another of ongoing academic debates. For a more in-depth understanding of these issues and controversies, readers are encouraged to refer to the endnotes and ample references provided.

The diversity of the chapters is a strength of this book. While the introduction aims to provide coherence between themes and links between chapters, each chapter stands on its own. We are not affirming one method or perspective over another. A few contributing authors were asked to reduce their manuscripts to comply with our word limitations, but they were not asked to cut anything that we did not agree with or thought would be controversial. Often we nudged authors to examine more deeply an action or incident we felt would cause some concern for our readers, but we did not censor their ideas, accounts, or terminology.

The focus on challenges and barriers to ethnography and how contributing authors overcame these challenges (or did not) is the heart and soul of this book. Whether or not we, or the readers, agree with every action, reflection, or strategy discussed in these chapters, we believe the authenticity of the writing will advance the field of ethnography, primarily because of the authors' honest portrayals of how ethnography played out in the field, as well as in their lives. We are proud of their contributions, and we thank each author for genuinely responding to our request to fill the gap between the "ideal" ethnographic field methods taught in research textbooks and the reality of fieldwork in unchartered landscapes with unforeseen challenges.

REFERENCES

Bourgois, P. (2003). *In search of respect: Selling crack in El Barrio.* New York: Cambridge University Press.

Goffman, A. (2015). *On the run: Fugitive life in an American city.* Chicago: University of Chicago Press.

Scheper-Hughes, N. (1989). *Death without weeping: The violence of everyday life in Brazil.* Berkeley: University of California Press.

Sterk, C. (2011). *Fast lives: Women who use crack cocaine.* Philadelphia: Temple University Press.

Whyte, W. F. (1943). *Street corner society: The social structure of an Italian slum.* Chicago: University of Chicago Press.

Introduction

Miriam Boeri and Rashi K. Shukla

LOOKING FOR ONE OF THE WOMEN IN MY *ethnographic study on suburban women who use methamphetamine, I drove with my research assistant to the rundown trailer park where I first saw her attempting to clean a derelict trailer so she could live in it with her son. Finding the stench of dog excrement and rodent droppings too overwhelming, she accepted an offer from a man in the park to live with him in another trailer that had also seen better days. I was worried when no one answered the door and became anxiously aware that the park seemed almost deserted. Hearing sounds from people at the back of the trailer park, which was situated between a lonely country road and the railroad tracks, I drove my car to the end of the dirt and gravel path. As I noted a dismal scene of abandoned rusty tin boxes that served as homes but with no signs of the living, it became evident that the former inhabitants were no longer around; however, my desire to find my study participant made me push on.*

"Stay here," I told my assistant. He was a young man with enough life experiences to make him a valuable helper to my study, but I did not want both of us to be in a vulnerable position. As I continued by foot to where I heard loud talking, I turned the corner and saw beer cans littered around four men with their chests bared to the warm evening. Old motorcycles were parked behind them. One man looked up when he heard my steps, and, unbuckling his pants as he walked toward me, called out in a slurred voice, "You ready to fuck?" I remember feeling disgusted at the sight of dirty grey underwear, and backing up slowly while keeping my eye on him, I yelled out to my assistant, who I could hear walking toward me on the gravel, "Get back to the car. Don't come down here!" (Paraphrased from field notes, Miriam Boeri)

FIGURE 0.1. Deserted trailer park in one of the field sites where the women lived when temporarily homeless. Photo credit: Miriam Boeri.

I got in my car and we left without incident. Later, I found the woman I had been looking for. She told me that the group of men I met there had called a sex worker to come down to the trailer park where they often partied after work. They probably thought I might be her. She told me this in the matter-of-fact way that indicated scenes like this were part of her everyday life.

In retrospect, that time in the deserted trailer park was a potentially dangerous situation, but most of my fieldwork is more like the day I drove for two hours and sat two more hours in a parking lot waiting for a scheduled interviewee to show up, only to have his "spies" come by to check me out first. I eventually ended up interviewing both the spies and the man who sent them, who became one of my trusted community consultants. Reflecting on similar experiences, I remember feeling more despair for the people I met than any fear for the sometimes risky situations I encountered.

Facing potential risks, learning to assess the situation quickly, and finding trusting and trustworthy participants are part of conducting ethnographic fieldwork among people who are hard to study. These are some of the challenges discussed in these chapters, described by ethnographers who overcame barriers and addressed unanticipated obstacles to their research among hidden populations.

ETHNOGRAPHY'S CONTEMPORARY CHALLENGES

What are the challenges associated with studying deviant, stigmatized, or criminal behaviors in the field? What happens when the best-laid plans go awry? How do ethnographers address Institutional Review Board (IRB) demands or lack of funding? This collection illuminates strategies employed in studies on stigmatized and illegal behaviors that take researchers into largely unchartered landscapes. Written for practitioners, academics, and students, the study snapshots presented in each chapter provide insights on the types of strategies and techniques utilized to address real-life difficulties and obstacles faced when using ethnographic methods.

The one common thread across the chapters is their focus on hidden and marginalized categories of people, often considered vulnerable populations. These include people who are incarcerated or formerly incarcerated, use illegal drugs, suffer from intergenerational poverty and structural inequality, have health issues or transmittable diseases, or engaged in activities that are unconventional in contemporary society. Understanding their experiences and representing their reality through ethnographic research takes empathy and compassion, but it can also take an emotional toll.

Ethnographic research is indispensable for an in-depth understanding of behaviors that are stigmatized, criminal, or considered deviant and often enacted in secret. However, what ethnography is and how to do it is debated even among the most successful ethnographers. Much of what happens while in the field is not revealed in print. Novice ethnographers wonder what to do when they face difficult situations they never read about in textbooks, while more experienced ethnographers remain anxious about how much they should reveal and to whom.

The purpose of this book is to reveal true-to-life challenges encountered during fieldwork that are rarely discussed in print. The ethnographers writing these chapters are using research methods outside the safety and comfort of clinical or academic settings. With raw honesty and introspection, they examine their own misgivings, sharing how they met, addressed, and overcame unanticipated challenges. They write contemplatively and deliberately, sometimes disclosing the emotional highs and lows experienced, other times offering judicious advice on how to avoid pitfalls and remedy missteps that may occur while in the field.

The diversity of the projects discussed is one of the strengths of this book. Ethnography is characterized by heterogeneity, flexibility, and adaptation; methodological strategies are adjusted for particular fields. The parameter of the studies described here were influenced by a number of factors, including the availability of resources and logistical constraints, among other considerations. Levels of experience and access to team members with diverse skills impacted the types of decisions made before, during, and after fieldwork.

Ethnographic methods rely more heavily on the experiences and instincts of the researcher than methods requiring a rigid adherence to standard data collection protocol and techniques of analysis. While both qualitative and quantitative data may be collected, the ethnographer becomes the tool of data collection (Schensul, Schensul, and LeCompte, 1999). Since ethnographers are not constricted by standardized procedures, they can make modifications when their plan is revealed to be flawed or when they discover new information that alters their direction. Such liberty is invigorating for many researchers, but it can also be intimidating for some, and perhaps frightening for newcomers.

The stories shared on these pages are meant to educate, inform, and inspire current and future researchers who find themselves motivated to engage in ethnography. The lessons and insights provide important information for those seeking to get close to people and behaviors in field settings. Ethnography can be practiced in a variety of ways within different disciplines, but it essentially involves in-depth interactions with people in settings where they live, work, or play.

While there is not one definition to pin to ethnographic methods, what counts as "real" ethnography is often debated (Agar, 2006). The variety of methods described throughout these chapters can be categorized by different labels. Those adhering to a traditional approach to ethnography might question if some of these studies are under an ethnographic umbrella. Is Robert Gay's study of life in a Brazilian favela as narrated by two of its members over thirty years an oral history or an ethnographic study? Does Eugene Soltes's examination of convicted executives count as ethnography or a case study? Ethnographic convention and styles change over time (Van Maanen, 1988, 5–6), and authoritative statements of what constitutes ethnographic research are ephemeral.

Ethnography adapts. Ethnographic research occurring within contexts of change and technological advancements presents difficulties and challenges, while also offering opportunities to invent new strategies that push ethnography beyond its traditional boundaries. Research methods cannot remain stagnant and be relevant, and ethnography is no exception. Flexibility is critical for advancing scientific knowledge on hidden populations. As shown in these chapters, contemporary ethnographers triangulate different methods, incorporate new technologies, and develop rapid forms of ethnographic research as they adapt to new fields and emerging problems.

Triangulation

Triangulation of data from various sources of information enhance efforts to understand complex human behaviors and provide researchers with additional avenues for assessing the validity of their research findings. While some of these data sources will be generated directly from study participants who are interviewed, observed, or who otherwise participate in research, as these studies demonstrate, there are more often than not multiple slices of data about any given problem. Each slice of data or indicator potentially provides unique or comparative information on the issue or problem being studied. Advancements in science and technology mean that scholars of this era have more opportunities for the types of information gathered and analyzed as part of an ethnographic approach.

Triangulation has been defined as the combination of quantitative and qualitative methods, as well as combining different strategies of data collection and analysis (Creswell and Clark, 2007; Lincoln and Guba, 1985, Malterud, 2001). Most ethnographers use multiple strategies in their ethnographic studies, or they combine ethnographic methods with other research methods. Mixed methods of data collection produce diverse kinds of data. All sources of data are limited and have potential flaws, but through triangulation of data, the view becomes clearer and more precise (Boeri, 2007).

The chapters in this book illustrate triangulation of different data and diverse methods. In his research into prison deaths, Joshua Price discusses the triangulation of disparate sources that involved government documents, health records, letters, online messages, and notes from secret meetings. Addressing the problems of what legally counts as criminal evidence, he confronts the "arbitrariness" and validity of these disparate documents. Are letters evidence? Are stories told to us evidence?[1] Are they less or more valid depending on their source? Why are stories told by a correctional officer evidence when stories from the prisoner or his/her family not considered evidence? His questions resonate with ethnographers who are challenged on the veracity of their sources and the validity of the data they use to support their arguments.

Incorporating Technology

Many of the contributors integrate alternative sources of information using traditional and more modern technologies. Heith Copes used photography to contextualize stories in his study of people in rural areas who use methamphetamine. Ana Lilia Campos-Manzo asked her young subjects to take virtual tours of their neighborhoods via Google maps, allowing the images to stimulate their memories as they narrated their stories. Price obtained information critical to his study on prison deaths via social media outlets such as Facebook posts and text messages. Using ethnographic findings in an intervention project, Avelardo Valdez, Alice Cepeda, and Charles Kaplan visually projected public health messages on town walls in community spaces, further illustrating the innovative and creative use of technology in their applied ethnographic study.

As researchers adapt their project design to incorporate new technologies, the notion of observation moves beyond traditional physical observation to include diverse forms of direct or indirect observation. Jason Fessel, Sarah Mars, Philippe Bourgois, and Daniel Ciccarone filmed videos of injecting activity to better study the sequence of injection behaviors. Marie Rosenkrantz Lindegaard started with traditional ethnographic methods, such as living in the communities where her population lived, talking with families and friends, and conducting interviews, but her methodological strategies were modified as the research revealed unexpected sources of data, such as the video recordings from the local television stations.

Rapid Ethnography / Rapid Assessment

Beyond the more traditional form of ethnography involving extended periods of time in the field, some of the ethnographers adopted a form of rapid ethnography. Rapid ethnography is used when there is a need for a quick assessment of an emergent problem, and it is particularly important for assessing social issues when they occur among people engaged in covert behavior.

Merrill Singer and J. Bryan Page discuss how they used "Rapid Assessment for Response and Evaluation (RARE)" in their studies among people who inject drugs to prevent the spread of HIV and hepatitis C infection (HVC). Fessel, Mars, Bourgois, and Ciccarone describe their rapid-assessment strategy as "focused short-term ethnography" to gain insider perspectives. Addressing the criticism of rapid ethnography, the authors show, for example, that contrary to what some critics say, ethnographers *can* gain trust and rapport with participants using this rapid ethnographic method.

RECRUITMENT CHALLENGES

Using a variety of recruitment strategies is a time-honored tenant of ethnography, and many of the more established recruitment methods are illustrated by contributing authors here. Less transparent recruitment processes, such as covert research, are examined critically from different perspectives. Also discussed are the different ways to involve people drawn from the community in the research process. Some authors employed people from the study population as part of the research team; others describe "gatekeepers" who helped with recruitment efforts or facilitated their entry to hidden settings where participants could be more easily recruited.

Covert Research or Concealment

Contributors had differing views on ethnographic covert roles. Elizabeth Bonomo and Scott Jacques candidly describe the covert ethnography conducted by Bonomo for her dissertation research. Bonomo chose to conduct covert research, which her supervisor, Jacques, did not recommend but did not discourage either. According to the authors, "a dissertation is about establishing yourself as an independent scholar, so it has to be a road mostly travelled alone ... guidance [Jacques] did provide followed a few general principles: don't get hurt; don't violate our Institutional Review Board (IRB) agreement; otherwise, do what needs to be done to finish the project, to the best of your ability, in a timely manner." Bonomo finished her dissertation project, eventually disclosing her research motives to the people she studied, learning critically important lessons about ethnography through firsthand trial and error.[2] She discusses this experience with insightful detail, making her chapter provocative as well as intellectually stimulating to read.[3]

In contrast, Singer and Page write: "ethnographers who are attempting to study covert behaviors firsthand should never go undercover. That is, they should never present themselves as someone other than who they really are . . . the ethnographer should avoid any kind of identity deception." These authors advise ethnographers to respond honestly, or they risk alienating the people with whom they are attempting to build rapport. Distinguishing concealment from deception, they view concealment as a "game" that is quite familiar and acceptable to people who are engaged in hiding their own activities. Recruitment strategies described in their chapter include months of "hanging out" in local bars, and, on other occasions, clandestinely watching people and their interactions on a public street from their rented study office window above. Meeting people that he had been observing for weeks, Page revealed his research interests to them when asked, skillfully avoiding any loss of trust. They suggest that protecting the researcher, the participants, and the research involves a wise and guarded process of revealing or withholding information.

Lindegaard, who at first perceived any withholding of information on her part as being dishonest with her participants, changed her views over the course of her research on violence in Cape Town. By the end of her study she concluded that what she thought was deception is part of the ethnographic process.

Community Consultants / Outreach Workers / Key Informants

A variety of terms are used to describe the people who help ethnographers with insider information as recruiters or as gatekeepers to the population under study. Called community consultants, outreach workers, or key informants, these terms refer to people from the community who are involved in the research through a paid or unpaid relationship with the ethnographer. Singer and Page refer to individuals who fulfill this role as "outreach workers"; Valdez and his colleagues called them "community field workers" in one study and "key informants" in another.

Fessel and his coauthors discuss key informants who are hired for security reasons, as well as members of a local harm reduction center they call "sponsors" who vouch for the research team and provide introduction to potential research subjects. Some harm reduction workers became part of their research team. The authors warn, however, that relying too much on one source of consultants, such as harm reduction workers (currently quite popular in drug research), can present what is called a "social desirability" bias: "There is always the danger, if you're accessing people through a harm reduction program, that people are going to repeat the harm reduction discourse . . . in a way that doesn't reflect their lived experience or the lived experience of most users or at least the users who are not plugged into the harm reduction world." The various roles discussed in their chapter represent community consultants at different levels of engagement.

Engaging community members in research is at the core of what is called Community-Based Participatory Research (CBPR) (Aguirre-Molina and Gorman, 1996), used by Honoria Guarino and Anastasia Teper in their study on young adults immigrants who use illegal drugs. Guarino and Teper discuss how key informants can be formally incorporated as part of the research team using a CBPR approach, in which members of the community hold well-defined roles in the study.

While the term *key informant* appears to be used across disciplines, it carries a negative connotation in many of the hidden communities where ethnographic research is conducted, particularly when these people are engaged in illegal activities. Police use "informants" as snitches to "rat" on their friends or family, a role despised by even law-abiding members of the community. The term *key informants* is therefore tainted by its link to the criminal justice system, and few people involved in hidden populations like to be called an informant.[4]

ETHICS AND ETHNOGRAPHY

Ethics are important in all scientific disciplines, but there are different philosophies driving ethical decisions (Israel and Hays, 2009). While ethical research activities are linked to wider debates about ethics, and also about the role of the self and relationships in ethnography, addressing ethical issues in research generally starts with gaining approval from external ethics committees.

In the United States, research is typically reviewed by an IRB. Although IRBs should be primarily concerned with the protection of human subjects, the power held by IRB members to mandate the details of this protection can expose the researcher and the subjects of research to unnecessary burdens and might shut down a research study entirely. For example, asking ethnographers to provide written consent for all participants is sometimes impossible when conducting ethnographic research with populations engaged in illegal activities. Although members of ethical committees are rarely privy to specifics of the ethical dilemmas and challenges ethnographers face in the field, burdensome demands may have to be met before ethnographers receive required IRB approval.[5] Ethnographers often question if members of these boards understand the nature of ethnographic research and whether ethnographic research should be exempt from ethical board approval (Gusterson, 2008).

Most ethnographers know that ethical perspectives from external sources can help to protect their study subjects in ways they might not have addressed sufficiently. Most professional societies and government agencies have established ethical guidelines that researchers must follow or be subject to serious consequences to their professional reputation, as well as to future research potential. Nevertheless, in recent years, the legitimacy of institutions to claim moral authority over research has been questioned, as perspectives on what is right or wrong ethically have differed depending on the kind of philosophical approach guiding authoritative decision-making (Israel and Hay, 2009).[6]

Conducting ethical research cannot be limited to written requirements and professional guidelines. Some ethnographers suggest that ethical concerns should be expanded for research with vulnerable populations. For example: "While in some types of social inquiry researcher responsibility may appear appropriately limited to the specific context of the risks or burdens produced by the research project, in ethnography the boundaries between research activities and other arenas of study participants' lives are blurred. As a result, anthropologists have tended to assume a much broader "contract" and set of moral obligations than may be the case in other research disciplines" (Singer, Heurtes and Scott, 2000, 392). The contributing authors in this book address ethical concerns in different ways. While focusing on minimizing the harm to their research subjects, whether through oversight from IRBs and ethical committees, or by deep introspection of their own moral obligations, their chapters reveal contemplative care and attention to the consequences of their research. But their actions and strategies are not consistent across studies, reflecting the reality of field research.

Some authors describe how they addressed ethical guidelines during the development of the research plan, through the process of gaining IRB approval, and in discussions on ethical concerns during research meetings. Others, however, addressed ethical difficulties more often while conducting research alone, or they reflected on ethical arguments after the research was completed and during the writing process, illustrating the difficulties of conducting ethnography.

Among U.S. contributors, some viewed the IRB process as a challenge to overcome. Their discussion of IRB issues provides insight on the regulatory requirements and reveal differences in institutional norms. In a few cases, IRB approval was not mentioned, which prompted us to question why not, highlighting the long-standing debate on what kind of research needs IRB approval.[7] Soltes was one of the authors who at first did not mention IRB in his chapter but later clarified that his research was a "case study" and therefore did not fall under the IRB oversight, which was consistent with IRB standards at his institution. Other types of research involving minimal potential harm to participants, such as oral histories, are exempt by some ethical boards but not by others.

Curtis Smith and Leon Anderson's discussion of their challenges with the IRB is an example of the incongruity between research experiences of most IRB members and the reality of an ethnographer's fieldwork. In Smith and Anderson's study, requirements imposed by the IRB impacted the timing of Smith's dissertation research, delaying it by some months. In their case, Anderson had built relationships with IRB members, making some of the restrictive problems with the IRB considerably more negotiable.

Ethical standards and procedures for research can vary widely across different countries. Sometimes reconciling the differences in ethical requirements can be challenging. Lindegaard is one of the international contributors who received approval from ethics boards in different countries. Based in the Netherlands but conducting her research in South Africa, she received approval for her research from the ethical commission of the University of the Western Cape *and* the University of Amsterdam, as well as from the South African Department of Education *and* Department of Correctional Services for her study on violent rape and murder. In contrast to Lindegaard, some of our U.S. contributors experienced more restrictions from their ethical boards for much less dangerous research, highlighting the differences between IRBs in the United States compared to other nations.

One of the challenges in the United States is the requirement to obtain a signed consent. Requesting participants to sign their names to a document after telling them their identity will not be revealed is a common problem for ethnographers studying people engaged in stigmatized or illegal behaviors (Sanders and Copes, 2013). Sometimes, the justification to ask for a waiver for the signature is approved by the IRB, but this varies by institutions. IRB requirements resulted in some restrictions for Guarino and Teper, who write how they addressed IRB requirements for a signed informed consent by obtaining a "Certificate of Confidentiality" from the federal government to help ensure their participants that, despite the need to sign their name on the form, all their data was protected from court subpoena.[8]

The chapter by Campos-Manzo on her studies among some of the most vulnerable populations (e.g., incarcerated parents and their children) devotes detailed attention to the process of obtaining IRB approval for her research, which is typically a very difficult and time-consuming procedure. Campos-Manzo provides comprehensive guidance on how to address IRB requirements that often mean delays to starting or finishing research. When she was questioned on why she chose to study such vulnerable populations, her response drew attention to her personal beliefs on moral obligations as an ethnographer: "My answer is that every human being deserves dignity and respect. Part of that is understanding their lives holistically. To achieve that understanding, one must listen to their voices. Any challenge then becomes just a pebble on the path to creating platforms for marginalized voices to be heard." Her chapter demonstrates how the IRB can be helpful in many ways, which is not always appreciated by researchers conducting ethnography.

Doing research ethically also means respecting what the subjects of a study are saying rather than ignore their claims when it clashes with commonly accepted scientific knowledge. The experiences and views of the subjects of ethnographic research might be more valid than knowledge generated by the scientific community working in labs and clinical settings. For example, Fessel et al. refer to an earlier study by Bourgois and Schonberg (2009), as they recall how the once popular public health recommendation that injectors should rinse their syringes with bleach was not being followed by the street injectors they met, who preferred to rinse with water instead. Integrating this "knowledge from below" with the medical establishment's "knowledge from above" led to the discovery that using bleach could be harmful to some injectors. The authors discuss why "social plausibility" found through qualitative research must be added to the more established "biological plausibility" for better analysis and outcomes. Their chapter informs readers on how ethnographers can address a discrepancy between what they find on the field and what is "known" by the experts, which is not as uncommon as one might believe.[9]

Difficulties with IRB requirements seem less onerous when considering ethnography's rich discourse on reflexivity. The fine line between learning about one's self while learning about the culture and people being studied is a common theme in writing on ethnography. Some have used the metaphor of jazz to describe the ethnographer's role: "Ethnographers are engaged in a dual quest for self-identity and empathy that is improvised in ways that resemble the 'conversation' that occurs between jazz musicians when they are playing jazz" (Humphreys, Brown, and Hatch, 2003, 6). Ethnographic research conducted among hidden and often vulnerable populations compels the researcher to reflect on personal motives, values, beliefs, actions, and moral obligations.

Engaging with their subjects as cointerpreters of the data and often cocreators of the findings, ethnographers are not bound by the standard of objectivity found in positivist research philosophies. Unlike scientists using positivist approaches, ethnographers typically do not claim to be objective.[10] Their findings are not meant to be representative in the positivist sense that the findings of their small sample is representative of the whole population. Instead the findings represent the ethnographers' interpretation of the data they collected. It is revelatory, taking science in new directions. It is evocative, suggesting the limitations of what we think we know. Ethnography has a tradition of providing a genuine representation—arguably more so than scientific methods using statistical analyses (Marco and Larkin, 2000). In the ethnographer's role, objectivity is replaced with reflexivity:

> The full meaning of reflexivity in ethnography refers to the ineluctable fact that the ethnographer is thoroughly implicated in the phenomena that he or she documents, that there can be no disengaged observation of a social scene that exists in a "state of nature" independent of the observer's presence, that interview accounts are coconstructed with informants, that ethnographic texts have their own conventions of representation. In other words, "the ethnography" is a product of the interaction between the ethnographer and a social world, and the ethnographer's interpretation of phenomena is always something that is crafted through an ethnographic imagination. (Atkinson, 2006, 402)

The contributors were asked to reveal the difficulties and unexpected challenges they faced with honesty and transparency. They responded beyond our expectations, illustrating the reflexive nature of their ethnographic work through self-knowledge and introspection, questioning their own assumptions and preconceptions, and showing more concern for the effects of their research on their study populations than for their personal sacrifices and sorrows.

Impact on the Community

Reflexivity through reflection, self-awareness, and engagement with the social world of the study population increases the authenticity of the findings (Malterud, 2001; Atkinson, 2006). One theme prominently discussed by our contributors was their consideration of how their work impacts the community they study. Valdez and his colleagues embedded reflexivity into their methods, with a specific goal: "Reflexive ethnography is immersion in the world that will eventually produce a participatory change in that world. . . . The critical feature of our methodology was a move from a methodology model based on a single ethnographer . . . to a team ethnography model that forced us to be reflexive in dealing with novel emerging problems." Their experiences in a multiethnographer study provides practical knowledge on how to ensure reflexivity is a shared component of team research.

The contributors using photographs and videos of their participants often expressed concern about when visuals can meaningfully represent findings beyond text. Copes used photos to "to draw readers into the world of rural users of meth," prompting him to reflect on "the emotional labor of working with people I grew to know and care about." Price shares his profound personal deliberations on whether using photos or videos when exposing suffering is a kind of voyeurism, and that by "putting racialized violence on display, one risks desensitizing people to violence." Will it lead to justifiable outrage? Does it relieve the suffering—or relive it? His questions do not end with answers, but they provoke reflection on the impact of visuals.

Bourgois, who uses videos of injecting practices in his research, described the ethnographer's plight in his previous writing: "We cannot escape seeing, feeling, and empathizing with the people we study. It impels us to raise problematic questions and confronts us ethically and practically with the public stakes of our writing" (2011, 6). There is no right answer to when using visuals helps more than harms, and the ethnographer must make those difficult moral, ethical, and emotional decisions for each ethnographic study.[11]

Danger and Personal Tolls

While all research impacts researchers, ethnography has the heightened ability to place researchers in the proverbial line of fire, exposing them to situations flooded with uncertainties and unknowns. Numerous types of personal costs can accompany ethnographic research. Personal costs extend beyond potential danger to life and economic costs, and include emotional and psychological tolls. These are referred to by various terms, including vicarious "post-traumatic stress" (Warden, 2012, 150), "secondary trauma" (Singer et al., 2001, 394), and "compassion stress" (Ragar, 2005, 426).

Ethnographers need not go into potentially dangerous situations blindly, but neither can they go in suspicious of everyone and everything. Bad experiences can happen, but they are the exception rather than the rule.[12] Ethnographic research is often a lonely endeavor, which increases its risks. Despite the abundant literature on how to avoid and protect against potential risks,[13] danger is "endemic in research on deviant behaviors" (Adler, 1993, 105).

Although many of our contributors described dangerous situations, few discussed the potential danger to themselves. Rarely is risk to personal safety discussed in detail.[14] The danger to which ethnographers can be subjected and how this is ameliorated, who has responsibility to and for whom, and how young or new ethnographers should be guided or supported in contemporary studies are areas that remain debated and generally part of the ethnographers discussion with their ethics boards.

Danger was ever present for Lindegaard when she traveled to Cape Town to study men who intentionally engaged in violent acts, and she discusses how she learned to address safety issues in her chapter. But instead of providing vivid details of the risks she was taking, she presents an introspective analysis of her long-held assumptions on the ethical and emotional aspects of ethnographic research. As a white European woman with no personal experience with violence, she was a complete outsider to her black South African male subjects who were incarcerated for violent acts. One warden advised her: "You have three things against you Marie: you are white, from far away, and you have a cute face, so watch out!" Lindegaard candidly revealed that she had no formal training in how to address the challenges she faced in South Africa, but she learned through the experience of doing ethnographic research. Her chapter discusses a number of textbook learned "ideals" that she brought to the field from the classroom, but she eventually had to reevaluate what was ideal and what was real. She learned through experience to find someone from the neighborhood whom she could trust to hire as an assistant for safety purposes. Singer and Page, who are more experienced ethnographers, refer to this kind of person as a "cultural guide," needed for safety reasons when conducting ethnography in unfamiliar places.

Personal tolls often go unrecognized and undocumented. Copes reveals his innermost struggles in his chapter on methamphetamine use in rural Appalachian towns with heart-wrenching honesty rarely seen among academics. Gay discloses his increasingly personal relationship with his subjects, revealing intimate details of his internal conflict over an unexpected friendship in his long-term study on Brazilian favelas. Price leaves us breathless with the honesty of his contemplation over the distressing situation he found while conducting ethnography on reported suicides in county jails and prisons. These chapters also reveal the emotional labor involved in this kind of work, sometimes accompanied with mental anguish and soul-searching struggles.

ORGANIZATION OF THE CHAPTERS IN THIS BOOK

The range of topics covered in this collection is broad. The writing styles are also diverse, representing differences across disciplines, as well as different points in the authors' careers. Three of the chapters are written by recent graduates recounting challenges encountered during their dissertation research. Others are written by authors with extensive experience in the field and significant publications. Some chapters are descriptive stories, while others embody a more academic writing style. Organizing the book from new ethnographers to the more seasoned ethnographers, we took a risk putting the recent graduates first. We hope the lessons learned by following this progression from the challenges of entering the field for the first time, to how teams of accomplished ethnographers overcome obstacles, to contemplating the meaning of a life career in ethnography is worth the risk.

Rather than identify one prominent theme in each of the many-faceted chapters, we based the organization of chapters on aspects of the ethnographers themselves and/or their research. Part 1 groups new ethnographers—both graduate students working on a dissertation with a mentor and a seasoned researcher making a switch to ethnography. Part 2 highlights the work of ethnography by experienced research teams. Part 3 groups two research studies with unusually vulnerable and hidden populations. Part 4 ends the book with three chapters illustrating the reflexivity inherent in ethnographic research.

Part 1: Becoming an Ethnographer

This section focuses on studies conducted by those new to ethnography, including doctoral students and a professor venturing for the first time into ethnographic research. Unique insight into challenges include a discussion of covert versus overt research, how to address IRB set-backs, and learning about the power of ethnography.

In chapter 1, Lindegaard exposes details of the difficulties she faced as she attempted to navigate her research journey alone in another country. In a powerful and unconstrained style, she describes her struggle to create a shared sense of meaning for actions she abhors. Revealing her tortuous path to success and the mistakes she made along the way, she provides insights that readers may use to guide their own research.

In chapter 2, Bonomo and Jacques outline some of the unique challenges that accompany the fieldwork of a novice researcher venturing into an unchartered real-life field setting. Conflicts regarding giving money to potential participants, apprehension over the romantic motives of key subjects, and questions about deception when playing a covert researcher role are shared with insightful self-awareness of Bonomo's novice role and Jacques' traditional approach to mentoring.

In chapter 3, Smith and Anderson take us through their personal journeys in their graduate student and mentor roles as they face unanticipated obstacles to finishing research essential for Smith's dissertation. The authors discuss challenges common in ethnographic research and provide a wealth of classic and contemporary literature on these topics. Their chapter offers a contrasting view to the previous chapter on the mentor role, underscoring the flexibility of ethnographic methods in the learning process.

In chapter 4, Soltes discusses the new strategies he learned as a researcher skilled in quantitative methods when he began studying business misconduct as a novice ethnographer. A political scientist grounded in positivist perspectives, Price takes us through his own discovery of ethnography and its surprising rewards.

Part 2: Team Ethnography

This section has three chapters written by experienced ethnographers who received external research funding and worked primarily in multidisciplinary research teams. These chapters discuss different perspectives on how to incorporate "rapid ethnography," illustrating the value of this strategy, particularly for applied aims.

In chapter 5, Singer and Page open their chapter with a discussion on the social construction of drug users as "monsters," which the authors refer to as a "chimera," drawing from Greek mythology. Their chapter highlights the impact of power dynamics in a society that creates the need for populations to become "hidden" and "hard-to-reach."

In chapter 6, Fessel and his coauthors provide detailed description of triangulating the data collected in their multimethod study. As a multidisciplinary team, they provide insights on the contributions of qualitative versus quantitative data. The chapter explains the sometimes difficult identification of when "saturation" is reached, and the thorny issues of confidentiality and IRB concerns when filming participants injecting.

In chapter 7, Valdez and his colleagues show how ethnographic research informed their innovative approach to using projection mapping technology in an applied research project. The chapter highlights strategies for rapid assessment and how to involve the community in the research process for better outcomes.

Part 3: Navigating the Unusual

This section includes two chapters that describe ethnography among unusually hard-to-find populations. The authors highlight numerous IRB challenges and how they overcame difficulties in gaining access to their hidden populations.

In chapter 8, Campos-Manzo discusses the benefits of the IRB oversight she received, and how she learned to embrace them as protectors of her research and her participants. Learning to appreciate the strict IRB guidelines, Campos-Manzo lays out in transparent detail how to address the ethical challenges involved gaining IRB approval, while sharing insightful lessons for ethnographers working with minor children and prisoners.

In chapter 9, Guarino and Teper describe their mixed-methods study, providing important detail on how to imbed a qualitative component into a quantitative study. Their targeted study sample represent a deeply hidden drug-using population that avoids places like harm reduction syringe exchange services, creating more barriers to recruitment and challenges on where to conduct interviews.

Part 4: The Emotional Impact of Doing Ethnography

While authors in all chapters were reflexive of their work, the three chapters in this section reflect more on the emotional challenges of doing ethnography. The realities of the personal toll of ethnographic research are rarely discussed. As a result, not all who venture into ethnography are prepared for the impact. These final chapters fill this gap in contemporary ethnographic literature.

In chapter 10, Gay, who had not intended to conduct an ethnography at all, continued a relationship with a Brazilian drug-dealing gang member and his family that became a liaison he could not break. His reflections on his travels back and forth from his safe home and work in an elite college in the United States to the Rio favela is written with uncommon candor as he discusses his own challenges and triumphs.

In chapter 11, Copes delves deep into his own disquieting dilemma arising from the emotional impact of listening to stories of suffering and knowing he cannot stop the misery he has seen and heard. Gut-wrenching accounts of despair and violence are vividly accentuated with visual evidence. Experiencing vicarious post-traumatic stress disorder, Copes holds nothing back, writing his thoughts with impressive humility, uncensored by scholarly decorum of objectivity.

In chapter 12, the emotional labor of Price's activist ethnography is powerfully exposed as he tries to "make sense" of death in jail and how it impacts his ongoing work among prisoners. Reflecting on this dilemma, Price explains, "the question at the core of this essay has been how to expose the state violence at work in killing black people without parading racialized torture and morbid, gruesome portraits of abject misery." Stymied at the end of his research, he has no suitable answer, in his mind, but encourages us to not despair of doing ethnography.

In conclusion, the chapters in this book reveal the underbelly of ethnographic research among hidden and hard-to-reach vulnerable populations. Our aim is to provide insights into ethnography as a method and to lay bare the reality of getting one's hands dirty in ethnographic fieldwork. If this transparency generates scholarly controversy, we have done our job.

The project describing the lives of women who use methamphetamine was supported by the National Institute on Drug Abuse Award R15DA021164.

1. For more on this topic of what counts as evidence, see Maruna's (2015) chapter on stories as evidence.

2. Jacques' decision to contribute to this chapter as a silent but present coauthor reflects his preferred function as a hands-off dissertation supervisor, which is a not uncommon in practice but rarely described in publication. Another chapter in this book, written by Curtis Smith, a graduate student, and his advisor, Leon Anderson, depicts a very different student-supervisor relationship than that of Bonomo and Jacques. Both chapters provide insight that are similar in some ways and different in others. While Bonomo wrote from the perspective of the graduate student, the Smith and Anderson paper has more from the perspective of the dissertation supervisor. Bonomo pursued fieldwork among a population she was unfamiliar with, while Smith used his previous experiences as a social worker to inform his study among homeless outreach workers. Both chapters are likely to inform graduate students conducting ethnography who are new to the field and those who hold a supervisory role as advisors.

3. Bonomo's honest portrayal of her covert research might generate criticism. Yet, her views are not unique among ethnographers, particularly those in criminology—we just don't read about it because of a tacit taboo on covert ethnographic research (Murphy and Dingwall, 2001), which has not always been the norm. A number of renowned ethnographic studies started as covert research, such as Adler's study of cocaine dealers (Alder, 1993). See Calvey (2018a, 2018b) for an overview of views on covert ethnography and examples of contemporary covert research.

4. The attempt to dissuade the use of the term "key informants" by ethnographers is a goal of one of the editors (Boeri) and does not necessarily reflect the views of contributors. Using the term *informants* to describe people from the community who help ethnographers conduct research potentially puts them in harm's way as well (see more discussion of key informants in Boeri, 2018).

5. See Sanders and Copes (2013) for perspectives of IRBs from ethnographers who study drug dealers and offenders.

6. This chapter only briefly touches on the topic of ethics; readers are encouraged to read Israel and Hay (2009) for a fuller discussion of ethics for social science research covering international perspectives and practices.

7. The U.S. IRB is guided by federal regulations that govern research with human subjects, known as the Common Rule. In 2017, the U.S. Department of Health and Human Services (HHS) announced a change to the Human Subjects regulations that would reduce oversight of studies posing no or minimal risks (Milton, 2017). The expansion was delayed and essentially neutralized (U.S. Department of Health and Human Services, 2018). The Federal Policy for the Protection of Human Subjects were "intended to better protect human subjects involved in research, while facilitating valuable research and reducing burden, delay, and ambiguity for investigators."

Retrieved from www.federalregister.gov/documents/2017/01/19/2017–01058/federal-policy-for-the-protection-of-human-subjects#104.

8. Application for a Certificate of Confidentiality (CoC) is open to all researchers who need one, even if they do not have a federally-funded grant. For more information on the CoC see: https://humansubjects.nih.gov/coc/index.

9. See Boeri, Gibson, and Harbry (2009) for a description of another incident in which study participant stories were at first discounted by professionals but later proved true.

10. For a better understanding of objectivity, see Kuhn's (1962) insights on science and paradigm shifts, claiming that no science is truly objective.

11. For an in-depth discussion of using photos of participants in ethnographic studies see Bourgois and Schonberg (2009).

12. The general consensus is that although "safeguards are balanced against the goals of research" not all negative situations can be anticipated (VanderStaay, 2005, 398).

13. See Williams et al. (1992) or Page and Singer (2010) for comprehensive description of strategies for avoiding and handling dangerous situations in ethnographic research.

14. For one of the increasingly rare examples of the extent of dangerous situations that ethnographers voluntarily enter, see Bourgois' description of his introduction to an East Harlem "shooting gallery" (Bourgois, 1998).

REFERENCES

Adler, P. A. (1993). *Wheeling and dealing: An ethnography of an upper-level drug dealing and smuggling community*. New York: Columbia University Press.

Agar, M. (2006). An ethnography by any other name. *Forum Qualitative Sozialforschung/Forum: Qualitative Social Research, 7*(4), art. 36. Retrieved from http://nbn-resolving.de/urn:nbn:de:0114-fqs0604367.

Aguirre-Molina, M., and D. M. Gorman (1996). Community-based approaches for the prevention of alcohol, tobacco, and other drug use. *Annual Review of Public Health, 17*(1), 337–58.

Atkinson, P. (2006). Rescuing autoethnography. *Journal of Contemporary Ethnography, 35*(4), 400–404.

Boeri, M. W. (2007). A third model of triangulation: Continuing the dialogue with Rhineberger, Hartmann, and Van Valey. *Journal of Applied Social Science, 1*(1), 52–48.

——— (2018). *Hurt: Chronicles of the drug-war generation*. Los Angeles: University of California Press.

Boeri, M. W., D. Gibson, and L. Harbry (2009). Cold cook methods: An ethnographic exploration on the myths of methamphetamine production and policy implications. *International Journal of Drug Policy, 20*(5), 438–43.

Bourgois, P. (1998). Just another night in a shooting gallery. *Theory, Culture & Society, 15*(2), 37–66.

——— (2011). Lumpen abuse: The cost of righteous neoliberalism. *City & Society, 23*(1), 2–12.

Bourgois, P., and J. Schonberg (2009). *Righteous dopefiend.* Berkeley: University of California Press.

Calvey, D. (2018a). Covert ethnography in criminal justice and criminology: The controversial tradition of doing undercover fieldwork. *Criminology and Criminal Justice,* online publication date February 2018. Retrieved from DOI: 10.1093/acrefore/9780190264079.013.296.

——— (2018b) The everyday world of bouncers: A rehabilitated role for covert ethnography. *Qualitative Research,* online publication date April 17, 2018. Retrieved from DOI: 10.1177/1468794118769782.

Creswell, J. W., and V. L. Clark (2007). *Designing and conducting mixed methods research.* Thousand Oaks, CA: Sage.

Gusterson, H. (2008). Ethnographic research. In *Qualitative methods in international relations,* Research methods series, ed. A. Klotz and D. Prakash, 93–114. London: Palgrave Macmillan.

Humphreys, M., A. D. Brown, and M. J. Hatch (2003). Is ethnography jazz? *Organization, 10*(5), 5–31.

Israel, M., and I. Hay (2009). *Research ethics for social scientists.* London: Sage.

Kuhn, T. S. (1962). *The structure of scientific revolutions.* Chicago: University of Chicago Press.

Lincoln, Yvonne S., and E. Guba. 1985. *Naturalistic inquiry.* Beverly Hills, CA: Sage.

Malterud, K. (2001). Qualitative research: Standards, challenges, and guidelines. *Lancelot, 358,* 483–88.

Marco, C. A., and G. L. Larkin (2000). Research ethics: Ethical issues of data reporting and the quest for authenticity. *Academic Emergency Medicine, 7*(6), 691–94.

Maruna, S. (2015). Qualitative research, theory development, and evidence-based corrections: Can success stories be "evidence"? In *Qualitative research in criminology,* ed. J. Miller and W. R. Palacios, 311–38. New York: Routledge.

Milton, J. (2017). HHS announces final changes to human subjects regulations, January 24, 2017. *Consortium of Social Sciences.* Retrieved from www.cossa.org/wp-content/uploads/2017/01/Common-Rule-Hot-Topic-Milton-Jan2017.pdf.

Murphy, E., and R. Dingwall (2001). The ethics of ethnography. In *Handbook of ethnography,* ed. P. Atkinson et al., 339–51. London: Sage.

Page, J. B., and M. Singer (2010). *Comprehending drug use: Ethnographic research at the social margins.* New Brunswick, NJ: Rutgers University Press.

Ragar, K. B. (2005). Compassion stress and the qualitative researcher. *Qualitative Health Research, 15*(3), 423–30.

Sanders, S., and H. Copes (2013). Speaking with ethnographers: The challenges of researching drug dealers and offenders. *Journal of Drug Issues, 43*(2), 176–97.

Schensul, S. L., J. J. Schensul, and M. D. LeCompte (1999). *Essential ethnographic methods: Observations, interviews, and questionnaires.* New York: Rowman & Littlefield Publishers.

Singer, M., E. Huertas, and G. Scott (2000). Am I my brother's keeper? A case study of the responsibilities of research. *Human Organization, 59*(4), 389–400.

Singer, M., et al. (2001). The challenges of street research on drug use, violence, and AIDS risk. *Addiction Research and Theory, 9*(4), 365–402.

U.S. Department of Health and Human Services (2018). Federal policy for the protection of human subjects: Six-month delay of the general compliance date of revisions while allowing the use of three burden-reducing provisions during the delay period. Federal Register,83(118), Tuesday, June 19, 2018, Rules and Regulations. Retrieved from www.govinfo.gov/content/pkg/FR-2018–06–19/pdf/2018–13187.pdf.

Van Maanen, J (1988). *Tales of the field. On writing ethnography.* Chicago: University of Chicago Press.

VanderStaay, S. L. (2005). One hundred dollars and a dead man? Ethical decision making in ethnographic research. *Journal of Contemporary Ethnography, 34*(4), 371–409.

Warden, T. (2012). Feet of clay: Confronting emotional challenges in the ethnographic experience. *Journal of Organizational Ethnography, 2*(2), 150–72.

Williams, T., et al. (1992). Personal safety in dangerous places. *Journal of Contemporary Ethnography, 21,* 343–74.

PART ONE

———

Becoming an Ethnographer

ONE

Going Native with Evil

Marie Rosenkrantz Lindegaard

WHEN YOU ARE AN ETHNOGRAPHER, ideally you go native by using yourself as a research tool to understand phenomena from an insider perspective. This implies putting yourself in the shoes of others by immersing yourself emotionally and physically in their lives. This is challenging when the aim of the study is to understand violent acts from the perspectives of those who committed the acts. When the people studied engage in what could be considered "evil" activities of intentionally inflicting pain and suffering on other human beings (Vetlesen, 2005, 2), some research ideals are challenged.

This chapter reflects on the ways the ideal of doing ethnography influenced me to compromise when "going native with evil." I conducted fieldwork with young South African men who intentionally engaged in violent acts. My aim was to understand the circumstances that made them commit violence and their experiences from an insider perspective. I started by considering participants as capable agents with the capacity to make bounded choices (Cornish and Clarke, 1987). While I acknowledged that they were victims of different forms of structural violence, such as historical inequality, racism, and poverty (Abrahams and Jewkes, 2005; Kaminer et al., 2008), I tried not to reduce them to victims. I was determined to figure out under what circumstances they appeared to have a choice, particularly in the vulnerable moments where they used violence. Although they might have been categorized by a variety of psychological categories of disorders, as an anthropologist schooled in the tradition of relativism, I avoided categorization and engaged with them without preconceptions. My aim was to create a shared space of intersubjective reflexivity that allowed us to create a shared sense of understanding (Tankink and Vysma, 2006).

Doing ethnographic research with violent individuals was a confrontative and sometimes painful experience. I struggled with my inability to live up to some of the most basic dictums of doing good. As an undergraduate student in ethnography, I was taught the following: "become one of them," "do not judge your participants," "do what they do," "accept that participants become friends," "include different perspectives on your topic," and "listen to local advice" (Hammersley and Atkinson, 1995). In this chapter, I reflect on how these ideals influenced me, and on how others may learn from my experiences and mistakes, to understand that making mistakes is a part of ethnography. I discuss these ideals by showing how they were integrated in my study, my response to the difficulties encountered when assuming these ideals could become reality, and the lessons I learned when reflecting on and questioning my ethnographic assumptions. The power of ethnography lies in the disorienting effects of the unknown and the willingness to get lost. To understand from an insider's perspective, you need to let go of preconceived assumptions, which can be a scary thing to do.

PURPOSE OF THE CAPE TOWN STUDY

The aim was to understand why young men in Cape Town use violence, and in what ways they avoid using it in conflicts in their daily lives. I was interested in understanding their experiences with using and avoiding violence, and in explaining their reactions as related to the broader contexts of their lives. By combining interviews and observations, I focused my attention on both what young men *said* about violence and what they *did* when in conflict situations. Following them into different contexts also provided insights into how narratives about violence were contextually related and may change, depending on the audience.

I engaged in fieldwork from 2005 to 2006, with follow-up studies in 2008 and 2017 (see Lindegaard, 2018). During this time, I conducted more than 130 interviews with 43 men, aged sixteen to twenty-five, in 2005 and carried out extensive participant observations with 30 of them. Ten were in prison for the entirety of the study, while three moved in and out of prison, and the remainder were outside. Participants had experiences with violent acts of varying degrees of severity (e.g., murder, attempted murder, rape, assaults, and armed robberies). Participants were recruited at high schools, via snowball sampling to include those not attending school, and in a prison during a

FIGURE 1.1. Sipho's front door in Gugulethu. Photo credit: Marie Lindegaard.

five-month period. Initially, participants showed me around their neighborhood taking photos of people and places that made them comfortable or uncomfortable. They showed me the photos and eventually took me the places where they had taken them in their neighborhood. After establishing rapport I spent more time with them, visiting friends and family, and going out to local bars, night clubs, beaches, and shopping malls (see fig. 1.1). I transcribed the recordings and wrote observation notes. Participants' were given pseudonyms. In 2017, I started using closed-circuit television (CCTV) camera footage to analyze interactions in violent conflicts. My research was approved by the ethical commission of the University of the Western Cape and the University of Amsterdam, and by the South African Department of Education and Department of Correctional Services.

As an ethnographer I was a clear outsider. I had had no experiences with violent acts. I am a woman, not South African; I have acquired higher-education and am white (most participants were nonwhite). As expressed by one of the warders in the prison where I conducted fieldwork: "You have three things against you Marie: you are white, from far away, and you have a cute face so watch out!" Despite obvious differences, participants' reflections were not so much about differences but about similarities. As one partici-pant, Drégan, recognized: "If you had been a man, Marie, and you had grown up on the Cape Flats, you would be just like me! You also like danger. Otherwise, you would not have done this kind of work. Some people might think you are a nerd but you cannot be a nerd and do this kind of work. You are just like me! You just happened to live in another part of the world." Drégan touched upon questions I grappled with myself. What made me dif-ferent from my participants? What caused our dissimilarities? To under-stand, my aim was to immerse myself emotionally and physically as much as possible into their lives. This led to confronting a range of inconsistent dogma regarding fieldwork and compromising on ideals to protect others and myself from danger (Ferrell and Hamm, 1998). Many compromises involved dilem-mas of being an outsider, not knowing when to express emotions, struggling with understanding my subjects, balancing judgments and generating trust, not knowing when to be honest and when to be less than honest. In retro-spect, I wish someone had told me that making compromises was not only wise but necessary when researching violence. The aim to understand and not judge people was the precondition for preventing violence.

IDEAL 1: BECOME ONE OF THEM

My predefined assumptions became apparent as my own emotional responses to engaging with participants emerged. In the beginning, I felt anxious and afraid. I tried to hide these emotions because I was worried that expressing them would endanger my ability to establish rapport and understand acts from their perspective. Fear and anxiety had to be suspended to access their points of view.

One example to illustrate this point is from an interview conducted with Drégan. While I wanted to know about the "evil acts" that he committed, at the same time, I struggled emotionally with handling the details about these acts because it challenged the relationship I was establishing with him. To relate to him and understand him, I needed to feel connected with him. However, my own fear and disgust of the details of his acts made me unable to listen to what he was saying without judgment. Instead, I tried to take control by posing too many, irrelevant questions.

I met Drégan while working for a nongovernmental organization in prison and interviewed him at his house upon release. I was in unfamiliar territory with a person experienced with killing and violence, and this caused me distress. Fortunately, his mother and sister were home in another room, and we whispered at times to prevent them from hearing our conversation. I tried to focus on his experiences but struggled to listen. His story made me upset.

D: So, one evening, I was sitting in the shebeen [illegal bar], this guy asks me for a kiss. I tell him, are you crazy; are you fucking crazy. The guy hits me with a beer bottle. I carried an axe at that time; a small axe. If it was not an axe it was a tagger or a knife; just something; always armed; it was part of the dress code. I take out the axe. Hit this guy but the guy is not alone. Now I am crazy and there is this whole gang. But I have a friend with me as well. He also has an axe but he is crumpling. I come back to that guy that I already knocked out. He is already away. When they see the state he is in, they get crazy. And they see I am all alone, Miss man.

M (*INTERRUPTING TOO QUICKLY*): Can you explain? I would very much like to hear every detail of when you hit this guy.

D: I was like crazy, Miss man . . .

M (*DEMANDING ELABORATION*): So what do you remember? Like almost every minute?

D: Like I say, I cannot even remember none of their faces man. The moment when that guy hit me with a beer bottle and I stood up and I hit the first person that I see. I just stood up with my axe. I do not even know if the guy that I hit was the guy that hit me with the beer bottle. They were like a group and I just hit the first guy.

M (*INSISTING*): And what do you remember from the moment where you hit him?

D: It just feels like everything goes slow.

M (*INSISTING*): What clothes did he have on?

D: I cannot remember none of that. Because two weeks after that incidence I went back there to look for the guys and we wanted to shoot them. But I did not know who these people were so I had to ask around. I probably spoke with them but I am like gone. I was drunk. I do not notice any-body. I am just in love with myself at the time.

M *(INSISTING)*: So where did you hit him?

D: In here. In his face.

M *(INSISTING)*: How hard?

D: Joh, very hard *(laughs nervously)*. With all the anger and power, you have in your body.

I tried to understand his experience as if I had been a part of it myself, but instead of allowing for elaborations I tried to stay in control by asking questions that at the time seemed relevant. I made the following remark about the interview in my notes afterward: "One of the things, which becomes clear from listening through the interview, is that I do not get all the points. Not because the story is actually that complicated—more because the whole topic makes me confused and emotionally unstable. I think I spend energy on putting myself together instead of focusing on what he says" (field notes).

The interview was highly distressing emotionally. The content would have been more valuable if I was quiet and listening. My own anxiety about the murder made me try to take control, which is not a fruitful approach when the aim is to understand.

In my reflections afterward, I described how it made me feel to put myself in his place:

I felt like throwing up, particularly in the situation with the axe. My stomach turned around and I had to focus on my breathing. After the interview, I felt very heavy. I felt like crying but I cannot cry. It feels like the tears are sitting right under my eyes but they cannot get out. When I got home, I walked up and down the floor unable to sit down. I feel restless and powerless. I am wondering if I violated him by asking him to move to what he called "the dark side." Am I supposed to cheer him up and handle his trauma? Does it make sense to see him as traumatized? (field notes)

My Response: Reflections on Emotions

The interview with Drégan made me doubt the feasibility of my study's aim of putting myself in the place of someone who had killed. After the interview, I realized that in order to continue in an emotionally engaged manner I needed to reflect on how emotions influenced interactions with participants.

I forced myself to recognize those emotions through relaxation exercises and weekly reflections with a psychologist. These interventions did not remove my anxiety but helped me to recognize and acknowledge it. Instead of denying my anxiety and outsider role, I started embracing it by emphasizing how little I understood.

Lesson 1: Express Emotions and Doubt

Hiding emotions may be necessary to understand the topic of research from a native point of view, because revealing them may expose negative judgments. However, one lesson learned is that saying aloud "this description makes me feel nauseous" or admitting "not to understand the logic of killing because of an argument" is more productive and does not necessarily involve judgment. After Drégan's interview, I started using our differences actively by saying things like: "I do not mean to be disrespectful but I really do not get this. To me it is not logical at all." Saying this aloud invited participants to be more honest about their experiences and emotions. Emphasizing differences rather than shying away is a way to understand the other better.

IDEAL 2: DO NOT JUDGE YOUR PARTICIPANTS

Acknowledging differences created more honesty in our exchange of thoughts, but sometimes honesty led to oversharing. One example occurred when I provided Devron, another prison inmate, with the wrong transcription. When I was transcribing, I always made two versions. One included the verbal exchange, observations of body language, emotional experiences during the interview, interpretations of participant emotions, and conclusions about the content in relation to the overall questions. Another included only the verbal exchange. When I provided transcriptions to participants, I always used the verbal exchange version, except on one occasion.

Devron was in prison for murdering a girl he knew from school. His story deeply influenced me. I described my experiences in detail in the transcriptions. Devron had not only killed a woman who had shown trust in him by allowing him to walk her home after they met in a local bar, but he also raped her with a friend. The rape was the reason they felt they had to kill her.

During the rape, she promised never to tell the police if they spared her. He explained to her that killing her was the only option. The transcriptions that I gave to him involved the following reflections that clearly involved judging Devron (marked in italics) in a way I tried to avoid in our interaction:

> When I saw Devron in the class [where I presented my research], I thought he was a soft guy. He seemed shy but intelligent. I am not sure why. When he started talking during the interview, I realized that *he was probably the most hard and "far out" I had spoken to so far.* He was sentenced for murder, and he was eager to talk about it. He literally said it would be a relief for him to get it off his chest. He explained he had raped and killed a woman in the area where he stays. *It made me sick to hear his story.* I kept thinking to myself, it is ok you think he is sick. The only way I could understand him was by thinking about his crime as a matter of provoking and crossing boundaries. *Devron came across as not particularly burdened by his activities. He did not show signs of being disturbed.* Kyle [another participant] yesterday could hardly get it out of his mouth. *Devron described killing as "these things just happen." For him violence seemed to be normalized as something he even felt obliged to do.* He had been in prison only three weeks. Perhaps he has not yet realized what he has done. *Perhaps he will never realize.* . . . The interview went easy. He was open and good in elaborating. He came across as strong in his body language. *Confident but also aggressive. I was for the first time happy about the open door [to the corridor].*

After I provided him with the wrong transcripts, I saw him in the corridor when visiting other participants. The way he looked and responded to me was different. He handed me a letter he had written. The letter made me realize I made a mistake, which Devron confirmed when I spoke to him the next day. In the letter, he responded to my comments about him with questions that required honest answers from me (marked in italics):

> I cannot believe that I was opening my dark side in me for you. It was nice talking to you, really, but I want to know: *Why did you feel uncomfortable when I was talking to you? . . . I wonder what goes through your mind when you look at me because you speak to a man that killed someone and you know what took place with the murder.* . . . I will think of you because I told you a story that nobody else knows about me. It is just you and Kyle that know.

I knew I had to step out of my ethnographer role and be honest about my interpretations. My main worry was that my honest perspectives would come across as judgmental and cause emotional distress that would be difficult for Devron to deal with alone in the prison. After consulting a friend and colleague, I decided to reply to Devron in a letter and organize access to immediate counseling for him if needed.

My Response: Generate Open Dialogue

This example had immediate consequences for my relationship to Devron and required a direct response. Even though one may argue that oversharing is not a problem but just generates new and more honest dynamics with participants, too much honesty may put researchers and participants in awkward positions. In a letter responding to his questions, I openly expressed my confusion about my interaction with him:

> For me it was shocking to get exposed to your "dark side." I never dared to move to that side before I got to know you. I felt uncomfortable because *I was afraid of both you and myself.* Knowing that you had raped and killed a woman, I was thinking: could he do it again? Why doesn't he do it to me when he was able to do it to someone he knew from school? Am I different from her? Am I safe? I felt related to you and your story, which made me think: *if someone like him, whom I feel connected with, can do this kind of "dark" stuff, then why not me?* (letter to Devron)

Devron replied with his own letter:

> But Marie, you must know that you must never, never think that I am that kind of person that will do that to you because *I shared something very important with you and this puts you in an important place in my heart.* In the part of my heart where you find all my best friends. And you will stay there because I will remember you, Marie. . . . I will end off with the words: live well, live well and if anyone tries to rob you remember what I said. Do not be scared. *Most of the robbers do not have a heart like me, who will stab a beautiful girl like you with a knife.* You must live well, Devron will think about you.

I later interviewed Devron again. This one differed from the first because he expressed confusion about his violent acts and himself as a person. It ended with him crying and asking for help. He got counseling, I continuously visited him, and we stayed in contact. My oversharing clearly triggered another aspect of Devron than our usual interactions, and this aspect would probably not have been revealed if I had not overshared my experiences. Perhaps my honesty triggered a reaction in him that he was not yet ready for given the unsafe prison environment. Devron eventually became a high-ranked prison gang member whose main task was to organize the sexual abuse of lower-ranked members.

Lesson 2: Be Honest but Do Not Overshare

It is impossible to be honest all the time because it may damage rapport with participants. Oversharing experiences changes the dynamics of interactions with participants, which may be positive but could also cause harm. The point at which expressions of honesty become oversharing is unclear. When the research involves engaging with people who have done evil to others, it is sometimes necessary to hide in the role of the understanding researcher, even when this role feels wrong. After the prison visit, this role often made me aggressive and frustrated. It felt wrong to just listen and not express disgust when participants were telling their stories. The lesson is that honesty is necessary because it makes you keep asking about aspects that you do not understand, but oversharing makes you vulnerable and may put participants in a difficult position.

IDEAL 3: DO WHAT THEY DO

An important aspect of ethnography is to participate in the lives of the people involved in the study (see fig. 1.2). In studies of violence, there are ethical and safety-related boundaries for how closely the researchers can or should participate and observe. Therefore, the ideal of participating in the lives of participants requires compromises. The dilemma with such compromises is that it is necessary to negotiate an ethnographer role as someone who would be capable of observing while at the same time clearly expressing unwillingness to actually carry out such observations. I negotiated a role as someone who would be there when the violence took place. At the same time, I was someone who had to leave or close my eyes if it actually happened. This complicated impression management led to confusion and confrontations (Goffman, 1959).

While interested in my participants' criminal activities, I tried to keep a distance by not wanting to know too many details about the exact places and times and about any future crimes planned. This constructed distance was sometimes confusing for participants, who seemed to have the impression that they could always count on me. Due to the ideal that I was supposed to

FIGURE 1.2. Drégan in the window of his bedroom in Delft. Photo credit: Marie Lindegaard.

participate as much as possible in their lives, I struggled with drawing boundaries when witnessing their involvement in violent activities.

Sipho had been involved in car thefts in the city center almost every night for a period of time. One night he phoned me after midnight asking me to pick him up. I ignored his calls because I thought he might be committing crimes. He phoned eleven times and I did not answer. Instead of honestly saying I could not pick him up because there were limits to my participation, I said my phone had been out.

Thabo disappeared and his family did not know where he was. His brother contacted me the day after, and we went to local police stations to check lists of arrested people. We found out he had been arrested for attempted murder and theft and was awaiting trial in prison. Due to my permission to conduct research in prison, I was able to find him and interview him about the accusation. Before the interview, I had paid for his bail from prison because I found it unethical not to do so if I had the option, irrespective of whether he was guilty. On average, my participants awaited trial for two years, and those parts of the prisons were notorious for being the worst because of sexual abuse, violence, gangs, emotional stress, and lack of facilities. It turned out that he and his friends had carjacked someone by threatening him with a gun. Thabo had been the one using the weapon. Even though I do not regret posting the bail, because I believe it was an ethically right decision, it raises questions of how to deal with being a witness to violence. Eventually the case against Thabo was dropped due to a lack of evidence.

My Response: Avoid Facts

After not answering Sipho's call, he involved me less directly in his criminal activities. He apologized for having asked me for help, and said he tried to avoid getting me involved when he was engaged in activities that would put me in a difficult position. Sipho became increasingly involved in crime and committed serious violent crimes. Eventually he got heavily involved in a gang and, tragically, was shot dead on a very busy street in his residential area (see Lindegaard and Zimmerman, 2017). Throughout my study, I knew about but avoided the details about his crimes. Until his death, he seemed to accept me in the role of being an "acceptable incompetent" (Hammersley and Atkinson, 1995, 99) witness to violence.

Bailing Thabo out had quite an impact on him because he felt he had to prove to me that it had been worth my money. He became a peer educator at his school and was doing his best to stay away from crime. He reflected on this pressure of the bail ten years later when I interviewed him again: "You gave me a push to do my best but leaving the gang was no option. Now I actually do the same. I keep up appearances at my work and with my wife and children up there [in another town] but on the weekends, I go down here [to Cape Town] and do my gangster stuff. I live a double life. It works for me. When you bailed me out, I realized I could do that" (February 2017).

Lesson 3: Accept Double Standards

Ironically, Thabo literally said I taught him to live a "double life" by bailing him out and thereby offering him a noncriminal role. When I made this role available to him, he realized that double standards were possible, enabling him to keep up appearances of living a life without crime while simultaneously being involved in it. In this way, researchers and participants sometimes have to deceive others via impression management. For me the tension was that I was involved in the lives of my participants in a role that enabled me to observe violent activities without actually being willing to participate. When going native with evil, the willingness to observe but not participate provides access to insider perspectives. A complication is that aspiring toward such a role requires heavy investment in impression management that is demolished by the refusal to participate when violence takes place. The lesson is that double standards may be necessary to access insider perspectives. It is necessary to keep up the illusion of being willing to participate in violence, while at the same time avoiding doing so for the sake of ethics and safety. Ethnographic fieldwork requires downplaying one's own opinions, beliefs, and sympathies for the sake of sustaining the "interaction ritual" (Goffman, 1972).

IDEAL 4: ACCEPT THAT PARTICIPANTS BECOME YOUR FRIENDS

Though I was aware of the problem of getting too involved with participants, I seemed to forget this because I was trying so hard to immerse myself. Establishing close relationships caused me to underestimate my own need for personal space. A few painful confrontations made me aware of the importance of establishing and safeguarding personal spaces and establishing transitional spaces to allow for "decompression" during transitions from one setting to another.

The need for personal space became apparent from a situation that occurred when I left Cape Town to go home for a break after eight months of fieldwork. Interactions with participants had started becoming very informal, with frequent occurrences of hanging out and bumping into each other coincidentally when out with friends (not participants). I had spent a lot of time with Drégan, also dancing with him and friends in a nightclub once, and it was therefore not strange when he asked me if he could come to the airport when I was leaving to say goodbye, since he had never been to the airport despite living next to it. He never dared going into the terminal because he felt out of place among all those "rich whities but with you it's different." I agreed to meet him there without realizing the impact it might have on me. I described the situation in my notes afterward:

> I was wearing my own clothes, something nice because I was going to see Willem [boyfriend] upon arrival so I wanted to look good. Drégan immediately noticed that I looked differently. He teasingly said "Oh, of course you want to look nice when you get home to Willem." I felt awkward and exposed, realizing how important my fieldwork clothes had been for my

feeling of protection. All eyes in the hall were on us. Drégan leaned over the table towards me whispering that they [friend and him] had drinks in their inner pockets, also for me. I ordered beers for all of us. When our glasses were empty, Drégan topped up with the ones from his pocket. He looked intensely at me and said with surprise, "You are nervous Marie. Oh my God, I have never seen you so nervous before. What's going on?" He knew about my flight anxiety. He tried to calm me down with jokes. He said, "Look at me. You just need to get drunk when you feel anxious. That's what I did before going here." We had a few beers. I felt dizzy and confused. I felt safe with Drégan and his friend but also completely out of place. By the second call for my flight, I rushed up the stairs and into the plane. I felt nauseous and distressed. When the plane took off, I started throwing up. It felt like I could not stop. I had to get it all out. (field notes)

Bringing Drégan into my personal space, dressed in my ordinary—not field-work—clothes, and exposing myself at a vulnerable moment when being in transit between my two homes (Cape Town and Amsterdam), made me confused and sick.

The importance of separating spaces also became apparent at a party at my house before leaving Cape Town. I had rented a room at the house of a white woman in the suburbs (close to the prison where I worked). She agreed to the party but would not take part. I invited my friends and a few participants, including one I had paid to be my assistant. Rumors had spread and uninvited participants showed up with friends in a rented minibus. Everyone was drinking, the music was loud in the bus, and soon the small group increased to at least thirty people, the majority male, black, and from the townships. The atmosphere was good, people were dancing, and conversations occurred between the township and suburban residents. At the end of the night, my housemate arrived and was distressed about the party. She went straight to bed, and we moved the party to a nightclub. A week later, there was an attempted break-in at our house. My housemate was convinced that some of the partygoers were involved. She was angry that I had brought participants to our house. In her eyes, there was a significant difference between my friends and my participants. She was trying to draw a boundary for my personal space that I had difficulties drawing myself.

My fieldwork site was so emotionally draining that it had started taking over my personal space. The prison environment was highly distressing for a range of different reasons. I started having sleeping problems, postponed leaving my house in the morning, and literally got lost on my way home from the prison, which was a fifteen-minute drive on one straight highway from my house. Sometimes I found myself driving on the opposite side of town after leaving the prison, without knowing how I ended up there. When I came home, I could smell the prison in my clothes.

My Response: Changing Clothes and Settings

My physical reaction to the stress I experienced by allowing Drégan into my transitional space, the distress of my housemate when her space was invaded, and reactions to the distress of doing fieldwork in prison are examples of underestimating my own need for personal space. My response was to create transitional spaces for myself that enabled me to decompress when I moved from fieldwork to my personal setting. After being exposed to high levels of stress, I needed to decompress in several stages to be emotionally healthy. Instead of going straight from my participants to my home, I created transitional spaces (e.g., go to a café or go running). I also changed clothes and took a shower to emphasize the transition. The process of decompression prevented me from bringing too much distress home. It helped me create distance and remain an outsider and thereby still be able to listen and attempt to understand when engaging with participants.

Lesson 4: Establish and Safeguard Your Transitional Spaces

I felt guilty about my need to decompress and get out of the space that participants had to deal with daily. I had to be able to deal with it if I really wanted to understand their lives from their perspective. When the aim was to understand and let go of my own assumptions in this study on violence, which can have such an impact on the researcher, I learned to establish and safeguard my transitional spaces in order to be able to connect and relate emotionally. When I violated boundaries, by inviting participants into my personal spaces, literally and emotionally, I was unable to function well enough to effectively listen and understand.

IDEAL 5: INCLUDE MULTIPLE PERSPECTIVES ON YOUR TOPIC

To understand the shifting behavior I observed, I tried to incorporate multiple perspectives on violent situations and behaviors. This ethnographic ideal of including insider perspectives from different points of view, however, turned out to be dangerous to participants and myself.

Ubeid told me that gangs had threatened him because he talked to me. He lived in a residential area, with many active gangs but tried very hard to avoid getting involved. Avoiding involvement meant greeting but not talking to them, staying inside, and focusing on school. In the beginning, I had primarily engaged with young men who avoided gangs, like Ubeid. At some stage, I wanted to include more perspectives and therefore started engaging with gang-involved youth. I became known as the researcher who was interested in gangs. For Ubeid, that reputation was a problem because his association with me made people expect that he aspired toward gang involvement. The gang-involved youth shared this expectation and started threatening him to become a member. This threat became so severe that Ubeid's mother decided to send him to stay with his aunt, who lived in another area. Due to the threat to Ubeid, I stopped engaging with gang-involved youth in his neighborhood. I moved into prison to recruit gang-involved youth.

In prison, I interviewed both inmates and warders about their perspectives on conflicts taking place within the prison to understand them from multiple perspectives, despite my primary interest in the inmates. The interviews with the warders often became personal because they struggled with threats while on duty. The interviews created rapport, and provided insightful perspectives. However, they also put me in a difficult position toward some of the warders because they felt betrayed that I was also speaking to inmates. In their eyes, inmates did not deserve a listener. Despite repeated explanations of my motivations for speaking to inmates, a few warders kept expressing their frustration, to a point where two of them suggested "forgetting" me inside the prison during the night: "When I signed in at Medium B, the two warders said, yes, just sign here but maybe you actually don't want to. It seems like you would really like to stay here all night. Apparently, you really enjoy speaking to inmates. Why don't you just stay here all the time if you're so interested? We don't mind forgetting about you [smiling]" (fieldwork notes, 2006).

During a follow-up study, the municipality of Cape Town provided me with the opportunity to use CCTV camera footage of violent crimes, including killings, providing a different perspective. I conducted fieldwork in the control room in the city center where operators followed what happened on city streets "live" with cameras that could zoom in and out. During one observation, a young man killed another in an alley in one of the townships that I knew well. We watched the whole event live from the first encounter between offender and victim, the period where the victim was on the ground but still alive, the actual death of the victim, and the police arriving at the scene. I came to realize that observing the act of killing was emotionally very difficult for me. When I interviewed offenders about killings, the image of the CCTV-captured killing overwhelmed me and made me unable to listen to their perspectives.

My Response: Divide Fieldwork into Phases and Sites

After I finished interviewing youth not involved in gangs, and to reduce the threat to Ubeid, I moved to a prison setting to recruit gang-involved youth. Although I kept meeting up more informally with the youth who were not gang-involved during that period, the clear separation of place and focus made being associated with me less risky for Ubeid and others not involved in the gang.

My supervisor wanted to report the two warders that had been threatening me to the head of the prison. I refused because I was worried it would make my work in prison impossible. Instead, I avoided doing interviews in the section where the two warders worked. I stopped interviewing warders to avoid the impression that I was taking their side. To express my awareness of their difficult working and living environment, I spent more time in informal conversations with them, and sometimes provided them with lifts to and from prison. This rapport ensured that I felt protected enough in the prison.

The challenge of observing the act of murder in the control room showed me the importance of separating the collection of offender perspectives from the observations of violence on CCTV footage. After watching the killing, I took a break from interviewing. The suffering of the victim I had observed dying made me unable to listen to the perspective of any offender. When I finished my observations in the control room, I took a break and returned to the interviews, listening to the perspectives of the offenders.

Lesson 5: Include One Perspective at a Time

Inclusion of multiple perspectives from the field is an important analytical tool of ethnography, but when going native with evil it can pose threats both to participants and researcher. While I highly recommend to include multiple perspectives (Lindegaard, 2010), the lesson learned is to separate engagement with conflicting groups and perspectives into different fieldwork periods. My experience shows emphasizing with one side or the other can be temporary, and should be clearly demarcated by field location and period in time.

IDEAL 6: LISTEN TO LOCAL ADVICE

Ethnographers rely on local advice to gain information they cannot directly observe and to incorporate local codes of conduct. In studies of violence in places that involve risk, this includes advice about the local conduct for safety. However, in my experience, local advice is not directly applicable for an ethnographer. My reaction to this realization was at first to ignore local advice. Eventually I realized that I had to observe local practices of safety rather than listening to local narratives about it, and I reformulated these practices into my own safety rules.

The first piece of advice I received from local researchers was to hire local nonwhite research assistants to do the research for me instead of doing it myself because they would know how to deal with safety issues. I did not follow this advice when I learned that the local researchers had never spent time in a township.

The second piece of advice was from friends living in township areas. When I asked them about safety in their neighborhood, I recognized a pattern in their answers. They said that in their close surroundings, about three blocks from their house, it was very safe. For example, Dasia, who lived close to a field where a lot of gang-related shooting took place, advised the following:

If you just stay on this side of the field, you will be fine. I never had any problems here, but on that side, you know by the robot, that is where everything happens. Yesterday they shot a gangster there.

Although Dasia lived at the center of where shootings took place daily, she thought real danger belonged to the opposite part of the neighborhood. Similar advice about safety revealed that places where my friends felt in control, and therefore they *felt* safe, were not places that would be safe for me.

The third piece of advice came from my participants, who brought someone along when feeling unsafe. For example, Ubeid explained how he was scared of walking to the library and would bring someone along to feel safe:

Sometimes, when I walk to the library to do a project or so, I sometimes feel threatened. That is why I always ask someone to walk with me. Though walking with someone will not stop the gangsters from killing us, I will feel more safe, if I am building up a conversation with someone. So, I normally walk with someone.

However, feeling safe was not the same as being safe. When I applied this rule, and asked my boyfriend to come with me, who made me feel safe, I was putting him in danger as well as myself.

My Response: Ignoring and Reformulating Safety Advice

I ignored the first piece of advice to "stay out of the townships" because I could not conduct an ethnographic study if I followed this advice. I learned that it is important to create a structure of safety that provides a feeling of control, but when I applied the third piece of advice, "bring someone along to feel safe," I realized that participants in my study were doing the same with me, which potentially put the person I brought along and myself in danger. Therefore, I reformulated this advice by bringing someone whom I trusted who was "streetwise" in these neighborhoods. I employed a friend from the township to accompany me in different neighborhoods, evaluate the situation, and inform me when I needed to withdraw for safety reasons. I also learned from him when to stay away from the townships, whom I could trust, and how locals developed their own safety rules.

Lesson 6: Develop Your Own Rules of Safety

When doing ethnographic research on violence, the safety of the researcher is a concern, but listening to local advice on how to address safety issues does not always work for someone from the outside. One lesson I learned is to develop my own rules of safety in the field. This meant observing local practices but also having someone from the neighborhood you trust to be with you, observe your surroundings as you interact with others, and teach you the local norms of street behavior. Developing my own rules of safety required acknowledging local advice while considering my position as an outsider.

CONCLUSION

Going native with people, who committed "evil" acts by intentionally inflicting pain on others required compromising on the ideals of doing ethnography. Even though I knew that ethnography is always about compromises because you have to adjust to others and be open and grateful for what people share, I experienced my compromises as confusing and at times counterproductive while being in the field. While I believe that the power of ethnography is the confusion and the willingness to get lost, I also believe that preparing better for fieldwork might help young scholars to turn the scary aspect of this into something productive and enlightening. Therefore, in conclusion, I provide the following advice for young scholars who are about to do ethnographic fieldwork.

First, accept that compromises to the ideal of doing ethnography, as taught at universities, are necessary. To prepare yourself for that realization, think carefully about what these compromises might involve in the fieldwork that you set out to do. In my case, I only came to this realization while I was in the middle of the fieldwork, and afterward when sharing with colleagues. My necessary compromises to my ideals of doing ethnographic fieldwork involved: (1) creating a personal space to reflect on emotional experiences of engaging with participants; (2) finding ways of generating open dialogue without oversharing; (3) consciously avoiding facts about activities of participants to protect all parties involved from ethical dilemmas; (4) demarcating personal space (e.g., changing clothes, settings); (5) dividing fieldwork into phases and sites to include multiple perspectives on the topic; and (6) developing your own rules of safety. For other researchers, with different topics, demography, background, and positionality in the field, this list might be quite different. Practically, I suggest making the list of expected compromises before leaving for fieldwork, adjust it during fieldwork, and eventually revise it after fieldwork while reflecting on the changes of the list with colleagues in all phases of the research.

Second, imagine the worst possible mistakes you could make while doing fieldwork and discuss with colleagues how you could deal with them in productive ways. In my case, examples of mistakes and challenges were the following: (1) the inability to listen to the crucial descriptions by participants due to being overwhelmed and disturbed about content; taking too much control of conversations for fear of what might come in responses to questions; (2) oversharing by mistakenly sharing transcripts that contained personal reflections about disgust toward a participant's actions; (3) drawing explicit boundaries as a witness of violence; (4) confusing differences between researcher and subject by allowing participants to become too much a part of personal spaces; (5) underestimating the impact of research on the lives of the participants; and (6) ignoring and reformulating local advice to develop my own rules of safety.

Third, reflect extensively on what your topic says about you as a person. Doing ethnography is a highly personal affair that makes researchers aware of painful and surprising aspects of themselves and their past. In my case, a common denominator of the fieldwork experiences and practices described in this chapter is my difficulty in drawing boundaries. By reflecting on my own confusion, challenges, and struggles in continuous dialogue with colleagues and significant others, I realized that my interest in violence might be related to my difficulties with boundaries. Violence by definition involves crossing personal boundaries. Violent acts transgress personal boundaries but they also demarcate them. People who use violence determine boundaries, they decide for others, sometimes even about life and death. Being reflexive before and throughout fieldwork, and seriously considering your own responses to challenges, mistakes made, and difficulties encountered, allows you to discover more about yourself.[1]

NOTE

I would like to thank Willem Rogier Boterman for being supportive during my fieldwork, Lidewyde Berckmoes for reflecting on fieldwork experiences and for helping me to structure my thoughts for the chapter, and Paige L.M. Copple, Amanda L. Dorman, and Cora M. Bradley for doing important editing of the chapter. The research was made possible by the Dutch National Research Council (NWO). Grant number: W 52–1085.

REFERENCES

Abrahams, N., and R. Jewkes (2005). Effects of South African men having witnessed abuse of their mothers during childhood on their levels of violence in adulthood. *American Journal of Public Health, 95,* 1811–16.
Cornish, D.B., and R.V. Clarke (1987). Understanding crime displacement: An application of Rational Choice Theory. *Criminology, 25,* 933–47.
Ferrell, J., and M.S. Hamm (1998). *Ethnography at the edge: Crime, deviance, and field research.* Boston: Northeastern University Press.
Goffman, E. (1959). *The presentation of self in everyday life.* Garden City, NY: Doubleday Anchor.
——— (1972). *Interaction ritual.* Harmondsworth: Penguin.

Hammersley, M., and P. Atkinson. (1995). *Ethnography. Principles in practice.* London: Routledge.

Kaminer, D., et al. (2008). Risk for post-traumatic stress disorder associated with different forms of interpersonal violence in South Africa. *Social Science and Medicine, 67,* 1589–95.

Lindegaard, M. R. (2010). Method, actor and context triangulations: Knowing what happened during criminal events and the motivations for getting involved as offender. In *Offenders on offending,* ed. W. Bernasco, 109–29. Cullompton: Willian.

——— (2018). *Surviving gangs, violence, and racism in Cape Town: Ghetto chameleons.* London: Routledge.

Lindegaard, M. R., and F. Zimmerman (2017). Flexible cultural repertoires: Young men avoiding offending and victimization in Cape Town, South Africa. *Ethnography, 18*(2), 193–220.

Tankink, M., and M. Vysma (2006). The intersubjective as analytical tool in medical anthropology. *Medische Antropologie, 18*(1), 249–65.

Vetlesen, A. (2005). *Evil and human agency: Understanding collective evildoing.* Cambridge: Cambridge University Press.

———————

Lost in the Park

LEARNING TO NAVIGATE THE UNPREDICTABILITY
OF FIELDWORK

Elizabeth Bonomo and Scott Jacques

AT A PARK IN DOWNTOWN ATLANTA, there is an area about the size of a boxing ring where people gather to play chess. Surrounded by low perching walls with flower boxes on top, there are four picnic-style tables with inlay chessboards. Across the street are restaurants, coffee shops, business offices, Georgia State University (GSU), and a police precinct. During the day, the area is bustling with activity. The chess players make moves, watch games, socialize, drink alcohol, smoke marijuana, gamble, and hustle.

Though the chess park may sound nice, students and professionals considered it to be a "no-go" zone inside an otherwise open city center. They walked next to the chess park on their way to class or work, but stayed to themselves. In part, this avoidance was due to perceiving the players as homeless, which they often were. They were usually dirty, and many carried large bags with all of their belongings. Students report feeling "uneasy and anxious" when near the players because they are "homeless and crazy," so they "might stop you and rob you."

I (Liz) began researching the chess park while taking Scott's qualitative research methods course during my third year of graduate school at GSU.[1] The course required us to ethnographically study a stigma of our choice (see E. Goffman, 1963). Over the prior semesters, I had become interested in the chess park and players. My curiosity stemmed, in part, from an invisible line dividing passersby and the players. They were a visible fixture of the downtown Atlanta scene, but deliberately not seen by most pedestrians.

This perception of the players as "homeless" was what I originally intended to study as the stigma. My thinking was people were scared of the players because they seemed homeless (see Snow and Anderson, 1993). However, there was another important characteristic of the players: they were black.

Passing observers cast the players as dangerous and criminal (Anderson, 1999, 2011; Duneier, 1999). The players, then, were not only stigmatized because they appear to be homeless, but also because they were black males.

This chapter describes my experience researching the chess players. The project lasted a couple years, was supervised by Scott, and approved by GSU's Institutional Review Board (IRB). By the end, I learned why they go to the park, what they do there, how they perceive themselves to be perceived by passersby, how that affects them, and their identities in and outside the park. That knowledge was a long time in the making, with many stumbling blocks along the way. This chapter discusses the problems I faced and how they were resolved during the course of my ethnographic study at the park.

FIRST MOVE

There are a variety of ways to access data and produce a sample (see Boeri and Lamonica, 2015). There is no one right way to generate cases because what is best depends on the population's characteristics and the ethnographer's resources (e.g., preexisting contacts, research monies). In my case, the players were not a "hidden population" and I had no preexisting ties to them.[2] Thus, the obvious path was to introduce myself to the players and then observe and speak with them.

Gaining access to such a group may seem simple, yet actually doing so can be quite difficult (see Bernasco, 2010; Copes and Miller, 2015; Miller and Palacios, 2015). While it was clear how I should approach the scene, the same was not true of how *exactly* to do so. The most straightforward approach would be to walk up, identity myself as a researcher, briefly describe what I want to know, and ask for their participation. Scott thought this would be fine since he did this for his own research. But I was apprehensive. I had convinced myself it was "their" park and it belonged to them. I viewed myself as an intruder and did not think I could just walk up to them and start asking them questions.

Instead, I wanted to covertly gain access. This approach requires the researcher to hide their true identity and intentions from the subjects. The researcher must develop a cover story, or plausible justification, for their ongoing presence in the setting while they secretly conduct their study. I felt it was unrealistic for me to be forthright with my study intentions, as overt research would have required. I assumed they would be wary of me entering "their" space and reluctant toward participating in the study. Additionally, I lacked confidence in my ability as a researcher and felt a sense of comfort in covertly approaching them. In some ways, it allowed me to put my doubt aside and focus on the role I needed to play to keep my cover in the field. I hoped to establish rapport with the players and, in turn, gain their permission to talk in-depth about my research interests.

Covert work requires a plausible cover story (Marx, 1989). Thus, I had to come up with an identity that the players would accept as a legitimate reason for me to be at the park.[3] This was made all the more difficult because my appearance prevented me from simply "fitting in" based on looks alone. I am female, white, and have a style that is the antithesis of "street." Such differences between observer and observed make covert work more difficult.

I had little control over how I looked, so the cover story would have to be especially convincing. Given that chess is the foundational activity of the scene, one approach would be for me to present myself as a chess player looking for a game. The problem with that idea is I did not know how to play. So, instead, I came up with the following idea for making contact. At a predetermined day and time, I would go to the park, say hello to some players, and start a conversation. When the planned time came, I went to the park, but I only had the courage to sit on the outside looking in, close enough to see but not hear what was going on. My anxiety stemmed from me feeling like an intruder.

The next day, I went into Scott's office to ask for advice on how to make headway. We decided that simply going to the park to have a conversation was an inadequate cover story. In truth, I later learned that this would not have been wholly implausible, albeit potentially problematic for another reason. Fast-forwarding a bit, once I had gained a place at the park (discussed below), many of the players thought I was a "snow bunny," defined by them as a white female who wants relations with black men (see A. Goffman, 2014). Nonetheless, that approach to gaining access would have been troubled. It could cause conflicts with players should they feel disrespected by being turned down by me, or jealous of those they think are with me. Also, using sex (appeal) to gain access is considered unethical in some circles, as is having an intimate relationship with a participant (see Goode, 1999).

Scott and I decided that since I did not know how to play chess, the next best option was to ask for lessons. The cover story was to pass as someone who wanted to learn chess and was solely there to get lessons. Not knowing how to play made it easier to pretend because I was learning in real time. In addition, a part of me was interested in learning the game for learning's sake.

However, this was largely overshadowed by my research intentions. Nevertheless, because there was an element of truth to this identity, that I had an interest in learning the game, we hoped it would reduce my anxiety about approaching the players.

I went back to the park a few days later and stood at the perimeter, observing and slowly building up my confidence to approach the men and ask for a lesson. On that particular day, there were two book vendors set up near the border of the park. I decided to stop by their table since it would bring me closer to the players. I made small talk with the vendors for a few minutes, but I was stalling. I was worried about how the players would respond, not sure if they would be willing to give me lessons. This was a defining moment for my fieldwork, and I did not want to mess up. After some minutes passed, I walked up to the nearest table and awkwardly blurted out, "So, who's gonna teach me how to play chess?" I stood there, looking at the players and hoping they would say something. To my surprise, without much hesitation, they started shouting, "Alvin! Alvin!"[4]

PAY TO PLAY

The players seemed excited as they were saying Alvin's name. They assured me he was the best at chess and therefore, he needed to be the one to teach me. I stood there as they got his attention and he made his way over to where I was standing. It happened quickly and I remember feeling relieved that they were being so receptive toward me.

As Alvin made his way over, the group informed him what was going on and he agreed to give me a lesson. He said he could teach me but it would cost five dollars upfront. I did not have cash on me, but I assured him I would pay him afterward. He refused. This took me by surprise in the moment, but in hindsight, it was silly of me to assume Alvin would trust me when he did not know me. I knew I needed to get the lesson and not delay it another day. I decided to go to a convenience store down the street and withdraw money from the ATM. I told Alvin and informed him I would be right back. Upon returning with cash in hand, Alvin and I sat down to begin our first lesson.

He began to teach me the basics, such as the names of the various pieces (e.g., queen, pawn) and how they are allowed to move on the board. We had side conversations throughout this first lesson, mostly me asking him a few questions about the park and himself. Toward the end of our lesson, he inquired about a textbook I had set on the table. I explained to him that I was in graduate school and it was the textbook for one of the courses I was teaching. As our first lesson came to an end, he knew a little about me as did I him. We made plans to meet again the following week. After I left the field this first visit, I remember feeling excited and proud by how well things had gone and was looking forward to subsequent visits.

For the next six months, I took lessons from Alvin multiple times a week. The lessons were of increasingly sophisticated strategies, such as which pawns to move and when to bring the queen out. I would occasionally forget something he taught me and he would make a comment, such as, "I told you this last time." He seemed slightly annoyed when I would forget, but he continued to instruct me.

Occasionally, Alvin would interrupt our lessons to play a game for money. The first time this happened, I was unaware that gambling was a common occurrence at the park. As a researcher, I wanted to learn more about this so I would always encourage him to play a money game if the opportunity presented itself. I made sure to emphasize that it would be educational for me to watch and it could help improve my game. I wanted to justify why we should stop my lesson without raising suspicion to my true research intentions.

Additionally, during our lessons, I used our time together to learn more about him. Playing chess allowed us the opportunity to have a casual conversation. Over time, we got to know each other better and I became more comfortable asking him questions about things he told me from his past, or about observations I made in the field. Alvin and I were forming a close bond and I was learning a lot about chess, but this relationship had problems, too.

An ongoing conflict between us concerned money. Alvin charged me five dollars for each lesson, which was a fair deal, given that they usually lasted one to two hours. After a while, however, Alvin began asking me for more than a proverbial tuition fee for the lessons.[5] He would take me aside or walk with me as I left the park, then ask for some extra money for a snack or coffee.

Early on, such monetary requests were rare and so not a problem to grant. Then they became routine. The more often Alvin asked for extra money, the more annoyed I became. I felt this was impolite, but, more importantly, I did not have money to give. I explained this to him, but Alvin persisted. He would even beg, saying I was better off than him. More often than not, I gave in, thinking that to do otherwise would upset Alvin and put my research in jeopardy. At the time, I was not confident enough in my standing at the park and I feared that if I refused his request, he might stop giving me lessons and deny my access at the park. I needed to be in his good graces, not only because he was my point of contact, but he had a lot of influence at the park. He was respected by the other players and they admired him for his level of play. In many ways, he had control over my access to the park.

To overcome this issue, I began only bringing five dollars in cash to the park, figuring Alvin could not expect to receive what I did not have. Yet, he was savvy enough to know the difference between what a person has on their person versus in a bank account. He began asking that we go to a nearby convenience store to purchase him a snack or drink with my ATM card. The first few times, I agreed, grudgingly. Then I worked up enough annoyance and courage to tell him to stop.

Upon hearing my proclamation, Alvin's stated it was nice to have a little extra money. In turn, I backed down a little, saying it would be okay if an occasional occurrence, not a regular feature of our encounters. Though I was using him to make headway in my research, I felt as though I was being used as a walking, talking ATM. Perhaps this was an effect of my covert role as a researcher. However, researchers in an overt role can face the same problem. Scott, for instance, was often asked for extra cash by participants who became recruiters, some of whom were of low economic status. Indeed, most any relationship marked by economic disparity is likely to produce requests for handouts. Like gaining access, there is no one right way to respond. It took me a long time to assert myself, but once I did, Alvin limited his requests for additional money. In return, I began bringing snack foods to the park (e.g., granola bars). Compared to one-off purchases at the convenience store, it was cheaper for me to bring items I already had at home, giving me more of control over our give-and-take relationship.

ALVIN'S PIECE

Alvin had become my primary contact at the park, which relates to the other major conflict between us. When I would show up at the park, the other players assumed I was looking for Alvin, so they would point me in his direction. I grew to know other players and vice versa, but, until Alvin disappeared, the vast majority of my time was spent talking and learning from him. This was a methodological problem, potentially. Common sense tells us that one person, namely Alvin, is unlikely to perfectly embody the population of chess players. So long as I did not assume Alvin's background, motives, and behavior to be exactly like that of everyone else, I was on safe ground. However, the goal of my study was not to learn about Alvin per se; it was to learn about all of the players.[6]

This problem stemmed from Alvin acting possessive of me. He disliked me talking with other players, as evidenced by him questioning me for speaking to them and reprimanding men who spoke to me. It is hard to say why he acted that way, there are probably multiple reasons. One possibility is that Alvin felt special by "having" me. Being my teacher not only validated his status as the park's best player, but it also meant he had something the other men did not—the attention of a female. Many of the men at the park, as I would later find out, lacked an intimate relationship with a partner. In some sense, that was what I represented to Alvin—an element of intimacy he and the others were denied. This likely played into his tendency to "want me" to himself because it allowed him to stand out among the others as the one "with" the girl. It is also possible that our relationship was viewed by him as a sign of him being more "manly" than the other men who did not have the attention of a female.

Alvin expressed his possessiveness of me in ways I did not desire. Perhaps because Alvin wanted to make it clear I "belonged" to him, or maybe it was truly his way of expressing affection, he went beyond traditional social boundaries one would expect of a teacher. He would call me "baby," hug me, kiss my hand, and make flattering but unwanted comments about my physical appearance. As with the money issue, I tolerated the sexual harassment because I feared doing otherwise could limit my access to the park and players. But that tolerance may have sent the wrong signal to Alvin, perhaps worsening his untoward behavior.

Additionally, Alvin's possessiveness of me may have been exacerbated by my identity as his mentoree. Like many professors, he may have disliked the feeling that his student was not fully engaged in the day's lesson. While lecturing, other players would stand around the table to make conversation with me. Alvin's facial expression turned to angry annoyance, and he would tell the conversationalists not to bother me.

Yet, Alvin was bothered by more than academic distraction. On one occasion, I arrived at the park, and before heading over to Alvin's table, I briefly stopped and spoke with other players. Upon seeing this, Alvin aggressively said to me, "Hey, why are you talking to him?" Another time, a player came over to Alvin's and my table and said hi. Alvin looked cross at him, to which the player said, "What? Am I not allowed to say hi to her?"

Because of such incidents, the players learned that Alvin wanted me all to himself. This put me in a tough position, both practically and academically. I wanted to speak with everyone at the park, but feared Alvin would consider this as an act of disrespect. Not only was I learning chess from him, but I saw my acceptance in the park as largely dependent on his acceptance of me. This became a cyclical process: I did not develop strong relationships with anyone but Alvin, so I relied on my relationship with him, who deterred me from gaining rapport with other players.

As the months went on, Alvin's possessiveness worsened. When players tried to interact with me, Alvin's words and facial expressions revealed increasing frustration. In turn, he suggested solving this "problem" by conducting lessons at a nearby coffee shop. From his perspective, that was a reasonable idea. He did not know that my major motive for coming to the park was research. I could have told him about this, but I did not feel ready to do so. Instead, I gave other reasons why I wanted to continue playing at the park, such as not feeling bothered by the other players, enjoying being outside, and wanting to be able to observe the ongoing games in an effort to learn and improve my own techniques.

ADJUSTING MOVES

Eventually, the possessiveness issue was resolved unexpectedly. About six months into the study, Alvin suddenly stopped going to the park. About a week after his disappearance, a player told me that Alvin was out of town, with an unknown return date. Thereafter, each time I went to the park but did not see him, it seemed more likely that he was not coming back.

Despite Alvin's possessiveness, or maybe because of it, I felt lost at the park without him. I did not anticipate his disappearance and was unprepared for how to navigate this new terrain. My relationship with him was far from perfect, but I did not have much of a relationship with any other player. By trying to respect Alvin, I had put myself in a bad spot. I thought about giving up the research, but decided to keep going back to the park. Each visit, I checked to see if Alvin was back and, more importantly, got to know the other players.

After Alvin left, the other players would ask me if I wanted to challenge them to a game. Until this point, I had not fully realized that they now saw me as a player, too. In their eyes, it was odd for me to be there and not play chess. I knew why I was "really" at the park, but they did not. After spending months taking lessons, I became a common fixture of the scene. I grew to understand their culture and social norms and I obeyed the unwritten rules that guided the behavior. I was no longer seen as an outsider, but instead, a trusted member of their group. I would never truly be one of them, but they treated and accepted me as a player. Although hiding my research intentions was somewhat problematic, being seen as a player showed that I had managed to overcome my outsider status.

After some prodding, I started to compete. This felt strange to me, as, until then, I had only played with Alvin. And I worried what Alvin would think when he got back. Maybe he would be upset that I was interacting with the other men and getting closer to them, or that I was learning about chess from someone else.

No matter what his reaction might turn out to be, my research depended on playing chess with others at the park. This would be the best way to familiarize myself with them, and vice versa. Thus, over the following months I visited the park a few times a week to play and watch games. Because I was knowledgeable of chess, known at the park, and not guarded by Alvin, I was able, finally, to focus on observing—that is, listening and watching—to the things that had drawn me there in the first place. I learned about the players' identities inside and outside the park, as well as how this affected their interaction and activities, including hustles and crimes.

At this point, I began seriously considering how to tell the players about my research. This was still a secret; not so much a lie as less than the whole truth. My secretiveness increasingly weighed on my conscious. The players had become not only my subjects, but also my friends. I cared about them, and feared that not being totally open with them would hurt their feelings.

My covert identity also posed methodological challenges.[7] I had to play chess with my left hand and take notes with my right, proverbially speaking. Even worse, I could not openly take any notes. Plus, I had to be careful about not asking the wrong questions, or too many questions. And there were times that it would have been best to put the game on pause and turn my attention to a noteworthy case, but this was precluded by my undercover identity. Therefore, when I left the field, I would write what I could about certain cases, recognizing that my notes might be thin or my inference incorrect due to my limited information. Later, after I observed subsequent events or developed a greater understanding about certain cases, I would make corrections or expand on thin sections. I would also make notes in my field notes when I was unsure of something, or write general questions for myself to think about on following field visits. Doing this served as a guide when I was in the field and allowed me to gain information to better address the interpretations I was making in my field notes. But I knew I wanted to go public so I could ask in-depth and probing questions to better understand and interpret what I was observing.

Nine months into the project, I partially disclosed my research to the players. I told them about wanting to do research on them, while leaving out that I had been doing this all along. This first came up with Damien. One evening, he asked me if I could help pay for his bus fare. I obliged and then decided this was a good time to ask for a favor in return. I briefly explained that I wanted to ask him some questions for a school assignment (i.e., my dissertation), to which he said, "Yeah, whatever you need." It could be asked if this approach was ethical in the sense that I used his financial request as a springboard for my academic request, which some not might not think is ethical. I would counter, though, that the bus fare was not contingent on his participation; I would have given it to him even if he had declined.

After Damien agreed, I asked if he thought the other guys would feel the same way. Damien reassured me, "Yeah, we know you're cool. Just tell me what you need." This conversation gave me a great sense of relief. It also made me more confident to have a similar conversation with other players. In the coming weeks, I told them what I had discussed with Damien, using it as a springboard to gain their approval of the research, too. Word traveled fast among the players and I quickly became known as the park's researcher.

SACRIFICE THE EXCHANGE

Once I went public with my researcher identity, I learned that obtaining the players' cooperation would require me to "go with the flow." I had to have an open, relaxed attitude toward the planning, timing, and completion of actions. Players thought this was an appropriate mode of conduct (see Anderson, 1999), though people from another subculture may think of it as haphazard, rude, or inconsiderate. Going with the flow was not an optimal strategy for me because it delayed my progress in the doctoral program. Without the necessary data, I was unable to move forward in a timely manner, which was consequential to graduating and getting a job.

I had little choice but to abide by this code.[8] I was dependent on the players for information, but they did not need me. Thus, I had to have a loose approach toward making a research-oriented itinerary with players, and be tolerant when they did not show up as planned. In fairness to my participants, their absenteeism is not unique among research participants. Part of being an ethnographer is waiting around for persons who agreed to talk at a particular time and place.[9] This is all the more frustrating when it is unclear if they are running late, or not coming at all; in the face of such uncertainty, the question becomes should I wait or is waiting a further waste of time?

Despite not taking offense to players' broken promises, these often disappointed and frustrated me. This would result, for instance, when players did not show up for scheduled interviews. When commitments are not kept, it almost inevitably results in negative emotions. This is particularly true when the activities are important—such as, in my case, completing a dissertation. I was easily affected by the players' lack of planning because I was not raised by the code of "go with the flow,"[10] which, again, prescribes a large degree of flexibility in when events take place. I am almost always present where and when I should be. Thus, I did not understand that this behavior was a cultural norm for the players.

A positive example of going with the flow concerns the day I found out the park was unexpectedly shut down following a fatal stabbing at the park the night before. I immediately reached out to the players via text message to make sure they were ok. I quickly learned the park was closed. I was told by a park official the park could be closed for three weeks; the closure lasted seven months.

By this point in my research, my goal was not only to learn about the park, but also the broader lives of players. The closure provided an opportunity for me to follow the players around as they relocated to other areas. Additionally, the shutdown served as a catalyst for many discussions with players. Perhaps because of their frustration with the closure, the players, some of which I did not have a strong rapport with yet, opened up to me in a way I had not anticipated. They shared details about the fatal stabbing and their reactions to how it was being handled, conversations that then branched off into other topics and provided me with a better sense of who they were.

Researchers often struggle with what data to collect, to what extent, and whether they are missing something. This was true for me, but with experience, I grew more confident not only in how to take notes, but also what to make them or not make them about. When I was in the field, my main method for taking jottings—short words and phrases that are later used to develop field notes—was through the use of my cell phone. I knew it would be unobtrusive as it is common, in almost any setting, to see someone on their phone. Therefore, I was able to use my phone and type notes without appearing suspicious. This allowed me to take jottings as events occurred, or soon thereafter. I would then expand on my jottings as soon as possible and make detailed field notes.

As I spent more time at the park, the quality of my field notes improved. In the beginning, my notes were thin and lacked the necessary depth and detail. This was due in part to the "newness" of conducting field observations. When I first started, everything was new and it was a sensory overload. This made it challenging to know what to look for or what was important. As I spent more time in the field, I became more aware and attuned to my surroundings, got to know the players better, and developed an understanding of the social world of the park. Also, I gained greater access as my insider status improved, and this allowed for richer field notes.

ENDGAME

I continued to collect data for four months after the park's closure. At that point, the future of the park was unclear and I had looming graduate program deadlines. I had a sufficient amount of data, so Scott advised me to get going on writing the dissertation. For two years, I had continually learned about players as I gained rapport with them. At first total strangers, we grew to tease each other, share things on our mind, and confide in each other. I enjoyed spending time at the park, and appreciated the meaningful conversations and moments shared with them. However, the good things that came from the research raised problems, too.

As true in almost any relationship, there were times that I had little desire to visit the players. Going to a scene is easy, but it is difficult to make the most of one's time there. It is mentally fatiguing to make observations, take jottings, be an active participant in the setting, and later write up extensive field notes. There are various ways to keep going, however (see Emerson, Fretz, and Shaw, 2011; Spradley, 1980). A practical example is making short- and long-term schedules with specific tasks (e.g., taking field notes, writing them up, analyzing them, etc.) with specific deadlines (e.g., finish taking *all* field notes and subsequent tasks). Motivationally, stay focused on the importance of data for telling people's stories. With that said, sometimes the best thing to do is take a vacation from the field.

A researcher who sets out to do fieldwork should realize that it may come to dominate their life. I am but one of many ethnographers to whom this happened. Other ethnographers academically delve into a life with which they are already accustomed, be it personally or through friends and family (see Boeri, 2017; Contreras, 2013). In either case, completing ethnographic research requires sacrifice. There is always a give and take between doing one thing versus another, but this is especially true of fieldwork because the researcher needs to be on the subjects' schedule—to go with their flow. In my case, I often wound up prioritizing the players and park over class assignments, prepping courses I was teaching, and my personal life. When the project began, I could not have foreseen that the research would envelope my life.

During the course of fieldwork, the researcher is affected by the field and experiences a range of emotions as they become entangled in the lives of their subjects and invested in their well-being (Coffey, 1999). Such was true for me, as I would occasionally try to help the players with their personal affairs, offering advice or gathering information for them. I frequently thought about them when I was not at the park and I found myself worrying about them, especially during cold nights when I knew some of them slept on the street. I would text message them to find out how they were doing, but, in reality, there was little more I could do for them.

I became part of a new social circle, but, ironically, this made me feel isolated among my academic peers. Not many graduate students in the department conducted ethnography, and no one at the time conducted a field study to this extent. This uniqueness (among other issues) made it difficult for me to talk with other Ph.D. candidates about my research. I did not think they would understand my relationships with and concern for the players, in part because they were so different from my peers' experiences. Going native can make a researcher feel like a stranger in their own world (O'Reilly, 2009). No amount of talking with a colleague, mentor, or other outsider can fully attenuate such feelings. So a small piece of advice, then, for people who undertake this sort of research is to take solace in knowing we are alone together.

NOTES

1. Although this chapter is from my perspective, Scott Jacques helped write it and is therefore a coauthor. As touched upon throughout, Scott supervised my

study. What it means for someone to be a "supervisor" greatly varies from person to person or project to project. Whereas some supervisors are very hands-on and directive, Scott is exactly the opposite. For him, a dissertation is about establishing yourself as an independent scholar, so it has to be a road mostly traveled alone. He always made it clear to me and others that this is my project, not his, and thus its success or failure is my doing. I had final say on what people and phenomena to focus on, how and when to collect data in situ, write up field notes, analyze them, and so on. The guidance he did provide followed a few general principles: don't get hurt; don't violate our Institutional Review Board (IRB) agreement; otherwise, do what needs to be done to finish the project, to the best of your ability, in a timely manner. The editors of this book requested more details about Scott's role be provided. We opted to let the story be told through my eyes alone.

2. On how these factors affect sampling, see Copes et al., 2015.

3. On identity issues in conducting qualitative research, see Wesley, 2015.

4. All subject names are pseudonyms.

5. On money-based conflict experienced by other ethnographers, see Duneier, 1999; Jacobs, 1998, 2006; Liebow, 1967.

6. On how ethnographic sampling designs affect results, see Katz, 2001; Small, 2009.

7. On the problems and prospects of various data-recording techniques, see Emerson, Fretz, and Shaw, 2011; Spradley, 1979, 1980; Weiss, 1994.

8. On problems concerning the planning, timing, and cooperation of research participants, see the methodological chapter of Jacobs and Wright, 2006.

9. For more on uncertainty and recruitment, see Jacobs and Wright, 2006.

10. Going with the flow is not all bad. After all, part of the logic behind this code of conduct is that an unplanned activity may turn out to be better than what could have been scheduled. Indeed, the notion of going with the flow meshes well with that of analytic induction: using data to continually refine what is being studied and the explanation of it (Katz, 2001). Part and parcel with that process is a fieldworker's task of figuring out what to observe and record, as it is impossible to attend to everything that goes on.

REFERENCES

Anderson, E. (1999). *Code of the street: Decency, violence, and the moral life of the inner city.* New York: W. W. Norton.

———— (2011). *The cosmopolitan canopy: Race and civility in everyday life.* New York: W. W. Norton.

Bernasco, W., ed. (2010). *Offenders on offending: Learning about crime from criminals.* Cullompton: Willan.

Boeri, M. (2017). *Hurt: Chronicles of the drug-war generation.* Berkeley: University of California Press.

Boeri, M., and A.K. Lamonica (2015). Sampling designs and issues in qualitative criminology. In *The Routledge handbook of qualitative criminology*, ed. H. Copes and J.M. Miller, 125–43. New York: Routledge.

Coffey, A. (1999). *The ethnographic self: Fieldwork and the representation of identity*. London: Sage.

Contreras, R. (2013). *The stickup kids: Race, drugs, violence, and the American dream*. Berkeley: University of California Press.

Copes, H., and J.M. Miller, eds. (2015). *The Routledge handbook of qualitative criminology*. New York: Routledge.

Copes, H., et al. (2015). Interviewing offenders: The active vs. inmate debate. In *The Routledge handbook of qualitative criminology*, ed. H. Copes and J.M. Miller, 157–72. New York: Routledge.

Duneier, M. (1999). *Sidewalk*. New York: Farrar, Straus & Giroux.

Emerson, R.M., R.I. Fretz, and L.L. Shaw (2011). *Writing ethnographic fieldnotes*. 2nd ed. Chicago: University of Chicago Press.

Goffman, A. (2014). *On the run: Fugitive life in an American city*. Chicago: University of Chicago Press.

Goffman, E. (1963). *Stigma: Notes on the management of spoiled identity*. New York: Simon & Schuster.

Goode, E. (1999). Sex with informants as deviant behavior: An account and commentary. *Deviant Behavior, 20*, 301–24.

Jacobs, B.A. (1998). Researching crack dealers: Dilemmas and contradictions. In *Ethnography at the edge: Crime, deviance, and field research*, ed. Ferrell and M.S. Hamm, 160–77. Boston: Northeastern University Press.

———. (2006). The case for dangerous fieldwork. In *The Sage handbook of fieldwork*, ed. D. Hobbs and R. Wright, 157–68. Thousand Oaks, CA: Sage.

Jacobs, B.A., and R. Wright (2006). *Street justice: Retaliation in the criminal underworld*. New York: Cambridge University Press.

Katz, J. (2001). Analytic induction. In *International encyclopedia of the social and behavioral sciences*, ed. N.J. Smelser and P.B. Baltes, 480–484. Oxford: Elsevier.

Liebow, E. (1967). *Tally's corner: A study of negro streetcorner men*. Lanham, MD: Rowman & Littlefield.

Marx, G.T. (1989). *Undercover: Police surveillance in America*. Berkeley: University of California Press.

Miller, J., and W.R. Palacios, eds. (2015). *Qualitative research in criminology*. New Brunswick, NJ: Transaction.

O'Reilly, K. (2009). *Key concepts in ethnography*. Thousand Oaks, CA: Sage.

Small, M.L. (2009). How many cases do I need? On science and the logic of case selection in field-based research. *Ethnography, 10*, 5–38.

Snow, D., and L. Anderson (1993). *Down on their luck: A study of homeless street people*. Berkley: University of California Press.

Spradley, J.P. (1979). *The ethnographic interview*. New York: Harcourt Brace Jovanovich.

———. (1980). *Participant observation*. New York: Holt, Rinehart, and Winston.

Weiss, R. S. (1994). *Learning from strangers: The art and method of qualitative interview studies.* New York: Free Press.

Wesley, J. K. (2015). Negotiating identity as a qualitative researcher: The impact of studying marginalized populations in criminology. In *The Routledge handbook of qualitative criminology,* ed. H. Copes and J. M. Miller, 144–56. New York: Routledge.

THREE

Unearthing Aggressive Advocacy

CHALLENGES AND STRATEGIES IN SOCIAL
SERVICE ETHNOGRAPHY

Curtis Smith and Leon Anderson

MOST DAYS AS I BEGIN the hour-and-a-half drive to the city in which I am doing my research with homeless outreach workers, I envision in my mind's eye what I am going to see. Lately the drive has been filled with dismal images. The city is in the middle of a crackdown on the homeless and other residents in the neighborhood that houses the large homeless shelter where the outreach workers I'm studying do much of their work. The block around the shelter is being turned into what many workers, drawing on prison imagery, call "The Yard," with cement blockades and a heavy police presence. There have been sixteen hundred arrests on the block in the previous six weeks—a mix of drug dealers and homeless individuals but mostly the latter. Most arrestees are being dismissed back to the block shortly after booking (where else are they going to go?), with one more arrest now on their criminal records—and one more mark against them as outreach workers try to get them housing. The demoralization of the outreach workers has been palpable of late. How could the city move in such a counterproductive direction? Don't they appreciate the record-breaking success that social services have achieved in housing the homeless here in recent times?

But, I dismiss these dark thoughts for now. Today I am going to have a more positive experience. I'll be shadowing Roberto, a longtime champion for the homeless, whom I will be accompanying as he visits rental units and negotiates with property managers to take in homeless clients. Roberto is a light in the darkness and I'm always buoyed up by his pragmatic can-do optimism. On my drive I recall the commitment and savvy he brings to his work. It will be a good day. But when I arrive at the scheduled meeting place and time, Roberto is nowhere to be found. Really, I'm not surprised. This is often the case. He is undoubtedly dealing with a client's emergency or making an unexpected housing inspection. I'll have to catch up with him later. Having driven an hour and a half to make this meeting, it's a good thing I have a Plan B. (Curtis Smith)

OVERVIEW

In this chapter we describe Curtis's dissertation research on what we term "aggressive advocacy" by social service workers seeking to get their homeless clients into permanent housing. We are coauthoring the chapter for two reasons. First, Leon, in his role as Curtis's faculty mentor and dissertation committee chair, has played an active role in guiding this ethnographic project both methodologically and analytically. Second, the challenges Curtis has faced in this research need to be situated in the context of his being an "ABD" graduate student at the time of the research.[1] While the challenges we describe here are in many ways key generic challenges faced by most ethnographic researchers, they are often exacerbated when the researcher is in the liminal position of a Ph.D. student managing the multiple and simultaneous demands of graduate student life—precarious finances, lack of autonomous control of research, juggling teaching responsibilities—all while pursuing employment on the academic job market. In keeping with the call of this volume to present an uncensored view of ethnographic research, we want to examine how Curtis's research developed while at the same time looking at the structural constraints imposed by his graduate student status. Given that his research has proven successful, we feel confident in offering not just a critical view of graduate student ethnography but also a set of lessons learned from the field that may be of use to other ethnographers, especially those pursuing dissertation research.

After years of work as a homeless outreach worker, followed by earning a master's degree in sociology from University of Texas–El Paso, Curtis moved to Utah State University to pursue a Ph.D. and ethnographic research related to homelessness, under Leon's mentorship. Like Craig Willse, the author of *The Value of Homelessness* (2015), who embarked on a Ph.D. after several years working as a social service worker with the homeless, Curtis brought a depth of professional experience to the table as we explored options for a research project that would make valuable contributions in the field of homelessness studies.

Over the course of the last century, a strong body of ethnographic research has focused on the topic of homelessness, primarily directed toward studying the experiences of the homeless themselves, including such well-known eth-nographies as Nels Anderson's *The Hobo* (1923), Samuel Wallace's *Skid Row as a Way of Life* (1965), David Snow and Leon Anderson's *Down on Their Luck* (1993), and Philippe Bourgois and Jeffrey Schonberg's *Righteous Dopefiend* (2009), to mention but a few key studies. While notable ethno-graphic studies devoted to examining the experiences of the homeless con-tinue to be pursued, we decided that Curtis's experience as a homeless service provider offered new directions for potential research. Our decision was consistent with work by a handful of other ethnographic researchers, includ-ing Prashan Ranasinghe, who has observed, "Despite emanating from a rich ethnographic tradition and offering sophisticated, detailed, and insightful analyses . . . most inquiries [focused on homelessness] are limited because they are largely one-sided. What they fail to explore and reveal is . . . the perspective of the personnel who work in these sites, that is, the service pro-viders" (Ranasinghe, 2017, 5). While a few ethnographic studies have explored the work of social service providers for the homeless (e.g., Marvasti, 2002; Spencer, 1994; Spencer and McKinney, 1997), with the exception of Jacqueline Wiseman's (1970) *Stations of the Lost* nearly five decades ago, most have pursued a fairly circumscribed analytic agenda. The studies cited above, for instance, focus specifically on the strategies used by social workers during intake interviews with homeless clients, or, in Ranasinghe's (2017) case, the management of a homeless shelter.

As valuable as those studies are, Curtis's previous outreach work with the homeless was much more multifaceted. Over the course of six years he had worked with thirty to seventy homeless clients at a time, in two large metro-politan areas. Each of the street outreach positions he held entailed aggressive outreach, building trust by contacting homeless individuals on the streets, under bridges, in parks, and in abandoned buildings. The outreach worker role also involved daily transport of willing homeless individuals from the streets to local shelters and services in an effort to connect them with resources distributed across the service archipelago. His various daily duties included assessing the appropriateness of clients for referral, negotiating appropriate actions in pursuit of housing or other resources, and optimizing the number of successful services for homeless individuals in order that agen-cies might make the case for sustained funding. In short, Curtis's previous work in the field extended far beyond the intake-interview activities that had been the focus of most ethnographic research on social service activities with homeless clients. Consistent with the frequent ethnographic advice to "start where you are" (e.g., Lofland et al., 2005, 3), we began playing with ideas to create a research project focused on social service workers engaged with homeless populations.

A clear research focus emerged as we read Michael Lipsky's *Street-level Bureaucracy: Dilemmas of the Individuals in the Public Services*—the C. Wright Mills Award winner in 1980, republished with new commentary in 2010. Lipsky challenges the stereotypical image of street-level bureaucrats (SLBs) as rule-bound unimaginative and uncaring pencil-pushers. He argues that street-level public-service employees face the practical challenges of aligning their experiences with clients to the mandates of legislative policy and organizational guidelines, focusing primarily on the ways in which public-service workers invoke discretionary power and routinize interactions with clients in order to ration relatively scarce resources within organizational constraints.

Our sense of the potential value of Lipsky's perspective for understanding social services for the homeless was heightened when we read University of Chicago political scientist Evelyn Brodkin's claims that Lipsky's analysis represented a call for "the ethnographic turn" in the study of social services (2017, 131). As Brodkin observes, Lipsky's analysis challenges the "compliance model of street-level bureaucracy" (2012, 941). Lipsky, she argues, advocates a view that embraces the recognition of street-level bureaucrats' competency within, and especially beyond, explicit policy. Put simply, Lipsky invites empirical investigation of how ground-level social service workers adapt to ambiguous or complicated bureaucratic social service policies. Curtis entered the field with this goal in mind.

CHALLENGES FACED: UNCERTAINTY

In this section of the chapter we consider four challenges that emerged in the course of our research: (1) the difficulties we faced in navigating the Institutional Review Board (IRB) process; (2) the challenge of adapting to often chaotic research contexts; (3) the effort to gain analytic focus through grounded theory; and (4) challenges related to a decision to broaden the scope of our "data" to include autoethnographic observations from Curtis's years in the trenches as a homeless outreach worker himself. Each of these challenges illustrates the uncertainty that often comes with ethnographic research.

But before we address these issues, we want to reflect on what many out-side observers consider perhaps the most significant challenge in street eth-nography: the physical dangers posed by fieldwork with marginalized, impoverished populations with high rates of substance abuse, mental illness, and criminal records. Many ethnographers have chronicled their challenges in protecting themselves in such environments, including Sanchez-Jankowski (1991) in his research with urban gangs, Maher (1997) in her ethnography of an urban drug market, and Inciardi, Lockwood, and Pottieger (1993) in their research for *Women and Crack-Cocaine,* among others. While it is always wise to have a clear understanding of dangers posed in a fieldwork environment—as well as strategies for maintaining safety (e.g., Williams et al., 1992), our experiences have been relatively free of perceived threats to personal safety during research. Curtis's research has required that he spend time in a part of town well-known for illicit drug use, sex work, and heavy police presence. On the walk from his car to the offices of social service pro-viders, he frequently encountered illicit activities, but was never accosted in a threatening manner. Part of his success and confidence in navigating the streets probably comes from his years as an outreach worker in similar con-texts, as well as the fact that he is an adult male. Similarly, during fieldwork for *Down on Their Luck* (Snow and Anderson, 1993), while Leon witnessed several bloody altercations among homeless men, he was never physically threatened by homeless individuals, although he was at one point arrested and jailed by the police.[2] This is not to say that danger was not present in the settings in which Curtis and Leon conducted their research, but rather, that dangers from street "deviants" were for the most part easily avoided. In con-trast, police involvement in our research settings did present potential ethical dilemmas, especially the possibility of being asked to provide law enforce-ment with information (such as observed criminal behavior), and the ethical challenge of witnessing unwarranted police actions. Luckily, neither of us was asked to reveal informant activities to law enforcement. On the other hand, Leon did face the dilemma of witnessing incidents in which police officers intimidated or humiliated homeless men. In only one instance, when a homeless man was ordered out of a convenience store for no apparent rea-son, did Leon raise concerns to the police officers involved. While the ethical challenge of deciding to intervene or to blow the whistle on more serious police violence was present, we fortunately did not face such challenges. Nonetheless, we acknowledge that such potential ethical dilemmas are, as Westmarland (2001, 531) has observed, "intrinsic methodological aspects" of ethnographic research in which police presence is common. On the other hand, the challenges discussed below, starting with navigating human subjects' review, represented more significant dilemmas in our research process.

While numerous qualitative scholars have bemoaned what they view as the misalignment of IRB policies and practices with ethnographic methods (e.g., Bosk and DeVries, 2004; Katz, 2006; Librett and Perrone, 2010), the IRB challenges faced in this research were more mundane. We were confident that we could negotiate acceptable human subjects' protection with our university's IRB, but we did not anticipate the time it would take to receive that approval. After passing his comprehensive exams, Curtis promptly wrote his dissertation proposal and submitted an IRB application. We had planned an eight-month window, from May through December, free from teaching responsibilities, for conducting the bulk of the fieldwork for his project. But the IRB process proved slower and more involved than we had anticipated. The first speed bump came when we were informed that the IRB would not review his application until his committee had approved it—which we were unable to arrange until late April. The second, and more anxiety-provoking bump came in the form of an email from the IRB chairperson notifying us that IRB full committee reviews typically took six to eight weeks and that due to summer staffing issues, no reviews would be done from May through August—meaning that it was possible that Curtis's research could be delayed by six months. Luckily we were able to be approved for "expedited review," which the IRB chair took charge of reviewing in May. Still, even the expedited review dragged on, and the research window began to narrow. We were asked to develop policies for handling a variety of issues, especially informed consent with virtually all individuals with whom we would come into contact. Originally we had planned to include interviews with homeless clients as part of the research, but we were informed that approval for that would require a full IRB review—which would have meant delaying the research by six months, to a time when Curtis would have significant teaching responsibilities and was planning to be on the job market. While we jettisoned the expectation of interviewing homeless clients, we were still required to create four different, informed consent procedures to cover members of different groups, including not only the outreach workers who were the primary focus of the research, but also homeless individuals and other social service workers with whom they had even cursory contact while we were observing them. While we were able to develop these forms and procedures, it took time, both to create them and to correspond back and forth with the IRB chair.

Ultimately, two anxiety-laden months elapsed from the submission of the IRB application for expedited review to its approval. Finally it was time to head into the field.

Once fieldwork was started, the next challenge was to adapt data-collection strategies to the social world under investigation. Virtually all ethnographers find that they must build rapport with those they wish to study as well as adapt to their informants' schedules and contexts. While it was relatively easy to build rapport, especially given Curtis's experience in roles similar to those he was observing, the task of adapting to the outreach workers' schedules was more challenging for two reasons. First, the outreach workers we were most interested in, those who are aggressive advocates for their homeless clients, tend to have chaotic work schedules with frequent unplanned events, such as handling clients' spur-of-the-moment needs or responding to landlords' unexpected calls and concerns. Second, the research site itself was an hour and a half from the city in which we lived. Not surprisingly, the vignette at the start of this chapter was replayed numerous times as Curtis arrived at a meeting only to find it cancelled or postponed—often without any explanation as the research subject was dealing with an unexpected brush fire and nowhere to be found.

A third challenge emerged as research got into full swing: how to organize and make sense of the wealth of information that was being collected? While we had decided to focus on the work experiences of homeless outreach workers, that work was varied and at times chaotic. Like much ethnographic fieldwork, we began with a broad focus, but became more focused as fieldwork progressed. Starting with an interest in all homeless service providers, as the research moved forward we decided to focus in more depth on the strategies and experiences of homeless service providers who were especially aggressive in their advocacy for homeless clients within the service organizations in which they were employed. These outreach workers clearly exemplified the creative discretionary power that Lipsky (2010) articulated in *Street-Level Bureaucracy*. Unlike the stereotypical pencil-pushing bureaucrat sitting behind a desk and denying clients services because they have not completed the required form in triplicate or do not have their Social Security card, these homeless service workers go the extra mile to help their clients complete the forms, track down documents, and at times even create documents or finesse their way around needing them. Still, the challenge remained of how to document and describe their aggressive advocacy for their homeless clients.

As we discussed Curtis's data and coding strategies, we could see an overlap between how he had approached his work with the homeless during his years as an outreach worker and the activities that he felt most drawn to documenting and analyzing in his current research. It was clear that he himself had profound relevant experience. While at first we partitioned his personal experience from that of his dissertation fieldwork, over time we came to question that decision. If he was observing and interviewing other outreach workers about activities that he had years of experience with, we asked ourselves, why not take advantage of his depth of experience and incorporate what Leon has articulated as analytic autoethnography (Anderson, 2006) into the research project? But this option raised new questions, both in terms of IRB review and dissertation committee approval.

CHALLENGES ADDRESSED: MANAGING UNCERTAINTY

Looking back at the various challenges and uncertainties we faced in the course of this research, it is comforting to know that we found ways to manage them, to build a successful research project. In this section we consider the strategies that we drew upon to address these challenges. The first challenge, that of responding to IRB demands and temporal constraints, required flexibility and disciplined persistence. As roadblocks appeared in the research, it was easy to see the allure of becoming what Jack Katz (2006, 501) has referred to as an "IRB outlaw" entering the field before receiving IRB approval. But for us, that was clearly not an option. We simply had to continue responding to IRB requests for explanations and create the forms and procedures they requested. As Librett and Perrone have noted, "most applications for institutional approval of qualitative research are eventually granted" (2010, 729). Ours was too, but it took more time and effort than we wanted to put into it. The frustration was compounded by financial and career constraints that Curtis faced in completing his graduate student requirements. We were fortunate that Leon had a modest personal, as well as a longer-standing professional relationship with the IRB director. This did not mean that we were let off easy in terms of IRB protocol, but it is our sense that the responses we made to IRB questions were treated with a relatively generous spirit of trust in our judgment. This somewhat personalized aspect of the review process, however, gave us little confidence that other qualitative researchers would be able to navigate the process as easily. As Katz has noted, "the private character of IRB decision making blocks researchers from learning about the accommodations that have been worked out by some of their colleagues"—which was us in this case. Katz goes on to note that IRB "discretionary interpretations do not constrain future decision making even within a given campus administration" (2006, 500).

The second challenge, that of adapting to chaotic research contexts, was made especially difficult by virtue of the fact that the research site was over eighty miles from home. The high likelihood that any prescheduled meeting or interview would end up being canceled or delayed meant that it was imperative to have a plan B—and even a plan C—for any given day. This required an open research plan. A linear research strategy, moving step by step from one focal issue to another simply was not an option. Any given day might require abandoning the original plan and pursuing some other component of the research, say spending the day with an outreach worker completing various intake forms rather than riding along to housing inspections—or just the opposite. This necessary flexibility required piecing together analysis from episodic observations, at times leading to worries that some important events or activities might be missed. In the end we placed faith in the ethnographic assumption that if something is an important aspect of the social world under study, it is likely to show up many times over the course of fieldwork. Happily, we feel confident that that was the case, but we also decided (as discussed below) to expand this project in ways that added significantly to the data available for analysis.

The next challenge, of gaining analytic focus, is a widely acknowledge aspect of the emergent nature of ethnographic research (e.g., Emerson, Fretz, and Shaw, 2011; Lofland et al., 2005). Undoubtedly, the most common approaches to developing analysis of qualitative data draw to varying degrees on grounded theory (e.g., Charmaz, 2014; Glaser and Strauss, 1967). We too relied on grounded theory to develop key analytic focuses. However, we acknowledge that our reading of Lipsky's and Brodkin's scholarship on the discretionary activities of street-level bureaucrats had sensitized us to some critical aspects of social service practice. While we had not yet developed the term *aggressive advocacy* to describe a range of SLB discretionary practices, we were keen to record evidence of such practices when it was observed. Further, Curtis's recollections of his experience as an outreach worker were rich with additional examples. As our data on aggressive advocacy accumulated, we decided to treat that concept as an "operational construct" and to intentionally search for new examples to expand our data on this practice. This methodological strategy has been referred to by Patton as "operational construct sampling," in which "one samples for study real-world examples (i.e., operational examples) of the constructs in which one is interested" (Patton, 2015, 238–39). "Sampling on the basis of emerging concepts," as advocated by Strauss and Corbin, aims to "explore the dimensional range or varied conditions along which the properties of the concept vary" (Strauss and Corbin, 1998, 73). As we conceptualized it, aggressive advocacy entailed a range of activities engaged in by some, but not all, homeless outreach workers to aggressively use their knowledge of social service bureaucracies, funding sources, and other support programs to secure services for their clients. It involves not just following bureaucratic rules, but strategically interpreting (or some would argue, intentionally misinterpreting) the rules to make clients eligible for housing and other services, as well as other activities intended to get their homeless clients into housing and help them keep it. As we amassed and coded field data we identified several specific kinds of aggressive advocacy, such as "fitting stories" through which social service workers "fit" their homeless clients into service eligible categories, such as "literal homeless" and "mentally ill" (Smith and Anderson, 2018).

As mentioned briefly above, while we developed our analysis of aggressive advocacy, Curtis could recall many experiences from his time as a homeless outreach worker in which he or his colleagues used various aggressive discretionary tactics to help homeless clients get and maintain services. Given the depth of his personal experience, we felt we could benefit significantly if he brought his personal experiences into the project as data in their own right. If he could interview a current outreach worker about his or her experiences over the course of several years and use the responses as data for analysis, why should his own experiences be any less appropriate for study? Indeed, Curtis's years of experience offered a wealth of additional information on which to form our analysis—provided, of course, that this information was acceptable as data for this research to our university's IRB and to his dissertation committee. We succeeded in expanding the data set in this direction by virtue of a very rigid definition of autoethnography at the IRB, on the one hand, and a flexible dissertation committee on the other. When we asked the IRB if using "autoethnographic data" from Curtis's past employment would be acceptable, we dreaded the anticipated reply, but we were quickly informed that autoethnography falls within the category of oral history which is not subject to IRB review (see also Katz, 2006). While the IRB viewed autoethnography as more aligned with the humanities than with social science, Curtis's committee had no reservations to accepting his autoethnographic recountings as valid sociological data. Indeed, committee members expressed views similar to that of Jack Katz statement that, "Blurring boundaries between personal and research life does not necessarily indicate an incapacity to plan research. It is a strategically valuable way to gain firsthand data on behavior in a range of social contexts at once diverse and mundane" (2006, 500). As a result, Curtis was able to comb his own experiences for various forms and examples of aggressive advocacy to further expand his data set.

REFLECTION

As we write this chapter, Curtis is completing the writing of his dissertation and we have published one journal article already from the data—with many more, and perhaps a book, to come. Reflecting back on the experience, it is clear that the anxiety we experienced along the way was in part the typical anxiety that comes with any new research project. But that anxiety was exacerbated by the limited timeframe Curtis had for conducting the research given graduate program funding and the pressure to find academic employment. Little has been written, at least that we are aware of, examining the specific challenges associated with pursuing ethnographic research within the constraints of doctoral programs. We hope this chapter spurs further discussion of that issue.

On a different note, while we consciously developed this research project to build on Curtis's past employment experience, we could not see until late in the research just how much that past experience could contribute to this study. Curtis has found the research findings both self-clarifying and self-validating. In the process of studying other homeless outreach workers and analyzing their experiences, he has found many ways that his experiences overlap with theirs. In the process, he has been able to move beyond his previously inchoate feelings about aggressive advocacy in social service settings to a well-articulated social science understanding. One clear example of this is his analysis of the value of a discretionary "underlife" (Goffman, 1961) in a bureaucratic social service agency. In his role as an outreach worker, Curtis had been tasked with two potentially conflicting responsibilities: (1) finding homeless clients who fit specific service eligibility criteria, and (2) maintaining high-enough numbers of recorded clients for the agency to justify continuing funding. During the course of this research, other outreach worker expressed this tension as well, including one who commented, "You know, if agencies are too stringent, then they don't help many people. The kinds of services they offer suffer because not many people actually qualify for services." When viewed from this perspective, the creative underlife activities in which outreach workers play loose with their interpretations of service eligibility criteria can be seen as embracing the "spirit of the law"—that is, the "ethic of care" on which social services are ostensibly based (Ranasinghe, 2017)—and the practical need for agencies to provide service numbers that merit continuing funding and perhaps even increasing it. Far from being organizational renegades, then, aggressive advocates are valuable, and at times indispensable, institutional players.

TAKE-AWAY ADVICE

In conclusion, we want to provide a few key "lessons learned" in this research. These lessons fall into two categories. The first relates to the meso-level structural contexts in which ethnographic research is embedded. The second involves the more personal aspects of successfully navigating the ethnographic enterprise.

Social science research does not occur in a vacuum. It requires various kinds of support, from broad cultural beliefs in the value of social science to private and public support for research activities. At the meso-organizational level of individual universities, opportunities for graduate student ethnographic research are significantly influenced by university funding policies, availability of faculty mentors, and the culture and practices of IRB gatekeepers. Sociology doctoral students interested in pursuing ethnographic research often find themselves in departments with strong quantitative biases, making it difficult to put together dissertation committees that are comfortable with and responsive to the needs of qualitative research. Few things are more important for graduate student ethnographic success than finding a mentor who will actively guide the project, both methodologically and institutionally. Faculty mentors have more experience and more institutional power in negotiating a path through potential financial and bureaucratic roadblocks. In Curtis's case, for instance, it fell to Leon to find funding for two semesters that Curtis could devote to field research, as well as to grease the gears with the IRB. Beyond a supportive mentor, it is critical to have a full dissertation committee that embraces qualitative research, ideally one that is open to eclectic data-collection strategies that often emerge in the course of ethnographic fieldwork. More than one promising and creative ethnographic dissertation project has fallen apart due to the objections of methodologically inflexible committee members. In our case, less flexible committee members might well have balked at incorporating autoethnographic recollections, despite our argument that it is very similar to interviewing any other research subject. Or they could have held firm to the need to include interviews with homeless clients, thus forcing a full IRB review that would have significantly delayed the start of the research.

Success in navigating ethnographic research—especially, perhaps, with marginalized or deviant populations—is also enhanced if the university IRB is knowledgeable and receptive to the methodological contexts of qualitative research. Furthermore, just as homeless outreach workers have discretionary power to interpret and invoke Institutional rules, IRB committees have considerable discretionary power in deciding when a rule should be enforced or when a workaround is acceptable. Decisions about whether written or verbal informed-consent procedures should be required, for instance, or how much latitude is acceptable for observational fieldwork in which people who are not the primary focus of the research are also present, represent discretionary decisions. Understanding the local IRB and its policies is vital to the process of "getting to yes"—and getting into the field. When possible, we believe it is a wise move to look for opportunities to get to know your IRB staff and committee members. While to some scholars it might seem cynical to suggest that a personalized relationship with IRB members could be beneficial, we would suggest that institutional discretionary power is not infrequently influenced by such relationships and that a savvy researcher will seek to build such support. Further, when the opportunity arises for qualitative researchers to serve on institutional review boards, we should see that as an opportunity to influence local IRB practices in ways that facilitate successful navigation of the IRB process for ethnographic research.

At the personal level, successful ethnographic research requires managing uncertainty at several levels. In this chapter we have described the uncertainty we faced during IRB negotiation, when entering chaotic research settings, and in the emergent process of gaining analytic focus. A certain level of bravado seems well-advised, even necessary, especially in the early stages of an ethnographic project. Indeed, we would argue that ethnographic research entails a significant degree of what Stephen Lyng (1990) has referred to as "edgework," or voluntary risk taking. Still, anxiety based on the uncertainty at the start of an ethnographic venture should not be interpreted as a sign of a poorly developed research plan and imminent failure. Rather, it needs to be recognized as part of the research process. We need to work through it to get where we want to go!

Additionally, while the methodological and analytic contours of any given ethnographic project may be unclear at the outset, the strategies of data collection and analysis have been honed by generations of qualitative researchers and provide a valuable roadmap for the process, if not the outcomes. Nonetheless, ethnographic research is an arduous and time-consuming endeavor. Like the homeless outreach workers we call "aggressive advocates," successful ethnographers recognize the need to get out of the office and into the streets—to "get the seat of your pants dirty in real research"—as Robert Park admonished his University of Chicago students nearly one hundred years ago (McKinney, 1966, 71).

In short, ethnographic research is not for the lazy or the faint-of-heart. It requires a working knowledge of ethnographic practices, but that alone is not sufficient. Ethnographic success is built on a foundation of structural support, personal commitment, and the courage to step into the unknown. In this chapter we have endeavored to portray this process in an open uncensored light, in the hope that our description of the challenges we have faced and the strategies we have used to address them will be of use to other scholars as they pursue the ethnographic adventure.[3]

NOTES

1. All but dissertation.

2. Aware of the frequent arrest of homeless individuals, the research team, headed by David Snow, had endeavored to be prepared for such possibilities by meeting with Austin Police Department officials to make them aware that they were conducting ethnographic research. Leon carried a letter, signed by the Austin police chief, with him at all times stating that he was a researcher and should be released at the booking desk if he should end up there. When he did end up being arrested with two homeless men on an open-container violation, the arresting officers and booking-desk sergeant dismissed the letter and booked him in jail until David Snow was able to bail him out. The arrest was later expunged from Leon's record and the two homeless men he was arrested with were released after a court hearing the next morning. Stories of Leon's arrest circulated among the homeless for several days, leading several homeless men to share their stories of arrest with him as well.

3. The primary research on which this article was based (Smith) was supported by funding from the Department of Sociology, Social Work, and Anthropology at Utah State University. The secondary research discussed (Anderson) was supported

by the Hogg Foundation for Mental Health at the University of Texas. We also wish to express appreciation to the homeless outreach workers whose endeavors to help the homeless are the focus of Curtis's dissertation.

REFERENCES

Anderson, L. (2006). Analytic autoethnography. *Journal of Contemporary Ethnography, 35,* 373–95.

Anderson, N. (1923). *The Hobo: The sociology of the homeless man.* Chicago: University of Chicago Press.

Bosk, C. L., and R. G. DeVries (2004). Bureaucracies of mass deception: Institutional review boards and the ethics of ethnographic research. *The annals of the American Academy of Political and Social Science, 595,* 249–63.

Bourgois, P., and J. Schonberg (2009). *Righteous dopefiend.* Berkeley: University of California Press.

Brodkin, E. Z. (2012). Reflections on street-level bureaucracy: Past, present, and future. *Public Administration Review, 72,* 940–49.

——— (2017). *The ethnographic turn in political science: Reflections of the state of the art. PS: Political Science and Politics, 50,* 131–34.

Charmaz, K. (2014). *Constructing grounded theory.* Thousand Oaks, CA: Sage.

Emerson, R., R. Fretz, and L. Shaw (2011). *Writing ethnographic fieldnotes.* Chicago: University of Chicago Press.

Glaser, B. G., and A. L. Strauss (1967). *Discovery of grounded theory: Strategies for qualitative research.* New York: Routledge.

Goffman, E. (1961). Asylums: Essays on the social situation of mental patients and other inmates. New York: Random House.

Inciardi, J. A., D. Lockwood, and A. E. Pottieger (1993). *Women and crack-cocaine.* New York: Macmillan.

Katz, J. (2006). Ethical escape routes for underground ethnographers. *American Ethnologists, 33,* 499–506.

Librett, M., and D. Perrone (2010). Apples and oranges: Ethnography and the IRB. *Qualitative Research, 10,* 729–47.

Lipsky, M. (2010). *Street-level bureaucracy: Dilemmas of the individual in public service.* Expanded ed. New York: Russell Sage Foundation.

Lofland, J., et al. (2005). *Analyzing social settings: A guide to qualitative observation and analysis.* 4th ed. Belmont, CA: Thomson/Wadsworth.

Lyng, S. (1990). Edgework: A social psychological analysis of voluntary risk taking. *American Journal of Sociology, 95,* 851–86.

Maher, L. (1997). *Sexed work: Gender, race, and resistance in a Brooklyn drug market.* Oxford: Clarendon.

Marvasti, A. B. (2002). Constructing the service-worthy homeless through narrative editing. *Journal of Contemporary Ethnography, 31,* 615–51.

McKinney, J. (1966). *Constructive typology and social theory*. New York: Appleton-Century Crofts.

Patton, M. Q. (2015). *Qualitative research and evaluation methods: Integrating theory and practice*. 4th ed. Thousand Oaks, CA: Sage.

Ranasinghe, P. (2017). *Helter-shelter: Security, legality, and an ethic of care in an emergency shelter*. Toronto: University of Toronto Press.

Sanchez-Jankowski, M. (1991). *Islands in the street: Gangs in American urban society*. Berkeley: University of California Press.

Smith, C., and L. Anderson (2018). Fitting stories: Outreach worker strategies for housing homeless clients. *Journal of Contemporary Ethnography, 47,* 535–50.

Snow, D. A., and L. Anderson (1993). *Down on their luck: A study of homeless street people*. Berkeley: University of California Press.

Spencer, J. W. (1994). Homeless in River City: Client work in human service encounters. *Perspectives in Social Problems, 6,* 29–46.

Spencer, J. W., and J. L. McKinney (1997). "We don't pay for bus tickets, but we can help you find work": The micropolitics of trouble in human service encounters. *Sociological Quarterly, 38,* 185–203.

Strauss, A., and J. Corbin (1998). *Basics of qualitative research: Techniques and procedures for developing grounded theory*. Thousand Oaks, CA: Sage.

Wallace, S. (1965). *Skid Row as a way of life*. New York: Harper & Row.

Westmarland, L. (2001). Blowing the whistle on police violence. *British Journal of Criminology, 41,* 523–35.

Williams, T., et al. (1992). Personal safety in dangerous places. *Journal of Contemporary Ethnography, 21,* 343–74.

Willse, C. (2015). *The value of homelessness: Managing surplus life in the United States*. Minneapolis: University of Minnesota Press.

Wiseman, J. (1970). *Stations of the lost: The treatment of Skid Row alcoholics*. Chicago: University of Chicago Press.

FOUR

Going into the Gray

CONDUCTING FIELDWORK ON CORPORATE MISCONDUCT

Eugene Soltes

FOR NEARLY EIGHT YEARS, FROM 2009 to 2016, I sought to better understand the decision-making processes and business cultures that surround and contribute to executives' engaging in corporate misconduct. This work culminated in my book *Why They Do It: Inside the Mind of the White-Collar Criminal* (Soltes, 2016). Beyond a few brief observations, the text does not describe the obstacles I encountered during the project. The rough-and-tumble, learning-by-doing process that characterized much of the fieldwork is largely unspoken.

As a business school professor studying once-prominent executives who had fallen into disrepute, I faced some rather unique challenges. In this chapter, I reflect on my fieldwork and some of the most significant obstacles I encountered exploring business misconduct.

A BUSINESS SCHOOL PROFESSOR HEADS TO PRISON

Scientific research typically begins with a hypothesis to examine or a specific question to investigate. By contrast, my work on corporate misconduct grew quite unexpectedly, out of personal curiosity and happenstance, while I was still a graduate student. Late one evening, while running some regression models on my computer, I flipped through the television channels as I awaited the computer's output. I came across a show, *Lockup,* where the producers spoke with offenders convicted of murder, assault, rape, and other violent offenses. In describing their crimes, the men discussed gangs, drugs, and troubled upbringings. As I watched the show, I thought about a different group of offenders—senior corporate executives—who had faced none of these hardships, but whose actions also led them to prison. As a business school student, the failings of such respected executives struck me as particularly disconcerting because similar figures are often upheld in M.B.A. pedagogy—implicitly and explicitly—as exemplars of good leadership.

While watching the show that evening, I wrote down a list of questions that I imagined asking some prominent former executives if I were to have a discussion similar to those depicted on the show. My questions were those of an engaged observer who had read their cases of corporate misconduct in the pages of the *Wall Street Journal,* rather than those of an academic researcher. I discovered that the addresses of incarcerated individuals were readily accessible online; the following day, I sent these questions to a number of executives who were serving lengthy prison sentences. I went back to my empirical research and effectively forgot about the letters.

To my surprise, nearly two months later I started receiving responses. Several executives responded in detail to my questions, while others offered to speak more in person if I visited them. I found their responses about how they managed pressure intriguing and some of their observations insightful. I noted how a number of the points they made contrasted with perceptions of white-collar crime often held in the media and academic research. Still, I regarded writing the letters as a personal endeavor and did not see them as part of my scholarly work.

When I joined the faculty of Harvard Business School, I mentioned these letters to several of my colleagues, who thought the executives' responses could spur an interesting discussion among students around leadership and integrity. The most thoughtful letter I received was from Stephen Richards, the former head of sales for Computer Associates, who reflected extensively on some of the challenges he faced. "Understand that unfortunately the world is not black and white," Richards noted in his letter to me. "[A] senior manager spends most their life in the gray regardless of their responsibility and that can be a dangerous and hard place to be" (Soltes 2009, 13). With encouragement from my colleagues, I created a case study by providing students a copy of Richards's letter along with some additional background material about his career and firm (see fig. 4.1). My colleagues and I discussed Richards's case in the final session of our financial reporting course for first-year M.B.A. students.

To my relief—and delight—the case was positively received by students and colleagues. A number of my colleagues asked me what I planned to do next with this material. As I didn't consider these letters a part of my

STEPHEN RICHARDS
71320-053 A1D
PO BOX 7001
TAFT CA 93268

BAKERSFIELD CA 933
MOJAVE CA
15 FEB 2008 PM 1 T

MR EUGENE SOLTES
UNIVERSITY OF CHICAGO - GSB
PhD OFFICE
5807 SOUTH WOODLAWN AVE
CHICAGO IL   60637

60637+1610

FIGURE 4.1. A letter from a prison case study. Courtesy of Harvard Business Publishing.

scholarly work, I did not have a particularly articulate response. As someone focused on quantitative hypothesis-driven research, I saw a litany of conceptual problems with using the qualitative assessments made by censured executives. I thought that these letters were hardly the seeds of a rigorous scholarly investigation.

In spite of my hesitation, I replied to several executives who had responded to my initial questionnaire, asking if they would be willing to continue a dialogue. I suspect that these initial interactions were motivated as much by my fear of disappointing my new colleagues, who were curious to see what could be learned from such interactions, as by my own curiosity. Yet, in the months that followed, my interest deepened as I observed the considerable disconnect between the intellectual brilliance of these former executives on the one hand, and the short-sightedness of their decisions on the other. Over time, I appreciated that despite the significant limitations of relying on commentary from white-collar criminals, there was still much to be gained by speaking extensively with these former executives.

I describe at length these details of how this project began because I believe that this unconventional start led to much of my ultimate success in gaining access to former executives at the heart of the project. Many of the executives I contacted had considerable pride and were initially hesitant to speak about their career in light of the often-sensationalized media coverage surrounding their cases. I suspect that many would have disengaged had I approached each simply as another research subject in a study.

In fact, since I did not feel that I was in the process of testing a particular theory, my investigation could best be described as "hypothesis building." In some ways, this felt even more authentic than my experience with quantitative work. Although few empirically focused scholars will admit it openly, much of this work is characterized by the desire to find evidence that supports a particular hypothesis. Nonresults are generally not publishable in leading journals, so we endeavor to demonstrate effects that we suspect are likely to be supported with data. Yet, such an approach immediately narrows the investigative process, since the researcher already has some understanding and expectation in advance of what he or she hopes to find. The desire to be curious and open to exploration is subjugated by a desire to provide evidence supporting a particular theory.

In most instances, my initial contacts with the executives began with mailing them a brief physical letter, in which I described my interest in better understanding both the successes and the challenges they encountered in their careers. In the cases where I received no response, I wrote additional letters, each slightly varied in presentation, generally a month after the previous letter was sent. Several executives later noted that my persistence encouraged them to respond.

Although I initially anticipated primarily speaking to incarcerated executives by meeting them in prison, logistical challenges made it infeasible to carry on extended dialogues over months and years in these settings. The dispersed location of correctional facilities across the country made visiting people on a regular basis impractical.

Gaining visitor's access to prisons was further complicated by the fact that wardens did not view me as a "researcher." In particular, I sought to speak with specific individuals whom I would identify by name. This differed from typical "prison research" that both anonymized subjects and drew them from randomized pools. In the view of correctional facilities, the objective of my work—a series of case studies on specific offenders—was ostensibly media-related. While the Institutional Review Board (IRB) does not similarly classify academic work as "journalism" or "research," viewed as individual case studies, my interviews with former executives also fell outside the scope of IRB. In this regard, the prison wardens' perspective on my work was formally consistent with the IRB.

Given these impediments to frequently visiting incarcerated executives, I relied heavily on telephone calls and email (via CorrLinks, the prison email system). Phone calls were set up at regular times, generally in the evening, and executives would call me collect. Especially for detailed and technical information that was difficult to convey orally, email turned out to be a particularly useful means of communication.

WANTED
U.S. POSTAL INSPECTION SERVICE

$100,000 reward for information leading to the arrest and conviction of Tomo Razmilovic

TOMO RAZMILOVIC

Violations:	Conspiracy to commit securities fraud, 18 USC 371. Thirteen counts of securities fraud, 15 USC 78j(b), 78m(a) and 78ff.
Case No.:	1144-1366960-FC(1)
NCIC No.:	W306000777
FBI No.:	none
Warrant No.:	Issued on May 28, 2004, by U.S. District, Eastern District of New York, Brooklyn, NY
Aliases:	none
DOB:	May 31, 1942, Split, Croatia
Description:	5' 11", 205 lbs., gray hair, blue eyes
Occupation:	Corporate executive
Misc. Info.:	Photograph taken September 1994

Tomo Razmilovic is the former CEO of Symbol Technologies, Inc., a public company. He is accused, with others, of carrying out a securities-related accounting fraud scheme wherein the investing public lost more than $200 million. He is now believed to be in Sweden.

TAKE NO ACTION TO APPREHEND THIS PERSON YOURSELF

FIGURE 4.2. Wanted poster for Tomo Razmilovic. Source: U.S. Postal Inspection Service.

Despite my best efforts to create a reliable communication channel with these former executives, I regularly encountered unexpected restrictions. For example, some prisons limited prisoners' phone and email time, while "events" (e.g., disturbances and violations) at others led to temporary cessations of phone and email communications. My meeting with the former Chief Executive Office (CEO) of Symbol Technologies, Tomo Razmilovic, involved the most complex arrangement. Mr. Razmilovic, among several executives from Symbol with whom I spoke, had been charged in a case of revenue recognition fraud. But unlike his colleagues, Mr. Razmilovic had fled the United States once charges against him were filed. By doing so, he became a wanted fugitive with a $100,000 reward for his apprehension (see fig. 4.2). I spoke with Mr. Razmilovic's attorney, who put me in touch with his client, then residing in Sweden. After consulting with an attorney about the risks of meeting a fugitive abroad, I met Mr. Razmilovic in Stockholm at a restaurant where we spent several hours speaking about his experiences. As he had effectively been in hiding and had not spoken publicly about his case, it was a unique opportunity to understand an executive's motivation, not only to commit fraud, but to flee charges as well. By being flexible in my approach to contacting executives, I was able to gather a diverse set of perspectives and a unique dataset from sources that would normally be viewed as inaccessible.

When I made contact with an executive, my priority was to figure out how to establish a rapport that would eventually facilitate a sometimes uncomfortable discussion about their career failures. With each, I would try to establish comfortable territory by finding a reference—perhaps a case study on their former firm—that could stimulate a neutral or even uplifting conversation about their former careers. Many deeply missed their professional lives, and our discussions often began as a kind of exchange between two people with a shared interest in business and financial markets. I also found executives "testing" me to see if I had a sufficient understanding of their firms and industries. It was clear to me in some instances, though it remained unsaid, that they would not continue our interaction until I demonstrated to them a fairly sophisticated knowledge of the economics and regulatory environment surrounding their firms. Knowing this, I would often spend significant amounts of time studying prior to each meeting.

In meeting nonincarcerated executives, I often sought to plan interactions over lunch or dinner, since meals facilitated opportunities to pause amid wide-ranging and challenging conversations. To make the interaction feel more like a casual dialogue than a research interview, I would often discreetly place a recorder on the table (with the executives' permission) to avoid note-taking during the meal. While this led to considerable transcription time after meeting, I believe the quality of the dialogue was much improved by making it more conversational.

After many interactions spread over weeks, or even months, focusing on an executive's successes, we would arrive at a natural point to discuss the challenges they faced. I did not rush to this point, but rather sought to indulge the executives' tendency to lead the conversation and offered as much time as needed. Ultimately, I hoped to develop a relationship where I could comfortably challenge the executives when I did not understand what they were saying, or if I believed their testimony was inconsistent with other information I had.

While a small number of former executives desired to focus exclusively on their professional careers, aspects of their personal lives often emerged during the dialogues. Their legal travails had deeply impacted and disrupted their personal lives, and for many this was the most consequential impact of the legal proceedings against them. While I initially focused exclusively on "them" during my fieldwork, over time I learned that sharing my own experiences—whether as a faculty member, as a husband, or as a father—enhanced relationships and led to more rapid and fruitful conversations. This realization emerged quite unexpectedly. My wife and I got married during the project, and we planned to honeymoon in a remote part of Africa with limited access to phone or email. Since I endeavored to be reliable and available to the executives amid our ongoing conversations, I explained to each why I would be unavailable. To my surprise, this spurred a number of executives to offer me their reflections on family and marriage, which enhanced my understanding of how they viewed their own relationships and the people around them.

One concern is whether I became too close to these former executives during the course of my project in the interest of getting them to open up. It was clear that numerous executives developed a personal connection to me. For example, one former executive sent my wife and me a long congratulatory note after we had our first child and, with some irony, offered advice on how to be a good father. As an even more poignant example, immediately after hearing news over the radio that his son had passed away, Bernard Madoff—who engaged in a Ponzi scheme and is serving a 150-year prison sentence—called to ask if I could read him his son's obituary. In these moments, I understood how deeply I had forged personal connections with these individuals.

At times, in these moments, I felt uncomfortable. Still, I saw the development of more personal relationships as important—even necessary—to earning these executives' trust and encouraging them to confide in me. I believe that had I strictly probed details tied directly to their professional lives, the project would have been far more superficial. In fact, I believe that my personal interactions with executives were among the most fruitful of the project (for instance, I describe Mr. Madoff's reaction to hearing his son's obituary read to him in chapter 14 in Soltes, 2016). At the same time, I realized that my extensive efforts to build relationships also risked potentially deemphasizing the genuine devastation they had inflicted on others. In the end, I sought to remain self-aware of these potential biases as a way to confront them, and left readers to be the ultimate adjudicators of whether the benefits of my approach exceeded the costs.

Many of the executives were represented by prominent attorneys, some of whom advised their clients to not speak about their case or experiences with anyone, including me. In several instances where the executives appeared to have ignored this counsel, I later received calls from their attorneys seeking special accommodations or requests to omit information. In one instance, an executive presented information to me that was part of an ongoing proceeding, and his lawyer requested that I destroy my record of the encounter and omit references to his client. Recognizing the potential consequence to the executive, who had entrusted me with his confidence, I obliged the attorney's request. In other instances, either an attorney or former executive would contact me after a conversation, to note that a piece of information they provided could have potential legal repercussions (e.g., a family member's salary). I evaluated each request and found that it was usually possible to accommodate such requests without compromising my work. It was at these times that I understood the potential repercussions of my work on the individuals involved, and recognized the need to balance my desire to convey a deep understanding of these men with an equal desire to not imperil their futures.

I decided at the start of this project that I would keep my conversations with executives private and my notes confidential. Unless I viewed a piece of information as portending some immediate harm or revealing an ongoing threat, I would keep sensitive and potentially detrimental information about these executives in confidence. From my perspective, since the executives were willing to voluntarily contribute to my work, I had a reciprocal duty to not imperil their well-being. At the same time, maintaining this position was occasionally uncomfortable. In one instance, a CEO casually joked about the need to practice expressing remorse with his $1,000-per-hour attorney, to make his case appear genuine for an upcoming parole hearing. Former executives would also occasionally say things that directly contradicted their legal testimony. Surprisingly, many even acknowledged this and characterized their prior testimony as an "oversimplification" to appease prosecutors who were seeking their cooperation. Though legally problematic, I often took these candid and unguarded remarks as indications that the executives were speaking frankly and with a degree of authenticity.

A number of executives, concerned about how they would be depicted by me, wanted to play a role in how they would be described. In business school cases, protagonists routinely have the opportunity to sign off on cases prior to their publication, giving them considerable power over the material. If executives do not like the depiction of themselves or their firm, they can often effectively kill the case so that it is not publicly released. From their prior experiences, some executives understood this aspect of the case-development process and sought similar sign-off conditions from me. While I modeled my approach to interacting with these former executives as a series of case studies, I did not consider it appropriate to cede control of my writing and interpretation to them, believing that this could compromise my integrity as a scholar. Nonetheless, since I challenged their assertions during our conversations, I felt it was fair that they would have the same opportunity with my writing. Thus, if asked, I offered to show the executives my writing about their cases prior to publication, giving them the opportunity to provide feedback. I was emphatic that I would have final control of the writing and would include or disregard any feedback they provided at my discretion. While it was a compromise, I felt comfortable that it would not undermine my final product, and, pragmatically, it was the only way to secure the participation of some prominent executives. To my surprise, the executives who reviewed their sections tended to make few, if any, suggestions, most of which were primarily technical in nature, such as the number of years earlier that an executive met his wife, a request to omit the first names of children after whom they named a financial structure, or the leadership awards they received. In several instances, they even sought to expand on comments that I feared would make them uncomfortable.

Academic researchers are often guided by strict routines and seek consistency in data collection. While these are valuable ideals from a research design perspective, when dealing with prominent individuals who often have teams of attorneys available for routine inquiries, sometimes research requires a more flexible approach. Beyond treating each executive respectfully and professionally, I spent considerable time understanding the details of their careers, firms, and cases (as discussed more in the subsequent section). I also sought to empathize with the challenges they faced: the disruption of family life, the tribulations of prison, and the stigmas they faced reintegrating into society after prison. I believe it was my willingness to adapt my process to each executive's personality and needs that secured the participation of so many in this project.

AN UNCONVENTIONAL ETHNOGRAPHY

Early in my project, I understood that there were several difficult conceptual challenges associated with studying corporate misconduct. Most crucially,

I recognized that I had been absent from the events I sought to understand, and would only learn about and speak to executives after they had engaged in misconduct. Unlike traditional ethnographic efforts, I could not observe these executives in their "native" work environments, making decisions as events unfolded. Instead, I would need to reconstruct their decision-making process and the cultural contexts after the fact. Furthermore, I also faced the problem that by focusing on individuals who were convicted of misconduct, I would miss the perspectives of executives who engage in misconduct but are never caught. I was acutely aware of these complexities and sought to adapt my process in several ways to mitigate their impact.[1]

Ethnography typically entails deep immersion and careful observation of the actions, communications, and unstated cultural artifacts of a group of individuals. Most often, ethnographers physically plant themselves inside the environments and in the midst of the activities that they hope to study. Yet, this is untenable for the study of white-collar misconduct, where among other challenges, the field site cannot be identified *ex ante*. To make this point clear, suppose that a researcher could identify a set of individuals prior to their engagement in criminal activity, and position himself or herself around those people. Even then it would still be challenging to document the crime, since most offenses occur over weeks or months, or even years, with the crime's "artifacts" dispersed over various modes of communication, including in-person conversations, phone calls, and email. One would have to adopt an omniscient view of all interactions to capture fleeting glimpses of actual malfeasance with certainty. Ultimately, studying corporate misconduct requires a different kind of ethnographic process where culture cannot be directly observed, but must rather be reconstructed.

Law enforcement and regulators often engage in the kind of observation unavailable to ethnographers. In the course of investigating allegedly illicit activity, investigators often acquire and later release copious contemporaneous records. These records permit a kind of ethnographic reconstruction of the interactions, dialogue, and actions surrounding crimes as they occurred. As an example of one such artifact, consider this email sent by the chief accounting officer at Beazer Homes (a construction company) to several colleagues (see fig. 4.3).

The language in the message directed colleagues to allegedly manage earnings as they approached the end of the quarter. In other cases, text messages and wire-tapped phone recordings provide further means to observe communication at the time of the misconduct. In some rare instances, there is

From: Mike Rand
To: Brendan O'Neill
Sent: Friday, June 30, 2000

I'm relying on each division to hit their revised forecast. It's dangerous to many involved- namely you and me if we strive towards something else. If you have more than 100k extra, hide it.

FIGURE 4.3. Email by the chief accounting officer at Beazer Homes.

FIGURE 4.4. Scott London photograph used as evidence in insider-trading case. Source: Federal Bureau of Investigation.

even photographic evidence. For example, Scott London, a former Klynveld Peat Marwick Goerdeler (KPMG) partner,[2] was photographed taking a payment from a friend after conveying confidential information about one of his clients (see fig. 4.4).

While contemporaneous documentary evidence can certainly be of value to researchers, there are several obstacles associated with using this type of evidence. In some instances, researchers will struggle to comb through the information due to the sheer volume. For example, in the database of Enron email communications, there were 620,000 messages. To digest such enormous amounts of material, I relied on selected groups of messages chosen by others who had large teams to support the careful analysis of each message (e.g., prosecutors, defense attorneys, bankruptcy examiners). This reduced the number of messages to read to hundreds, from hundreds of thousands. Yet, each of these parties chooses material to represent and support their particular position, thereby introducing some bias into the subset that I accessed. Prosecutors, for instance, select records to show the potential guilt of individuals. Bankruptcy examiners seek to cast blame to maximize recovery. And defense attorneys select records to mitigate responsibility or cast doubt on intent. An ethnographer mining this archive of evidence needs to consider the biases that underlie the initial selection of evidence in these legal processes. Synthesizing different sources of evidence, I tried to reconstruct the cultural context surrounding a crime, in order to better understand the meaning of communications.[3]

Oral and written communications offer a glimpse inside organizations and into executives' decision-making processes, though the picture is often incomplete. To better interpret the meanings contained in these communication records, I needed to reconstruct some of the corporate culture in which the messages originated. Sometimes this is because the record's language is ambiguous or incoherent outside of the particular discourse from which it came. For example, an apparently jestful comment in communications may carry a greater or an entirely different double meaning. In another example, bankers concerned that their emails were coming under scrutiny began using acronyms like "LDL" for "let's discuss live" to avoid placing anything that could be perceived as incriminating directly in email. This example underscores the need for the researcher to decode jargon and cryptic language, and further to toggle between different media (e.g., written and oral records), in order to reconstruct communications in their fullness. To achieve this, in some cases I needed to interview individuals at affected or related companies who were not involved in criminal activity. My goal in doing so was to construct a picture of the cultural context and broader discourse in which incriminating communication records were embedded. Understanding the meaning of a communication often requires understanding the perspective of the individuals who created the messages.

Another challenge in the ethnographic study of white-collar criminals is verifying statements made by individuals known for engaging in deception. Could I trust such individuals to be truthful in their conversations with me, even in their self-assessments? Even if they sought to be honest, researchers have also documented the human tendency to misremember events.[4]

Given my awareness of these limitations, I approached these conversations with a healthy degree of skepticism. I viewed the executives' descriptions as merely one piece of a larger puzzle. While the piece could be entirely accurate, it could also be biased or incomplete. I sought to develop a rapport where I could challenge the former executives to provide additional verification of evidence if they offered details that seemed to differ from other documentary evidence I had access to. As an example, a former partner who previously worked at a well-respected consulting firm noted that consultants were not prevented from engaging in assignments outside the firm—a point that the consulting firm had publicly denied. As the firm's policy seemed sensible, I expressed doubt to him about the veracity of his claim. In response, the former partner provided me with a copy of his confidential employment contract that stated the firm's policies. To my surprise, the former partner who faced a lengthy prison term, rather than his well-respected organization, had more accurately described the specific firm's policy.

The availability of copious legal records reduced the need for—and often the value of—dialogue with former executives about the details of their own cases. In many instances, the primary value of speaking with executives about their cases was to see how they reacted when I presented information that was already documented. Did they choose to overlook, sidestep, or talk around the most damning pieces of evidence? Did they seek to rationalize actions or attribute blame to others? In the context of our conversations, even a lie, dissimulation, or distortion of the truth could be revelatory as I constructed a picture of their lives and personalities.

A considerably more valuable aspect of interacting with former executives was asking them more introspective questions about their feelings surrounding their work and actions. How did they view their relationships with their colleagues and clients? How did they view their own actions and the impact of those actions on others? Since I was inviting their subjective assessments, they were not bound by the same limitations as when they were sharing the details of their own cases.

Once I saw that executives would respond differently and provide more nuanced perspective when not talking about themselves, I increasingly spent time speaking with them about case studies, books, and articles in the media. I sent copies of Max Bazerman and Ann Tenbrunsel's *Blind Spots* (2012) and Francesca Gino's *Sidetracked* (2013)—two books that carefully investigate personal biases and tendencies to engage in and overlook dishonest behavior—to several of the former executives. Although the books highlight the broader human tendencies associated with unethical behaviors, many reacted defensively to the evidence and sought to describe how they were "better" than others. I found that our conversations around news headlines offered insights into how they viewed and empathized with the predicaments of others. I heard some express sorrow when a natural disaster occurred, for instance, while others derided such victims for not taking better precautions. I heard some express glee at the failures of others, while some seemed to appreciate with humility the similarity of those failures to their own. I found these more casual and less structured discussions to be among the most illuminating in the project.

In contrast to the politically correct and neutral statements many offered as executives under public scrutiny, in our private discussions they offered unvarnished and often blunt descriptions of their own actions. For instance, many executives described how they did not feel that their conduct was harmful. One said, "It didn't damage anybody . . . it was, in my mind, a very small thing dealing with small dollars." Another stated, "You can't make the argument that the public was harmed by anything I did. Give me a theoretical victim . . . there were no victims." These comments tended to be made as asides, signaling their views of their own cases, in the context of discussing others.

The value for me in speaking with executives was not to debate or reaffirm the record as described in the legal cases. Rather, the objective of speaking with former executives was to learn about their personalities and the cultures that they often created around themselves. It was this time-consuming effort that made this project more ethnographic than archival in nature. My goal was not simply to renarrate prior events, but instead to understand how people in such positions think and view the world around them. In this way, I sought to capture how these former executives respond to the world and events around them today as much as I sought to understand how they responded to different predicaments in the past.

Another major conceptual issue I faced was how to select executives to participate in the project. The experience of executives who are caught by regulators and prosecuted may differ in key ways from the experience of executives who engage in misconduct but elude detection. By focusing only on those executives who are prosecuted, I could be limiting my inferences to executives who engage in misconduct and are caught.

Conceptually, this problem is especially difficult, and one I often regarded as a catch-22. To some, such as those in the legal community, only executives convicted of crimes are actually white-collar criminals. Put simply, actions that are not successfully prosecuted are not crimes. However, as long noted by criminologists and sociologists, different circumstances—regulatory capture, limitations in regulatory resources, and failures by regulators to successfully prosecute—often lead to "criminal" actions not being prosecuted.[5] Nonetheless, opening the definition of white-collar crime up to include any action that someone could view as deviant has the potential to extend white-collar crime into a Pandora's box and catch-all for virtually any business activity. Should, for example, Michael Dell, the computer systems firm founder who settled without admitting or denying fraud charges in 2011, be viewed as a white-collar criminal? What about an individual like Anthony Chiasson, whose conviction of insider trading was later overturned by an appeals court because of a different interpretation of illicit insider trading? Would a single remark in email, made perhaps sarcastically, be sufficient to make an individual a white-collar criminal? The scope of what constitutes white-collar crime, if one moves away from the legal standard of guilt, could encompass a significant portion of regular business activity, and would require strong normative positions on what should or should not be considered a violation.

I sought to address this challenge pragmatically by acknowledging that some noncriminal cases still represented illicit conduct. Specifically, I expanded my working definition of "white-collar crime" to include some regulatory violations in addition to the wide range of criminal violations. Thus, I included a range of deviant conduct captured in civil cases, administrative proceedings, internal compliance proceedings, and certain criminal cases that were later overturned on technical grounds. I felt that this appropriately expanded the range of issues I could explore without injecting significant normative judgment or forcing me to adjudicate which actions ought to have been violations, but were never publicly judged as such. However, the difficulty in trying to appropriately expand the focus of my inquiry beyond those criminal judgments that were upheld was underscored to me when one of the former executives I spoke with called me after my book was released to express his frustration with the book's subtitle: *Inside the Mind of the White-Collar Criminal*. This individual's conviction had been overturned, and thus he felt that discussing anything related to his case in my book, alongside people whose actions were still felonies, unfairly characterized the judgment in his particular case. In fact, his main point of dispute was not anything in regard to the discussion of his case or my characterization of his actions, but simply his case being included in a book with "white-collar criminal" in the title, since he noted—correctly, from a legal standpoint—that he was no longer one.

Despite my efforts to broaden the scope of my study to executives who engage in regulatory violations rather than only those criminally convicted, executives who commit the "perfect crime"—those who are neither detected nor charged—remained outside my sample. I believed that this was an

From: XXXXXXXX
Sent: Thursday, June 29, 2017 10:23 AM
To: Soltes, Eugene
Subject: Need to speak with you if possible today.

Something in my office today took me back to your case study on Computer Associates. I'm in London but if you can spare two minutes I'd appreciate it immensely. Need to decide what I'm going to do before this goes too far down a road.

FIGURE 4.5. Email from a former participant of an executive education program.

inevitable limitation, and resolved that I would not be able to study those who engage in undetected violations. Yet, I realized later that I actually was surrounded by and already informally collecting data related to such actions.

One critical difference between a business school professor who studies corporate misconduct and an anthropologist or sociologist who studies a "foreign" community is that I permanently live in the same community that I study. That is, I am surrounded by both the culture and the decision-making processes that I investigate. Participants in my executive education programs as well as former students often contacted me to discuss challenges they were facing.

As an example, figure 4.5 shows an email sent to me by a former participant in one of my executive education programs, who was concerned about some dealings within his firm.

As the time the email was written, the individual was the chief executive of a firm in the midst of capital fundraising, and was about to close the quarter. He became aware of a potentially fraudulent contract that boosted earnings, but reminded him of a case study (on Computer Associates) that I had taught in class several years prior, in which executives were ultimately sentenced to lengthy prison terms for a similar fraud. He was struggling to decide how to act: should he proceed with a fraudulent contract (but one that was likely to be successfully resolved a few weeks later), or should he address the issue directly with the board, thereby potentially setting in motion a tumultuous series of events for the firm?

Examples like this are regularly brought to my attention. Through them, I observe how people wrestle with dilemmas involving both personal and professional ramifications. While at first I saw this as part of my teaching and mentoring, over time I incorporated insights from these conversations anonymously into my own study of how misconduct occurs. Through these interactions, I have been able to observe the decision-making process directly and in real time, not only in retrospect and through the prism of a regulatory or investigatory intervention.

In this way, my study of corporate misconduct is not just about executives I formally approached or ones who have been sanctioned. Rather, much of my understanding of deviant business conduct stems from my frequent—though more informal and unplanned—interactions with people in the business community. From an ethnographic standpoint, when exploring "hidden" processes that do not readily lend themselves to external observation, it is immensely valuable to be viewed as a fellow community member in whom other members can confide.

THE EMPIRICIST AND THE ETHNOGRAPHER

While research on corporate misconduct spans a variety of academic fields, the majority of the work is either large sample-based, with hundreds or thousands of observations, or firm-based, meaning the unit of analysis is firms, not individuals.[6] While these studies have substantially advanced our understanding of misconduct in important ways, they are relatively weak at elucidating the motivations behind manager- and executive-level forms of misconduct.[7] Ethnographic work can fill this gap.

Ethnographic methods can be effective at capturing mindsets, decision-making processes, and the richness of the cultural contexts that surround individuals and influence and inform their judgments. Such deep observation is usually untenable in large-sample empirical analyses that rely on homogenously coded, structured, and publicly accessible data. At the same time, while ethnographies tend to generate greater detail about individual lives and motivations, they also tend to lose some of the generalizability and precision that a quantitative analysis can offer.

Narrowly, one could say that empiricists are in the business of "theory testing," while ethnographers are "theory builders." However, it would be understating the value of ethnographic observation and analysis to say that they do not permit inferences to be drawn. To appreciate this, consider that when an airplane disaster occurs, a team of investigators from the National Transportation Safety Board (NTSB) travels to the scene to document the accident. Since airplane failures are relatively infrequent events, investigators would be poorly served by a regression that includes every flight and that models variables that could impair planes. Instead, NTSB investigators engage in a form of ethnographic research that involves not only picking piece by piece through physical wreckage but also understanding the human context surrounding the particular flight in question, including the pilots, the passengers, and air traffic control. In the end, the investigators both create hypotheses of why a disaster occurred (i.e., theory building) and seek to draw inferences from the data they collect, even if they are necessarily unable to test that theory by reproducing the exact same conditions. In this way, the line between "theory building" and "theory testing" is perhaps not always as clear as it is often conceptually believed to be.[8]

NOTES

1. Cressey (1953) relied exclusively on testimony of perpetrators and did not have contemporaneous evidence (e.g., emails) with which to compare their commentary. Observers could have dismissed Cressey's study as not being relevant to how all embezzlers engage in their crimes. However, one of the most important ideas in fraud theory, known as the "fraud triangle," would emerge, suggesting that these methodological limitations do not necessarily impede significant observations from being drawn.

2. KPMG is one of the largest international auditing firms, providing auditing, tax, and financial advising services.

3. The interpretation of culture serves to define what a culture is. Thus, the reconstruction of a culture is itself creating and defining what that culture is (see Van Maanen, 2011).

4. The difficulty of relying on memory has been explored extensively in Loftus and Ketcham (1991).

5. See Sutherland (1949), and Soltes (2016, 23–25), for background on the controversy.

6. Fraud is one form of corporate misconduct; for an excellent survey of the fraud literature see Amiram et al. (2018).

7. Notable exceptions include Schrand and Zechman (2012) and Davidson, Dey, and Smith (2015).

8. I would like to thank Paul Healy and Krishna Palepu for their helpful suggestions and feedback on this essay and, even more significantly, the underlying work described here.

REFERENCES

Amiram, D., et al. (2018). Financial reporting fraud and other forms of misconduct: A multidisciplinary review of the literature. *Review of Accounting Studies, 23*(2), 732–83.

Bazerman, M. H., and A. E. Tenbrunsel (2012). *Blind spots: Why we fail to do what's right and what to do about it.* Princeton, NJ: Princeton University Press.

Cressey, D. (1953). *Other people's money*. Glencoe, IL: Free Press.

Davidson, R., A. Dey, and A. Smith (2015). Executives' "off-the-job" behavior, corporate culture, and financial reporting risk. *Journal of Financial Economics, 117*, 5–28.

Gino, F. (2013). *Sidetracked: Why our decisions get railed, and how we can stick to the plan*. Boston: Harvard Business Review Press.

Loftus, E., and K. Ketcham (1991). *Witness for the defense: The accused, the eyewitness, and the expert who puts memory on trial*. New York: St. Martin's Press.

Schrand, C., and S. Zechman (2012). Executive overconfidence and the slippery slope to financial misreporting. *Journal of Accounting and Economics, 53*, 311–29.

Soltes, E. (2009). A letter from prison. HBS no. 110045. Boston: Harvard Business Publishing.

——— (2016). *Why they do it: Inside the mind of the white-collar criminal*. New York: Hachette/PublicAffairs.

Sutherland, E. (1949). *White-collar crime*. New York: Dryden.

Van Maanen, J. (2011). *Tales of the field: On writing ethnography*. 2nd ed. Chicago: University of Chicago Press.

PART TWO

———

Team Ethnography

FIVE

_____

Hide-and-Seek

CHALLENGES IN THE ETHNOGRAPHY
OF STREET DRUG USERS

Merrill Singer and J. Bryan Page

STUDYING A CHIMERA: THE SOCIAL
CONSTRUCTION AND STIGMATIZATION OF
STREET DRUG USERS

Individuals who use illicit drugs on the streets of urban centers around the world gained public, media, and political notice during the height of the AIDS epidemic once it was established that the sharing or serial use of syringes were significant routes of HIV transmission. While street drug users were being studied to a degree by anthropologists and other social scientists before and independent of the AIDS epidemic (Agar, 1973; Carter, Coggins, and Doughty, 1980; Preble and Casey, 1969), the sudden, widespread, and ultimately global appearance of a potentially lethal infectious disease changed public health understanding of the urgency of this kind of scholarly investigation.

Because gaining useful knowledge about the specific assemblage of behaviors that puts this population at risk for infection came to be defined by national research institutions and other research funders as critical to prevention, anthropologists and other qualitative social scientists were recruited in notable numbers to implement detailed ethnographic research programs. Of concern were routine behaviors and drug-use technologies, social and risk environments, cultural understandings of drug use and drug-involved social lives, drug selection and polydrug use mixing patterns, involvement in drug distribution, relations with dominant institutions in society, and related matters, leading ultimately to a considerable expansion in the detailed behavioral literature on this previously somewhat obscure group (Carlson et al. 2009).

In carrying out this work, which today continues in new forms, especially in the study of pharmaceutically produced but illicitly consumed opioids like the semisynthetic opioid oxycodone and synthetic drugs like fentanyl and its analogs, researchers have had to confront the challenges of entering unfamiliar but socially marginalized landscapes in an effort to find, build trust with, and develop evidence-based understanding of socially tainted individuals. A fundamental influence on the conduct of this work was the constructed complex formed, on the one hand, by the criminalization and demonization of those deemed to be "dangerous drug addicts," and, on the other hand, by the collection of subculturally constituted strategies and knowledge used by drug users to minimize social opprobrium and survive on the streets, acquire drugs, and use them in public or semipublic spaces. The purpose of this chapter is to examine social science's approach to ethnographic fieldwork that developed under the thrall of the socially erected chimera of street drug users and their efforts to cope with the stigmatization, social control, and disciplining regime aimed at them.

We refer to the social construct that informs the portrayal of drug users in the news and entertainment media, in the social justice system, and in the policy arena as a chimera because it is a fabrication, a useful if harmful social invention supported by various "technologies of exclusion" (Anselmi and Gouliamos, 1998). Notably, the original use of the term in Greek mythology was a fire-breathing monster composed of incongruent parts. As applied to street drug users, the notion of chimera references the historic tendency to depict them as "monstrous persons" and "this mythology plays an important role in determining the way in which [they] are handled" by social institutions and people in society generally (Lindesmith, 1940, 199). Illicit drug users "are often labeled as dangerous, immoral, and unproductive members of society who engage in behaviors detrimental to themselves and others" (Lutman, Lynch, and Monk-Turner, 2015, 58). Demonic threats to the social fabric, drug users are blamed for most street criminality jumps, when they occur, in violent crime rates, the demise of the quality of urban life, and even terrorism. While research does not support these assertions, they are nonetheless influential in society. As Ferrell, Hayward, and Young (2008, 25) assert, "ideas do not emerge from nothingness; they occur and recur at particular times and places, in specific cultural and economic contexts." As we have argued elsewhere (Singer and Page, 2014), by labeling drug users as useless burdens on society, they paradoxically become useful in the prevailing social structure in multiple ways, including as deflective objects of blame for social ills, as sources of very cheap and disposable labor (on the street and in prison), as justification for the need for increasingly militarized police enforcement practices that help bolster social hierarchy, and as rich sources of dramatic distraction through the entertainment media.

A consequence of the making of the chimera of the "monster drug user" is the experience among drug users of an intense pressure to develop tactics to limit detection, harassment, and arrest, played out on a fraught stage of enduring drug craving and the consequent need to "score" drugs while avoiding the recognized health risks of drug use, from infection to overdose. The result is that the constantly evolving project designed to gain ethnographic access to understanding the daily world and health risks among street drug users emerged as a social performance of hide-and-seek.

BEING HIDDEN: A CONSCIOUS ACT OR A CONSEQUENCE OF EMERGENT SOCIAL NEED FOR IDENTIFICATION?

While approaches to the systematic study of hidden and hard-to-reach populations have gained purchase in the literature on the developing toolkit of ethnographic and related methods of social science research, aspects of which will be discussed in greater detail in the next section, less explored has been the social production of hidden populations as well as the actual nature of clandestinity.

Researchers (e.g., Agar, 1973; Koester, 1994; Page et al., 1990) have found that some people actively seek to minimize their social visibility, especially to individuals or social agents perceived as explicit threats (e.g., the police, immigration officers, social service officials, process servers, landlords, personal enemies) or to minimize experiences and settings known to cause suffering (e.g., street violence, stigmatization, incarceration). Others people may not actively disguise themselves but only come to be designated as hidden or at least hard-to-reach when they are defined as a distinct population in need of finding by an empowered social institution. A population—defined as a group of individuals that share at least one nontrivial characteristic—tends to gain research interest when their shared characteristic comes to be seen as putting themselves or others at health, criminal, or other risk. The wealthiest one percent of the U.S. population, for example, can, if it chooses, remain reasonably well hidden from public view, and is certainly hard for social science researchers to access, but this barrier to research availability is not defined broadly as a social problem in need of solving by dominant institutions.

While the extent of white-collar and corporate crime, and the level of social suffering and victimization they create, might suggest the super-rich should be a population of keen interest (Croall, 2009), according to statistics compiled by the Transactional Records Access Clearinghouse at Syracuse University (2016) the number of white-collar criminals even brought up on charges is small and has been dropping over the last twenty years, as have the number of convictions. Some researchers, nonetheless, have adopted the term "corporate violence" to label the extensive level of harm done to people or the environment through the actions of corporations (Friedrichs, 2009; Klein, 2014; Singer and Baer, 2008). Yet corporate officials rarely are targets of criminal justice agents and institutions, and certainly are not regularly subject to incarceration, because they are not deemed or constructed as a social group that presents recognized risks to the wider population, all evidence to the contrary. As this suggests, the power to create and enforce labels is critical to the designation of a group as a hidden population. So too is the ability to shape the cultural content associated with undesirable social labels. For example, because wealthy individuals and families frequently are able to shield embarrassing or even criminal behavior from public view, many social problems, including illicit drug use, come to be conceived of as inherent characteristics of the poor, a stratum with far less social capital to expend on image management.

Active concealment takes many forms and is highly influenced by the resources available to a population to disguise itself and its behaviors and everyday locations. Often for street drug users, a group with meager fiscal resources, concealment involves simply a matter of "blending in." For example, during research on the implementation of a mobile syringe exchange program as an AIDS prevention strategy, Singer conducted ethnographic research at the locations where a syringe exchange van made its stops during its first days of operation. While there had been considerable advance street publicity about the van's exchange sites throughout the city, what was most apparent prior to the arrival of the van at any location was the ordinariness of street activity to be observed there. People acted as they always did prior to the initiation of the exchange program; they were shopping or seeming to shop at local stores, talking with acquaintances on the street corner, crowded in small groups working on cars parked at the curb, or enjoying a cold drink and observing the world around them. And then the van arrived. Quickly some people—who were not particularly distinctive visually from others—detached themselves from what they had been doing and moved to where the van had parked, lined up, exchanged their used syringes for sterile ones, and moved promptly away from the area. With limited financial or other resources, hiding in plain sight was a key tactic of street survival for these illicit drug users. Other street drug user masking strategies include not carrying syringes while "taking care of business" (i.e., moving about the streets, purchasing drugs, and acquiring other resources), identifying isolated or secluded locations for rapid drug consumption, adopting in-group jargon to communicate about drugs, avoiding locations where they might be spotted, and limiting the depth of relationship they develop with most fellow drug users (cf. Koester, 1994; Page and Salazar, 1999).

Over time, in addition to populations engaged in active concealment, there emerge new populations of sudden interest to dominant institutions that also are defined as hidden. During the rise of the AIDS epidemic, various new populations came to be defined and labeled as hard-to-reach. A focus on women drug users, for example, developed when it was realized that they were "less visible in semipublic settings because of the widespread pattern of men copping [buying] drugs for use in private" with their partners (Gross and Brown, 1993, 447). Similarly, another new "group" that came to light (i.e., was constructed as being of interest) were the sexual partners of street drug users. As Hunt and coauthors note, "there is ... another perhaps even more hidden population at risk for HIV infection [than injection drug users]: their sex partners. Partners of those injection drug users who are not injection drug users themselves are often not connected with traditional sources of contact with drug users [e.g., drug treatment providers]; nor are they always part of the injection drug user world in which some information is shared about human immunodeficiency virus (HIV). They are the wives [or husbands] and lovers of injection drug users who may or may not be fully aware of their partner's intravenous drug use" (Hunt et al., 1993, 465). Artificially produced groups like sex partners of drug users may be particularly hard-to-find because they are composed of labeled "individuals who happen to share a particular kind of experience" or relationship but they are not necessarily linked together behaviorally or emotionally with other members of the "group" nor does the label placed on them constitute part of their social identity (Kane and Mason, 1992, 212). There are no enduring social settings in which the sex partners of injection drug users gather, communicate, or engage in social exchanges "as sex partners of injection drug users" (although this may occur if two individuals discover this shared characteristic has produced troublesome consequences for each of them). Moreover, there are no institutions that the sex partners of drug users routinely visit in their social role as drug user partners, or public programs that seek to assess their numbers, monitor their characteristics, or determine their distribution in the wider population. They "became a group" and a hidden or hard-to-reach target at a certain time and place and in a specific cultural and economic context when a social need developed (i.e., preventing the spread of AIDS, and soon thereafter, other sexually transmitted diseases). Fundamental to the operationalization of this need was the ability of an empowered social institution to label them and initiate research on them.

As this discussion suggests, being designated as hidden or hard-to-reach is a reflection of prevailing social structure. The conceptions of those who are so labeled are likewise embedded in the public imaginary, steering the enforcement behavior of social agents, and directing the policy initiatives of lawmakers.

HOW TO PLAY THE GAME OF "HIDE-AND-SEEK" SUCCESSFULLY

Approach to the Neighborhood of Interest

The first thing that an ethnographer tries to find out in beginning to study a complex of behavior is the location where people engage in the behavior of interest. Even the most covert of behaviors has some location known to people in the vicinity as a zone where you can find participants in the behavior in question, be it gambling, sex trade, drug dealing, or fencing stolen merchandise. The chimeric image of these persons engaged in covert behavior (especially drug consumers and dealers), as we described earlier, does not deter the experienced ethnographer from entering that territory, because the ethnographer enters every ethnographic task with a firm belief in the civility and gentility of most human beings. Ethnographers engage people in conversations that have the potential to lead to positive interactions and perhaps fruitful collaborations. A principle of reciprocity drives the activities of an ethnographer working among people who may be engaging in socially disapproved trade or commerce. If the ethnographer can deliver the message that she or he has scientific curiosity about some aspects of the behavior under study, she or he has begun to succeed in drawing practitioners of that behavior into further study.

The process described above requires patience, especially if the ethnographer is new to the area and is unknown to any of the local inhabitants. Page's entry into the southern barrios of San José, Costa Rica took about four months of hanging out in bars, talking to anyone who would speak to him (Page and Carter, 1980). After the locals had had enough time to assess his story for verity and check his other personal attributes, residents of the barrio began to allow him to approach and ask questions. This patience is a requirement, not because of the ethnographer's need to become familiar with the neighborhood, but rather for the neighborhood to become familiar with him or her. Once they were ready, the natives of Barrio Cuba came forward with useful information. In many cases, they had been aware of Page's presence weeks earlier, but they avoided him until they could be certain of his true intentions (Page and Singer, 2010).

Similarly, Page's assignment in Little Havana in Florida required months, not days or weeks (Page, 1990). In his approach to the task of studying street-based drug use among Cubans in Miami, he first chose a site where people from the surrounding neighborhoods went for certain kinds of goods and services (e.g., the barber shop, coffee stand, grocery stores, Chinese restaurant, Cuban style ice cream store, and Cuban bakery). Before renting a site he would use as the project office, Page interviewed drug treatment specialists to ascertain the possibility of finding drug users in that location, and they confirmed that it was an apt zone for this purpose. The office was on the third floor of a building that overlooked a small shopping center. The building's tenants included physicians, accountants, businesses, but no psychological or counseling clinics. This variety provided a cover for any visitor to Page's office for purposes of an interview or brief visit. Observers could not assume that people entering or leaving the building were involved in Page's study of drug use.

The office's ceiling-to-floor picture windows offered a panoramic view of the entire shopping center and some of the surrounding neighborhood. From this vantage point, Page could observe people in pursuit of their daily business, noting behaviors outside of the standard errands and shopping. While he recorded field notes describing the neighborhood and his visits to treatment centers, Page watched the shopping center for people "hanging out" or who were otherwise constantly visible. People of interest included a slender, middle-aged man who reliably took positions at one end or the other of the shopping center, a tall, attractive woman of mixed ethnicity who appeared regularly in front of the barbershop until a car would come by to pick her up, a boy of about eleven years of age who either skated or walked up and down the shopping center's sidewalks, and a young man in his twenties who sometimes appeared to be intoxicated.

Each of these people potentially could have contributed to Page's understanding of the neighborhood, and in time, he spoke to all of them, formally interviewing three of the four. Despite Page's presence for two years in that location, the middle-aged man never agreed to an interview. Not all of the "hidden" consent to emerge from hiding, regardless of the skill of the ethnographer. The other three required time to be approached productively. In the case of the sometimes intoxicated young man, Page had an encounter with him about a week after he had observed him stumbling through the shopping center looking disheveled and having trouble with his gait. He asked if Page had seen him last week, and when the answer was affirmative, he began to apologize for his behavior. In fact, that had been the purpose of his visit to this locality. Page told him that his purpose in Little Havana was to study drug use among Cubans. This statement seemed to interest the young man, who almost immediately began talking about his drug experience. The intoxicated episode of the previous week had involved eating a flower from chalice vine, a psychotropic plant (*Solanea nitida*) native to South Florida that contains scopolamine, which in medical form is used to treat motion sickness.

This young man, whose family had lived in this neighborhood for nearly two decades, eventually introduced Page to twenty-three individuals from the neighborhood who had varying degrees of involvement in illegal drug use, predominantly consumption of marihuana and cocaine. The tracing of that informant's network of informal social relations revealed that the people who were visible and perhaps identifiable as potential drug users through his picture windows were really only the most visible individuals in the network. The contacts introduced to Page subsequently by the initial contact would otherwise not have been identifiable. The young boy who was constantly hanging out in the neighborhood had two older brothers whom Page met through him, after the initial contact vouched for Page to the young boy. None of the three were of majority age, but Page eventually obtained permission from their mother (their father was deceased) to interview them separately. Of the twenty-three contacts linked to the initial young man, who was twenty-two years old at the time of contact, eleven were under age eighteen, but Page successfully obtained consent from the parents of six.

The Importance of Networks

In both of the experiences described above, the utilization of networks of informal social relations among drug users proved crucial to the efforts to find and recruit participants in the study of illegal drug use (Page, 1990; True et al., 1980). This use of networks in furtherance of recruitment was admittedly heuristic in both cases, and not based on theory about network linkage or morphology. Rather, the network method used in these cases was based on the fundamental concept that, in order to find a population of human beings who seek to engage in socially disapproved behavior, the investigator must ask for introductions to new contacts within an established contact's circle of friends and acquaintances. These introductions by people already accepted in their communities as trustworthy are remarkably powerful; they help the investigator to extend the range of people willing to participate in her or his study. Each new contact requires some additional cultivation, but the effort involved in the process of including additional participants is not nearly as great as that expended for the first few.

Eventually, weeks after finishing the field work phase of their studies, both Page and True (coworkers on the same project, but working on different dissertations) began to examine some of the works on networks among people in urban environments. Some sociological researchers had begun to consider the concept of networks in urban environments as early as the late 1930s (cf. Page, 2002). The anthropologist who pioneered the study of urban networks was Elizabeth Bott, who studied working-class men in London (Bott, 1955).

Her approach stimulated J. Clyde Mitchell (1969) to explore the concept of interpersonal networks in Africa. The rapid formation of cities that included many ethnicities provided fascinating laboratories for studying and characterizing networks of informal social relations. In attempting to make sense of highly complex lives in adaptation to suddenly urban ways of life, Mitchell contributed two summary insights: (1) that people participating in a network may have more than one reason for establishing a network contact (linkage), and (2) that the dominant forms of network (morphologies) observed in African cities were centralized networks and amorphous networks. True et al. (1980) used these features to characterize the lifestyles of Costa Rican marijuana smokers and nonsmokers. The study of Costa Rican marijuana smokers eventually entailed a total of three follow-up studies of the same group of study participants (Fletcher et al., 1996; Page, Fletcher, and True, 1988). In each case, the investigators' knowledge of the linkage among the participants and the morphology of the networks facilitated the task of tracking down these eighty-four individuals. Linkage, however, was the key feature for refinding the participants. If there were several kinds of linkage between them, for example working in the same business and living in the same neighborhood, the participants were relatively easy to find. If the linkage between a found participant and a sought participant only consisted of shared interest in obtaining marijuana, however, it was often difficult to locate the sought person. True et al. (1980) learned that the more kinds of links that existed between network mates, the easier it was to find them after several years of no contact. Conversely, if the linkage in the network was based only on the drug use links between members, it was often difficult to find the participants in this kind of network.

Mitchell (1969) described two principal kinds of network morphology: centralized, and amorphous. In the former kind, one or a few people had dominant roles in the network, as people who primarily had links with the central person(s) made regular contact with those persons. Some contact and linkage could be found among the people who constantly visited and communicated with the central person(s), but their main business was with the central person(s). Marijuana dealers, understandably, often operated in this kind of network, where they served as the central figures. People came to them to obtain their product, and they developed ongoing relationships with some, but not all of these clients. Among the Costa Rican marijuana users, amorphous networks had no central actors commanding the attention of many contacts, but they often had multiple ties between actors. Consequently, the participants in these amorphous network structures were repeatedly easy to find. Their contact with each other was so regular that establishing contact with one led quickly to contact with all.

Singer and his colleagues also used social network approaches in their studies of street drug users in Hartford. One approach they adopted was to recruit users through street outreach, and if they agreed to participate, ask them to try to recruit two of their drug-using associates into the study. These individuals, to the degree they were motivated to come to the research office by their associate, also were interviewed about their drug use behaviors. In this way, small amorphous networks of street drug users became visible to the researchers. One of the issues examined in this way was the role of violence in drug users' social networks (Singer et al., 1999).

Because the environment of drug use and trafficking involves violence used to enforce compliance with rules of transaction and comportment, the safety of field researchers has been a concern during the era of drug ethnographers (1970 to the present). Page and True, in the context of the study of Costa Rican marijuana users encountered a notably nonviolent system of drug trafficking and use, which resulted in their having a gentle introduction to street ethnography of drug users. In other contexts, such as Little Havana and Liberty City in Miami, violence was much more salient than it had been in Costa Rica. In fact, Page (1982, 1990) was conducting his research in Little Havana as the Cocaine Cowboys wars were in progress (1978–80). In that environment, as well as in other neighborhoods, Page adopted a strict policy of never showing the least interest in the process of trafficking and sale of illegal drugs. The process of participant observation inevitably revealed many aspects of drug procurement from the point of view of drug users, but the field researchers never asked any questions about these topics. The logic behind this approach involved avoiding situations in which the street informants recalled the ethnographer's pointed questions about traffickers whom police coincidentally later arrested. As outsiders recently allowed into networks, the first people suspected as informers would be the ethnographers if they had asked many questions about drug distribution of any kind.

These experiences can be summarized in four briefly stated principles:

1. People living in cities and engaging in socially disapproved behavior often rely on networks of informal social relations to pursue those behaviors.

2. Once a researcher has established a trusting relationship with one of these people, his or her introduction and vouching for the investigator are highly valuable in the recruitment of interviewees and study participants.

3. The networks formed among people engaged in covert behavior often take one of the following two forms: centralized or amorphous. The former is easy to recontact, but the linkage tends to be thin. The latter may have stronger, denser linkage than the former.

4. Linkage between participants in a network is the key to the network's longevity and reliability. The more varied links there are between members, the more durable the networks will be. Ten years after original contact, a network with dense patterns of linkage will remain organized.

Principle 2, above, drives the process that is called rapid assessment. When an emergent health related phenomenon needs ethnographic attention, there may not be time to engage in the classic anthropological procedures of establishing contact, building trust with key informants, and then investigating the problem of interest. Scrimshaw and her colleagues (Cifuentes et al., 2006; Scrimshaw and Hurtado, 1987) conceived of a set of procedures designed to address emerging health crises as they begin to have impact on their communities of origin. In these procedures, the principle of introduction becomes central, because it helps an ethnographic research team to gain rapid entry into the communities where urgent health problems are emerging. Representatives from the community, upon inviting the rapid assessment team to address their pressing problems, help the team to identify, engage, and train individuals living in the community. Their training gives them the basic tools of the field ethnographer, and, given their lifelong presence in the community, they have almost immediate access to activities and phenomena that would take the outsider months to discover. They work with the anthropologists on the assessment team, collecting open-ended interviews, conducting field observations, and meeting regularly to discuss and analyze findings. This system has proven useful in dealing at the community level with dengue outbreaks, water sanitation, and many other health problems.

Rapid assessment also proved valuable in efforts to characterize the nature of the HIV epidemic, especially among people engaged in covert behavior—injecting drug users, men who have sex with men, and sex workers. If people from the community affected by the health risk ask for a rapid assessment team to help understand and prevent further spread of the infections of concern (especially HIV and HCV) they can broker the identification and recruitment of people embedded in the groups of interest. These individuals can be trained in a matter of days in the skills necessary to become rapid assessment semiethnographers of covert behavior. Needle et al. (2003) used this approach in communities of color throughout the United States to identify areas of risk in drug use, HIV infection, and HCV infection. Invariably, the communities that conducted rapid assessment in this form (called

RARE—Rapid Assessment for Response and Evaluation) were able to identify new problem areas and deploy responses to these problems on the strength of what they learned (Browser, Quimby, and Singer, 2007). Singer worked together with fellow anthropologist Robert Trotter to affirm the validity and value of rapid assessment with health issues among drug users (Bates, Singer, and Trotter, 2007; Trotter and Singer, 2005).

SAFETY WHILE IN THE FIELD

Ethnographers who are attempting to study covert behaviors firsthand should never go undercover. That is, they should never present themselves as someone other than who they really are. Police do that often, and because of their attempts to deceive people who have something to hide, the ethnographer should avoid any kind of identity deception. Most important, deception opens the possibility of violent reprisals if the ruse is uncovered. Perhaps equally important, however, is the possibility of opening the sociologic imaginations of the people being studied. If the ethnographer is constantly introducing herself or himself as a social scientist who is trying to understand self-injection behavior, or sex-for-drugs exchanges, or HIV risk behavior, opioid addiction, or overdose risk, eventually, some of the people contacted in this way will begin to think of their own behavior in terms of its larger implications. People whose sociologic imaginations have become active may have particularly insightful things to say about what they do. They also may become energetic helpers and facilitators for the ethnographer's basic tasks. In the case of Juan Gamella's study of HIV spread in Spain (1994), one of his key informants shared his life story, resulting in a powerful book about the transition from Franco's dictatorship to Spanish democracy (Gamella, 1989). Singer (2006) based his analysis of a life of suffering using in-depth interviews with one of his key informants in a study of injection drug use. While the ethnographer is in the field, it is difficult to tell when the sociological imagination will be unleashed or what expression it will take. Sometimes it results in published life histories; at other times the unleashed individual throws him or herself into helping the ethnographer's study any way she or he can. Page's first key informant in Little Havana maintains some contact, although he now lives in North Florida. In all cases, the people so affected seem to grasp the transcendence of research and analysis beyond simply living the life.

Other aspects of safely conducting this kind of field work include:

1. Never indicate the least interest in trafficking or traffickers. Your identity may still be object of suspicion by some of the participants. If you ask a lot of questions about where the drugs or trafficked sex workers come from, and a trafficker is subsequently arrested, as an outsider not completely accepted yet, you become the prime suspect.

2. When study participants volunteer information about trafficking, stashes, and headquarters, let them know explicitly that you are not taking down that information, because of number 1, above.

3. Dress appropriately for the field situation. Never go to a shooting gallery or hot zone looking like you have anything worth stealing. Never hang out with the corner crack dealers wearing shabby jeans and a raggedy tee—that is potentially insulting. Wear some culturally fashionable warm-ups and decent kicks.

4. Bring a cultural guide (a person known to you and familiar with the venue to be visited) to all unfamiliar venues. This is a specific application of the principle of the introduction.

5. Always approach the people in the area of interest as you might approach a stranger on the street. Make no assumptions about their rapacity or ferocity or cruelty. Speak without hesitation and with genuine curiosity.

CONCLUSIONS

Given the fear and loathing that often taints discourse about drug use and drug users, our experience of direct, longitudinal contact with people who use and/or traffic in drugs has stripped away their "Chimera-ness." Furthermore, we have found their humanity and their capacity for empathy compelling. Having looked deeply into the background and origins of their systematically disapproved behaviors, we have found that much of their behavior can be interpreted as self-medicating behavior—responses to protracted suffering. When they engage in defending their life choices, they do so because their way of life is besieged on all sides.

When we recruit people involved in covert behavior to give us their life histories, their responses usually are enthusiastically positive. Once they begin to talk into the recording device, they often contribute astonishingly open, personal, and thorough accounts of their lives to date. As if they had been waiting all of their lives to have this kind of a conversation, the study participants speak volubly, seeming to take pleasure in the discourse. They may be hiding from unwanted attention, but when the attention is interested and nonjudgmental, they open up like flowers in the sunshine. Many comment that no one previously has been interested in them or their lives. Often they blame their addiction and other problems on themselves, and it is a relief to know someone wants to hear their story, their reality, their place as legitimate and respect-worthy people in the world.[1]

NOTE

This chapter draws from lessons learned by the authors in completing research funded by the National Institutes of Health, particularly two institutes: The National Institute on Drug Abuse (NIDA) and the National Institute of Mental Health (NIMH). Both had the perspicacity to recognize that ethnographic perspective was essential to understanding the behavior of people who of necessity hide their behaviors. Program officers such as Ellen Stover (NIMH), Willo Pequegnat (NIMH), Michael Backenheimer (NIDA), Beatrice Rouse (NIDA), Mario de la Rosa (NIDA), Eleanor Carroll (NIDA), Richard Needle (NIDA), and others provided encouragement and support for our endeavors, and they deserve credit for this, and much of our other work.

REFERENCES

Agar, M. (1973). *Ripping and running: A formal ethnography of urban heroin addicts.* New York: Academic Press.

Anselmi, W., and K. Gouliamos (1998). *Elusive margins: Consuming media, ethnicity, and culture.* Montreal: Guernica.

Bates, C., M. Singer, and R. Trotter (2007). The RARE Model of rapid HIV risk assessment. *Journal of Health Care for the Poor and Underserved, 18* (3 Supplement), 16–34.

Bott, E. (1955). Urban families: Conjugal roles and social networks. *Human Relations, 8*(4), 345–84.

Browser, B. P., E. Quimby, and M. Singer, eds. (2007). *When communities assess their AIDS epidemics.* Lanham, MD: Lexington.

Carlson, R., et al. (2009). Reflections on 40 years of ethnographic drug abuse research: Implications for the future. *Journal of Drug Issues, 39*(1), 57–70.

Carter, W. E., J. C. W. Coggins, and P. L. Doughty (1980). The Problem, in *Cannabis in Costa Rica: A Study of Chronic Marihuana Use,* ed. W. E. Carter, 1-12. Philadelphia: ISHI (Institute for the Study of Human Issues).

Cifuentes, E., et al. (2006). Rapid assessment procedures in environmental sanitation research: A case study from the northern border of Mexico. *Canadian Journal of Public Health, 97,* 24–28.

Croall, H. (2009). *Corporate crime.* Vols. 1–3. Thousand Oaks, CA: Sage.

Ferrell, J., K. Hayward, and J. Young (2008). *Cultural criminology: An invitation.* London: Sage.

Fletcher, J. M., et al. (1996). Cognitive correlates of chronic cannabis use in Costa Rican men. *Archives of General Psychiatry, 53,* 1051–57.

Friedrichs, D. (2009). *Trust criminals: White-collar crime in contemporary society.* Belmont, CA: Wadsworth.

Gamella, J. (1989). *La historia de Julián: Memorias de heroína y delincuencia.* Madrid: Editorial Popular.

——— (1994). The spread of intravenous drug use and AIDS in a neighborhood in Spain. *Medical Anthropology Quarterly, 8*(2), 131–60.

Gross, M., and V. Brown (1993). Outreach to injection drug-using women. In *Handbook on risk of AIDS*, ed. B. Brown and G. Beschner, 445–63. Westport, CT: Greenwood.

Hunt, D., et al. (1993). Outreach to sex partners. In *Handbook on risk of AIDS*, ed. B. Brown and G. Beschner, 464–82. Westport, CT: Greenwood.

Kane, S., and T. Mason (1992). "IV drug users" and "sex partners": The limits of epidemiological categories and the ethnography of risk. In *The time of AIDS: Social analysis, theory, and methods,* ed. G. Herdt and S. Lindenbaum, 199–224. Newbury Park, CA: Sage.

Klein, J. (2014). *Corporate violence. The encyclopedia of theoretical criminology.* Hoboken, NJ: Wiley.

Koester, S. (1994). Copping, running, and paraphernalia laws: Contextual variables and needle risk behavior among injection drug users. *Human Organization, 53*(3), 287–95.

Lindesmith, A. (1940). Dope fiend mythology. *Journal of Criminal Law and Criminology, 31*(2), 199–208.

Lutman, B., C. Lynch, and E. Monk-Turner (2015). De-demonizing the "monstrous" drug addict: A qualitative look at social reintegration through rehabilitation and employment. *Critical Criminology, 23,* 57–72.

Mitchell, J. C. (1969). *Social networks in urban situations.* Manchester: Manchester University Press.

Needle, R. H., et al. (2003). Rapid assessment of the HIV/AIDS crisis in racial and ethnic minority communities: An approach for timely community interventions. *American Journal of Public Health, 93*(6), 970–79.

Page, J. B. (1982). A brief history of mind-altering drug use in prerevolutionary Cuba/Breve historia del consumo de drogas que alteran la mente en Cuba prerevolucionaria. *Cuban Studies, 12*(2), 55–71.

———— (1990). Streetside drug use among Cuban drug users in Miami, Florida. In *Drug use in Hispanic Communities*, ed. R. Glick and J. Moore, 169–91. New Brunswick, NJ: Rutgers University Press.

———— (2002). Networks of informal social relations and HIV: Problems in characterization and analysis, bioinformatics and cybernetics; From gene expression to social interaction. Sixth World Conference on Systematics, Cybernetics, and Informatics, Orlando, FL.

Page, J. B., and W. E. Carter (1980). Smoking environment and effects. In *Cannabis in Costa Rica: A Study of Chronic Marihuana Use,* ed. W. E. Carter, 116–44. Philadelphia: ISHI (Institute for the Study of Human Issues).

Page J. B., J. M. Fletcher, and W. R. True (1988). Psychosociocultural perspectives in chronic cannabis use: The Costa Rican follow-up. *Journal of Psychoactive Drugs, 20*(1), 57–65.

Page, J. B., and J. Salazar (1999). Use of needles and syringes in Miami and Valencia: Observations of high and low availability. *Medical Anthropology Quarterly, 4*(4), 413–35.

Page, J. B., and M. Singer (2010). *Comprehending drug use: Ethnographic research at the social margins.* New Brunswick, NJ: Rutgers University Press.

Page, J. B., et al. (1990). Intravenous drug abuse and HIV infection in Miami. *Medical Anthropology Quarterly, 4*(1), 56–71.

Preble, E., and J. Casey (1969). Taking care of business: The heroin user's life on the street. *International Journal of the Addictions, 4*(1), 1–24.

Scrimshaw, S. C. M., E. Hurtado (1987). *Rapid assessment procedures for nutrition and primary health care: Anthropological approaches to improving program effectiveness.* Los Angeles: University of California Latin American Center Publications.

Singer, M. (2006). *The face of social suffering: Life history of a street drug addict.* Prospect Heights, IL: Waveland.

Singer, M., and H. Baer (2008). *Killer commodities: Public health and the corporate production of harm.* Malden, MA: AltaMira/Roman Littlefield.

Singer, M., and B. Page (2014). *The social value of drug addicts: Uses of the useless.* Walnut Creek, CA: Left Coast.

Singer, M., et al. (1999). Violence in the lives and social networks of street drug users. *Bulletin of the Alcohol and Drug Study Group, 34*(3), 8–11.

Transactional Records Access Clearinghouse. (2016). *White-collar crime convictions continue to decline.* TracReports. Retrieved from http://trac.syr.edu/tracreports /crim/421.

Trotter, R., and M. Singer (2005). Rapid assessment strategies for public health: Promise and problems. In *Community Interventions and AIDS*, ed. E. Trickett and W. Pequegnat, 130–52. Oxford: Oxford University Press.

True, W. R., et al. (1980). Marihuana user lifestyles. In *Cannabis in Costa Rica: A Study of Chronic Marihuana Use,* ed. W. E. Carter, 98–115. Philadelphia: ISHI (Institute for the Study of Human Issues).

SIX

Into the Epistemic Void

USING RAPID ASSESSMENT TO INVESTIGATE
THE OPIOID CRISIS

*Jason N. Fessel, Sarah G. Mars, Philippe Bourgois,
and Daniel Ciccarone*

EPIDEMICS CAN PASS THROUGH MULTIPLE historical phases. The United States is currently in the third phase of a long crisis of drug overdose mortalities (Ciccarone, 2019). In the first phase, which began in the 1990s, increased access to pharmaceutical opioids was an outstanding causal factor. In the second phase, heroin use also started to rise substantially with related mortality increasing steeply from 2010 to 2014 (Warner et al., 2016). Since then a third phase has emerged, characterized by rapid and unpredictable shifts in the active ingredients of "heroin." This exceptional volatility has largely been due to widespread adulteration with a variety of synthetic opioids, most notably fentanyl and its proliferating analogs (Ciccarone, 2017; Mars, Ondocsin, and Ciccarone, 2017). Chemical analysis, with its power to recognize and measure the hidden ingredients of drugs sold as "heroin," has been inconsistently implemented, subject to delays in dissemination, and impeded by the introduction of novel psychoactive substances (Ciccarone, 2017; Lucyk and Nelson, 2017). The unstable and poorly surveilled heroin-fentanyl supply of this third phase leaves users and public health providers alike in an epistemic void, ill-prepared to make knowledge-based adaptations. Lack of knowledge about the shifting ingredients of street heroin, therefore, is a distinctive risk factor in this current phase of the overdose crisis.

Although death from overdose (OD) is a well-known risk of heroin use, the scale of the current situation is historically significant, with OD-related mortality even outstripping HIV-related mortality at the height of the AIDS epidemic (Katz, 2017). In 2016, sixty-four thousand people died from drug overdoses in the United States, mostly related to fentanyl, heroin, and other opioids. Each phase of the opioid epidemic has presented different challenges

TABLE 6.1 Heroin in Transition Study Rapid Assessment Project Visits, 2015–17

2015, November	Baltimore
2016, February	San Francisco
2016, March	Baltimore (second visit)
2016, June	New Hampshire and Massachusetts
2016, September–October	Chicago
2017, February	West Virginia pilot (1-day visit)
2017, May	Portland, ME, pilot (2-day visit)
2017, September	West Virginia

for those attempting to intervene and for the users themselves. The diverted prescription opioid pills salient in the first phase presented few mysteries about their active ingredients. By contrast, the present iteration is characterized by exceptional lack of knowledge about the shifting make up of street "heroin" and users' adaptations.

This chapter explores the use of "rapid ethnography," or "rapid assessment projects" (RAPs), as part of a cross-disciplinary approach to understanding these recent developments. RAP, a form of focused short-term ethnography integrated with other research methods, is an existing methodology which was also taken up for the study of HIV during the 1990s. Although used internationally, in the United States it was particularly employed to address viral transmission disparities among urban African-American and Latinx populations (Needle et al., 2003; Trotter et al., 2001), being well adapted for documenting health risks among hidden and stigmatized populations. RAP was adopted by various research teams in the drugs field to research HIV, particularly in England (Fitch et al., 2004; Rhodes et al., 1999). It has often been favored by those sympathetic to harm reduction approaches due to its emphasis on gaining an insider perspective. The model of RAP used here is largely qualitative, with quantitative questions explored by the Heroin in Transition study outside the RAP to inform the overall picture.

In this chapter, we consider the ideas underpinning the research design of the NIH-funded Heroin in Transition (HIT) study (principal investigator, D. Ciccarone), what worked successfully for ethnographic data collection, and some of the practical, ethical, and philosophical challenges arising. For this account, we used as sources the HIT study's field notes and retrospective reflections of five field ethnographers on their experiences visiting seven sites over nine visits across the country (see Table 6.1). To begin, we trace the genealogy of our specific model of RAP which focuses on street-based, out-of-treatment users interviewed in a conversational but semistructured format as expert sources of information on emerging drug use.

The HIT study developed from earlier research on the two predominant types of heroin available in the United States and their varying effects on users' health. Since the 1980s, powder heroin has been exclusive to the eastern United States and "black tar" heroin to the western United States states with the Mississippi River marking the divide between the two markets (Ciccarone, 2009). Our earlier research used San Francisco and Philadelphia as exemplar cities for the Mexican-sourced black tar and the Colombian-sourced powder heroin respectively, with traditional long-term ethnographic research in each city.

Research evidence from our project and others had started to form a picture of regional differences in health risks corresponding with the geographical distribution of heroin source-types. Both qualitative and quantitative findings showed that black tar injectors in western states suffered more from vein damage, skin and soft tissue infections, and infection with tetanus and botulism, while HIV risk and overdose were higher among powder heroin users (Bardenheier et al., 1998; Binswanger et al., 2000; Ciccarone and Bourgois, 2003; Ciccarone and Harris, 2015; Ciccarone et al., 2001; Ciccarone et al. 2016; Mars et al., 2015; Mars et al., 2016; Murphy et al., 2001; Passaro et al., 1998; Unick et al., 2014; Werner et al., 2000).

However, by 2012 there were indications that heroin types in the United States were diversifying, creating important new research questions. "Gunpowder" heroin, a speckled, chunky powder of reputedly higher purity than black tar, was reported along the West Coast. Additionally a potent white powder sold as heroin had appeared in San Francisco, possibly fentanyl (Mars et al., 2016), while white Mexican-sourced heroin that mimicked Colombian powder heroin showed up on the East Coast. Next to nothing was known about their chemical characteristics, marketing and organized crime distribution networks, appeal to users, and particular health implications.

In order to investigate these novel and evolving heroin types and users' experiences of them in context as they emerged across the United States, the HIT research project required a nimble and responsive ethnographic approach. RAP would allow a single team to gather data from multiple locations across the country in a short time, also allowing comparative observations across sites.

The trend in rapid qualitative research emerged in the late-1970s within the applied social sciences. The approach responded to practical social and institutional needs in ways that reflected a belief that social interventions can be more successful when they take into account local knowledge and values and facilitate local participation (Beebe, 2001; Manderson, 1992). Rapid qualitative research has tended to be applied rather than academic, aimed at supporting governmental and nongovernmental intervention programs. Its earliest uses involved questions concerning both agricultural development and public health (Beebe, 2001, 146; see also Hildebrand, 1979, 1981; Scrimshaw and Hurtado, 1987; Shaner, Philippe, and Schmehly, 1982). Perhaps because of this heavy emphasis on the production of applied knowledge, the first published academic accounts to focus on rapid qualitative research methods did not appear until the late 1980s (Trotter et al., 2001). Rapid assessment was not touted as a replacement for longer-term ethnographic research but rather as a method serving quite different purposes. The long-term focus of traditional ethnography could provide neither the swift deployment, flexibility, wide geographic scope nor the scale sometimes required by aid agencies.

The HIT research project was conceived in 2012–13 at a time when heroin use in the United States appeared to be rising in the wake of an enormous expansion in opioid pill prescriptions. However, due to data lag time, the scale of the emerging heroin-fentanyl epidemic was not yet evident. As heroin- and fentanyl-related overdose deaths climbed into the thousands, the need for on-the-ground knowledge to address this public health emergency became particularly urgent and directed the choice of site visits. Site selection was an ongoing process informed by reports coming from contacts in the field of unusual forms of heroin circulating or particularly high rates of overdose; some visits were in response to invitations from concerned local service providers who expressed a need for more information. Once the location and dates were agreed upon, the size of the team was determined and logistical preparations made. A fine balance had to be struck between the planned recruitment of subjects through services and unstructured time that allowed for serendipitous encounters and fieldwork opportunities.

The semistructured interviews use a question guide from which each interviewer can digress to ask follow-up questions and explore intriguing responses. The guide is revised as part of an iterative process before each RAP in the light of previous findings and if there are particular local conditions or phenomena to investigate. For instance, after the first RAP in Baltimore, where several users described injecting small "tester shots" (partial doses injected to monitor potency before committing to a full dose), a question on this topic was added for all subsequent interviews (Mars, Ondocsin, and Ciccarone, 2018).

FIGURE 6.1. Pink "heroin" observed in Huntingdon, West Virginia. Photo credit: Daniel Ciccarone, M.D., M.P.H.

Heroin usually ranges in color from blackish brown, to pale tan and white. In the first Baltimore RAP, users described a startling range of colors in which the traditionally white local "Scramble" heroin had appeared, including blue, orange, and pink (Mars, Ondocsin, and Ciccarone, 2017). We then started showing users paint swatches, asking them to identify the colors of the heroin they had been using. This resulted in a surprising motley of heroin hues from across the study sites, suggesting unusual and unstable forms of adulteration. Figure 6.1 shows pink "heroin" observed in West Virginia.

AN EVOLVING MULTIMETHOD COLLABORATION

Although it is not unusual to find ethnographers working with epidemiologists on public health research, qualitative research is typically subservient to the quantitative (Ciccarone, 2003; Maher, 2002). Just why quantitative research enjoys evidentiary supremacy within the biomedical establishment is a question perhaps best left to historians of science (Daston, 2007), but in the HIT study's design, epidemiology and ethnography are on a more level footing. The benefits of combining ethnography with epidemiology and other quantitative approaches was particularly advocated by researchers trying to understand the HIV/AIDS epidemic (Agar and Kozel, 1999; Koester, 1996). Interest among senior team members in integrating these methods on a mutual, bidirectional basis originated with a serendipitous ethnographic finding in 1997.

At that time, Philippe Bourgois was engaged in ethnographic research among a group of San Francisco's homeless black tar heroin injectors. He was alarmed to discover that they believed rinsing their shared syringes with water protected them from HIV transmission (Bourgois, 2002; Bourgois and Schonberg, 2009). This went against public health hygiene recommendations of the time, which called for rinsing with bleach to kill the virus. As a research anthropologist committed to public health work among marginalized populations Bourgois dropped the anthropological position of cultural relativism and noninterference and attempted to intervene ethically and pragmatically. The homeless injectors accepted the free sterile syringes and bottles of bleach he delivered from the needle exchange but immediately lost the bleach bottles. They became offended by his repeated entreaties to rinse with bleach, ordering him to, "Shut-up Philippe ... Water works ... If you don't like it leave" (Bourgois and Schonberg, 2009, 107, 108). Reengaging with anthropology's hermeneutic of respect for local belief systems, Bourgois took seriously the biological plausibility of their claim and sought out the biological advice of a community physician, Daniel Ciccarone, who had experience treating HIV positive patients and was studying anthropology and epidemiology.

Bourgois noticed that the black tar users he was observing in San Francisco typically rinsed repeatedly with water to remove viscous residue before sharing a syringe. This contrasted with his observations of minimal syringe rinsing on the East Coast, where the heroin was an easily dissolvable powder. The comparison led to an ongoing cross-disciplinary collaboration. Together, Ciccarone and Bourgois hypothesized that syringe rinsing habits corresponding with the different regional source types could explain the lower HIV prevalence on the West Coast compared with the East Coast. They tested the hypothesis using epidemiological and laboratory evidence, mapping HIV sero-prevalence across the country with data on the distribution of black tar heroin and powder heroin. The resulting map of differential HIV prevalence rates among injectors matched the distinct distribution of Mexican black tar heroin and Colombian powder heroin across the country (Ciccarone and Bourgois, 2003).

Qualitative and quantitative approaches ask fundamentally different kinds of questions and productive dialogue between these different spheres of knowledge is crucial in the current opioid overdose epidemic. Neither kind of approach by itself could hope to account for the range of interrelated problems arising in a complex phenomenon such as an epidemic. Bringing into dialogue knowledge "from above" and knowledge "from below" has the potential to produce better analyses.

In epidemiology, the "biological plausibility" of a claim is often regarded as a necessary condition for establishing a causal relationship between a predictor and a health outcome. Yet while biological plausibility is indeed a crucial analytical category, it is not sufficient without a parallel "social plausibility"; qualitative research adds the missing dimension of "social plausibility" (Ciccarone, 2003). Bringing ethnography into a nonhierarchical working relationship with epidemiology makes qualitative data more generalizable and quantitative data more focused and relevant. Similarly, the significance of local qualitative findings becomes clearer when interpreted alongside macrolevel contextual epidemiological trend data, resulting in more relevant analyses all around.

REFLECTIONS ON THE RESEARCH PROCESS

Entrée to the Study Population

The project is led by the principal investigator, Daniel Ciccarone, a medical doctor with anthropological training and two decades of experience working in harm reduction (Ciccarone, 2012). Philippe Bourgois, an anthropologist known for his in-depth ethnographic studies of crack dealing and heroin injectors (Bourgois, 2003; Bourgois and Schonberg, 2009), provided methodological guidance and training to the team of ethnographers. Sarah Mars, with a background in oral and archival history and qualitative analysis (Mars, 2012; Mars et al., 2014), directed the qualitative research and analysis.

Like the project leaders, the team of ethnographers was similarly diverse in disciplinary and occupational backgrounds, including a history graduate, Jeff Ondocsin, and a bilingual (Spanish and English) Costa Rican anthropologist, Fernando Montero, who had been working as an ethnographer with Philippe conducting participant-observation fieldwork on Philadelphia's open-air inner-city heroin markets (Karandinos et al., 2014). They were joined on the team by two seasoned harm reduction workers, Mary Howe and Eliza Wheeler. Mary Howe directs the San Francisco Homeless Youth Alliance,

FIGURE 6.2. Ethnographer and participant in San Francisco. Photo credit: Daniel Ciccarone, M.D., MPH.

which provides syringe exchange and other services, while Eliza Wheeler works for the Bay Area's "Dope Project," providing overdose response training and naloxone distribution. All had experience working with drug users. Figure 6.2 shows Mary with a research participant in San Francisco.

With criminalized and hidden populations, long-term ethnographic immersion allows for a gradual approach to developing trust and acceptance in a community. The sudden appearance of individuals asking drug users questions can cause suspicion and distrust, particularly due to fears of undercover police or other law enforcement investigations. When doing long-term ethnography with hidden populations, ethnographers might establish trust by making themselves visible community members for several weeks through ordinary daily activities such as shopping in a supermarket, repairing their cars, and walking around with friends and family (Bourgois, 2003), before initiating contact with possible research participants (White, 1998). However given the inherent time constraints of RAP, there were some questions about the extent to which trust and rapport could be gained with the users that the team hoped to involve.

To deal with this problem, two approaches were used. First, where the team had no personal contacts on the ground, as in Baltimore, a more formal method of gaining access through local harm reduction services (syringe exchanges) was used. The project's emphasis on health and its links with public health services helped to reassure people that the researchers were not undercover police. Unlike other forms of intervention, harm reduction activists have a history of acting as proxy representatives for the interests of drug users and their numbers often include former users.

The second approach involved contact with local harm reduction workers already known to members of the research team, some of whom worked "underground" or unofficially. These key contacts acted as "sponsors" (Whyte, 1955), people trusted by the research subjects who could vouch for the trustworthiness of the team. This more personal mode of introduction allowed the research team to move outside of syringe-exchange facilities. This was important for checking against bias from potential influence of the harm reduction setting both on the sample and the content of the interviews.

Data collected solely within harm reduction settings could suffer from a "social desirability" bias where interviewees tailor their responses according to social pressures. (Krumpal, 2013). There could also be a selection bias, as these services may attract users who are more concerned about their health and exclude those who have trouble finding available services, whether due to language or other barriers. At all the sites, the study used convenience samples which are nonrandom and may be unrepresentative of users more widely. Fernando observed,

> There is always the danger, if you're accessing people through a harm reduction program, that people are going to repeat the harm reduction discourse for example on fentanyl, and so in a way that doesn't reflect their lived experience or the lived experience of most users or at least the users who are not plugged into the harm reduction world or the services that syringe exchange sites provide. But we made efforts pretty much in every place we went to escape the sphere of influence of harm reduction that we visited: homeless encampments, we observed injections, we interviewed monolingual Latino users who can't communicate with English-speaking harm reduction activists so they probably don't share the harm reduction discourse. So it's a matter of incorporating those safeguards into the methodology to make sure you're really getting a diverse sample of users to represent more accurately the general population of injectors.

The Development of Trust and Rapport

A recurring theme among the team's researchers interviewed for this chapter was their surprise at the relative ease of finding people willing to participate and the speed at which rapport developed. As Fernando put it, "Thanks to Eliza and Mary and Dan we had local contacts on the ground who had excellent access to the population we wanted to access and a great deal of trust—harm reduction activists—so we never had any trouble recruiting people. In fact we had to reject people in some places. . . . I feel like every interview I did reached a pretty surprising level of depth. I was actually pretty impressed how well the methodology worked." In addition to the valuable introductions from local contacts, there were a number of other reasons for the speed of acceptance and easy rapport, including the composition of the team, their knowledge and life experiences, and shared concerns about the overdose crisis itself.

Several different types of rapport could be observed during research encounters based on researchers' knowledge, skills, and life experiences. Interviewees might be motivated to ask for informal medical advice from physician Dan Ciccarone, or tap into other team members' knowledge of the heroin supply elsewhere. A special rapport developed with the team's "insiders," who have worked with drug users on a daily basis. As Fernando pointed out, "the fact that Mary and Eliza have so much ground-level experience gives us a lot of credibility." As a former homeless injecting heroin user, Mary was perhaps the team's most "inside insider." She reported that "most of the people I interviewed all could pick up on the fact that I was a former user also," and that some interviewees confided very intimate or traumatic experiences, sensing a sympathetic listener with a shared history. It is also possible that gender norms could have contributed to this comfort level and inclination to discuss intimate experiences. Eliza's East Coast origins and experience in harm reduction on both coasts contributed to the team's understanding of their contrasting cultures.

Public health researchers, harm reduction workers, and heroin users all seek answers to similar questions, and with the perceived urgency of the situation, this may have contributed to the rapport established so quickly between participants and ethnographers. Jerry (pseudonym), in Lowell, Massachusetts, who had been using heroin on and off for twenty years, said the following: "Now the dope is fentanyl and it's killing people left and right. I have over the years, I've watched friends—but on average, it was three [fatal overdoses] a year. Now the last three years it's been an average of twenty [per year]. I feel like I'm back in a combat state and I feel like I'm fighting for my life right now." The RAP methodology's short time scale might seem to be a hindrance to the development of rapport and the gathering of reliable data from the research population, but the ethnographers reported that the opposite could also be the case. Because of the lack of follow-up opportunities with those interviewed, the team's encounters offered an anonymity and lack of longer-term consequences that could be freeing to both parties. Interviewers could ask questions that were perhaps more direct than they would have asked if seeking to develop an ongoing research relationship gradually or aiming to provide harm reduction services, while interviewees could also feel freer. As Mary remarked, interviewees "have nothing to lose by being honest with me. . . . When people are compensated and given the freedom and anonymity to say whatever they want they'll be brutally honest." The lack of follow-up possibilities could also weigh on the interviewers. Jeff commented "I think about some of the people we've interviewed and I guess what's hardest is that we don't know anything about them now. They could have overdosed and died."

As well as concentrating on how to build rapport, the team also considered factors that might negatively affect this. It is well understood that the order of interview questions contributes to this sensitive process (Doody and Noonan, 2013), and the opportunity to revise the questions through the iterative process of repeated RAPs was helpful in this respect, as another ethnographer noted:

> I think that asking the "ethnicity/race" question early on has a negative effect on the development of rapport. ["Can you tell me what ethnicity you consider yourself?"] In addition to all the baggage that comes with race/ethnicity, I suspect that the question makes people feel they are being put into a box, rather than listened to as an individual. Sometimes there would be a sigh from the interviewee after it was asked, so we moved this question from the beginning of the interview to the end, when we hoped that some rapport has already developed, and it can be asked as a formality, rather than something that sets the scene for the whole interview. ["For our records, can you tell me how old you are and what ethnicity you consider yourself?"]

Research among hidden populations, especially those involved in illegal activities, can raise concerns about safety risks for both researchers and research participants. Considerable precautions, discussed below, are taken to ensure that interviewees are not at risk from participating in the research. For the researchers in this study, a balance had to be struck between staying inside the safety zone of harm reduction services, whose organizers can vouch for the team's trustworthiness, and carrying out research beyond their potential influence. A major concern is being mistaken for undercover law enforcement and, to a lesser extent, theft of cash or equipment.

The researchers work in pairs, dress in clothes that do not draw attention, and, in case of attention from law enforcement, carry with them copies of the Federal Certificate of Confidentiality. They check in with the other pairs by text and also take common-sense precautions such as avoiding showing cash in public. In some situations, key informants who are particularly interested in the research and have good local knowledge are hired to act as security or crowd control for the day, especially if valuable equipment is being used.

Despite precautions, there is always some risk. In Lawrence, Massachusetts, a regional center for heroin distribution, two of the researchers had an encounter that exemplifies the potential dangers of such research. Sitting in a car with an interviewee outside the town's needle exchange, they were approached by a man carrying a sock that appeared to be filled with a hard object for use as a weapon. He asked who the researchers were and seemed suspicious of the questions they were asking. At one point, he threatened to take one of the researchers away in his car, but was eventually satisfied with their account and, apparently convinced that they were not a threat, left the scene. This happened on the last scheduled afternoon of research in Lawrence. Two months after the RAP team's visit, a milling operation in Lawrence, Massachusetts, was seized by law enforcement, where heroin and fentanyl were being mixed together and processed into cylinders ("fingers") for midlevel sale (Drug Enforcement Administration [DEA], 2017). While the researchers had no knowledge of the DEA's operations there, it is not surprising the local suppliers were concerned about people asking questions.[1]

The "Epistemic Crisis"

Unlike prescription opioid pills, where the content of the supply is pharmaceutically produced and regulated,[2] what is sold on the street as "heroin" is known to be unpredictable in potency and adulteration. Unpredictability of street heroin has long been a recognized risk factor for accidental overdose, and there are reasons to suspect that the enormity of the current crisis correlates with dramatic supply volatility (Darke et al., 1999; Ciccarone 2017; Ciccarone, Ondocsin, and Mars, 2017; Mars, Ondocsin, and Ciccarone, 2017).

Supply instability makes it especially challenging to know what to expect and what precautionary adaptations to make. Users have the most at stake, facing the daily challenge of relieving withdrawal symptoms while trying to safeguard against overdose. Increased volatility has made this all the more risky. The HIT study has documented vernacular methods of judging the presence of fentanyl in heroin prior to use, which rely on appearance, taste, and smell. These methods need to be validated with toxicological testing and, if reliable, could be shared as methods of harm reduction (Ciccarone, 2017). Currently, fentanyl test strips are sometimes available to users. Although these are potentially helpful, they indicate neither the amount nor the specific fentanyl analogs present.

For researchers, insufficient data about supply volatility makes it difficult to understand mortality and morbidity trends. For harm reduction workers responding to the epidemic, the general lack of knowledge about the shifting ingredients of street heroin makes their work all the more challenging. Although we know that the heroin supply has been particularly unstable in recent years, we do not know how, why, or at what stage in the process of production the supply is being adulterated. There is a lack of up-to-date public health surveillance and source-type testing over time and region (Ciccarone, 2017). In addition, the production processes that have resulted in this period of heroin supply instability are a "black box" to public health researchers. Lack of reliable practical knowledge is thus an important characteristic of the current heroin-fentanyl overdose crisis.

EXPERTISE AND KNOWLEDGE PRODUCTION

RAP, as used in the HIT project, draws on different types of knowledge and expertise, along an "insider-outsider" continuum. As diligent monitors of the fluctuations and changes in street heroin, users themselves are a unique source of expert knowledge. User accounts link different kinds of embodied drug experiences with other noticeable shifts in the street supply. Embodied experiences are represented in their own terms in the research findings. Multiple corresponding user accounts can reveal a common reality and are taken as indicators of the currently circulating heroin supply. Thus informed by insider perspectives, the RAP integrates an "epistemology from below" (Renkin and de Beer, 2017). Knowledge from below seeks not only local specificity but also an understanding of relevant underrepresented views of the marginalized. Consistent with the anthropological tenet of cultural relativism, field workers aim to understand the local logics underlying risky practices. They observe the heroin itself, how and where it is prepared and used, and its apparent effects on the users. This includes heating (or not heating) the drug solution, methods of injecting, rinsing injecting equipment, bodily injection sites, and other potential risks or protections to health.

Beyond the embodied experience of using heroin over a period of time, users draw from a range of sources to synthesize their own understanding of the changing supply. This might include discussion with peers, media reports, medical and harm reduction efforts, and receiving the results of toxicological testing. For the ethnographers, knowledge may be drawn from across other RAP sites, previous research or harm reduction experience, published scientific literature, government reports and informal sources, as well as the media. At times, users' beliefs may be at odds with those of the interviewers. In analyzing the data from users, and reconciling possible contradictions, primacy is given to firsthand accounts. For instance, users' accounts of their own heroin use are given the greatest evidentiary weight, whereas speculation about the heroin's country of origin would require triangulation with other sources.

There are a number of established techniques for improving the reliability of qualitative data, including triangulation across data sources and the attainment of "data saturation" where no new answers are received to the same questions when repeated (Strauss and Corbin, 1990). While complete data saturation is an ideal, unattainable goal, each RAP aims to achieve an approximation of this on the key points of inquiry. However, we found that in some research environments, this was particularly challenging.

In small communities, such as Charleston, West Virginia, a relatively consistent picture emerged after nineteen interviews, a handful of videoed injection sequences and neighborhood tours; whereas, after thirty interviews, eight videos, and some neighborhood tours, a clear picture of Chicago's heroin scene remained elusive with multiple contradictory accounts. For large cities and/or places with multiple sources of supply, RAP may require repeated visits before data saturation is a possibility. As Dan observed, "I mean the biggest mistake we made in Chicago. . . . Chicago is a big, complicated city with multiple different—with a diversity of neighborhoods, you know the culture within any one of these neighborhoods is so different from another neighborhood that we would have been better just going to one neighborhood in Chicago instead of trying to go to four. And so that's where the RAP study comes up short and that is when you're working with complicated cities one wishes for multiple repeat business, or just longer immersion, you know, two to three weeks."

Part of the RAP ethnography involves filming injection sequences. Since heroin use is currently criminalized, filming potentially puts the user at risk of identification. The team implemented procedures to minimize that possibility, weighing the risk against the potential public health benefits. Loss of access to veins is a well-documented problem for long-term injecting drug users (Stein, 1990), particularly those injecting cocaine or black tar heroin (Ciccarone and Bourgois, 2003; Ciccarone and Harris, 2015; Mars et al., 2016). Recording the preparation and injection of heroin allows the team to examine and compare the microrisks of injecting behavior in detail after research trips. This might include measuring the cooking time for the drug solution, the number of needle "pokes" involved before an injector successfully administers the drug and other details. Such data has been used to inform mathematical modeling of HIV transmission by Georgiy Bobashev as part of the HIT project.

For some of the researchers, filming injection sequences was one of the more challenging aspects of the fieldwork. Although some injections go smoothly, and the injector finds a usable vein quickly and easily, at other times a long struggle ensues that increases the potential propagation of blood and heightens infection risk. Empathetic observers, concerned about health risks, have to assess how to engage respectfully with the injector, whose priority is to complete an intravenous injection. This elicits a complex ethical and pragmatic quandary about when and how to introduce harm reduction messages to high-risk injectors.

If the ethnographer decides to intervene with a sanitary message, the injector may become alienated and possibly even retreat from harm reduction services. In such tricky field situations, ethnographers need to weigh biomedical priorities against real practical challenges and judge carefully how to intervene in a manner that is not high-handed. To this end, ethnographers rely on their understanding of the local logic behind injection drug use practices. This is an excerpt from a collaboratively written field note from the San Francisco training session, February 8, 2016. The italic text was written by Eliza and the roman text by Sarah.

Dave is chatting and is watching as Morgan prepares his shot and starts trying to find a vein. Morgan does not prepare his injection site with alcohol, but just begins trying to find a vein on his left forearm. It is a long, bloody process that takes about thirty minutes. He repeatedly wipes his bleeding arm on his pants, and they get more and more covered in his blood above the knee. He licks the needle several times, and he seems to be sticking the needle straight in [perpendicular] to the vein instead of at an angle. Eliza asks him at one point if that technique usually works better for him than going in at an angle and he says [he has to push the needle deep] because of the scar tissue. It's difficult and painful for us to watch. Each time, he pushes the needle deep into the arm to what would appear to be below the level of the vein but *he finally registers, and at this point, the whole room goes silent as he finally is able to do the shot after spending so much time working the area.*

Watching the prolonged injection sequence was a disconcerting experience, and Sarah and Eliza were glad to take a break afterward and reflect on what they have observed.

Jeff also reflected on these predicaments:

I've felt uncomfortable in a few situations where it was really difficult for some-one to inject and there were some long, tense moments where people are pok-ing themselves and you're filming them . . . it's tense and feels stressful, because they're getting more frustrated. Probably my presence and the camera is contrib-uting to some of their nervousness, if they're nervous, and . . . if it goes on and they continue to fail to inject, the tension just gets higher and higher.

Direct observation of injection practices can be uncomfortable and raise pragmatic ethical questions for the ethnographer, but it provides crucial data on the logic underlying unsanitary practices. Direct observation also enables systematic documentation of the pharmacological micrologistics of heroin use, including its packaging and physical appearance. This can contribute to a better understanding of the "microrisks" that may have population-level effects. Direct observation allows ethnographers to ask detailed questions about socially taboo and otherwise hidden processes of preparation and use, and reciprocally to answer injectors' questions that can promote less harmful practices.

The videos remain confidential to the research team, and like the rest of the data, are protected by a Federal Certificate of Confidentiality issued by the National Institute on Drug Abuse (NIDA). This protects the research participants from involuntary disclosure of any of the data gathered by the researchers, especially to the police and the courts. Other measures to protect their confidentiality include the use of oral rather than written consent to participate in the study and the storage of all study materials on a secure server. The University of California San Francisco's Institutional Review Board has given ethical approval for the study.

DISCUSSION

The use of RAP in the midst of the current overdose crisis allowed the research team to take into account local knowledge from some of the user populations most affected. However, the knowledge gained highlights the public health significance of what still remains *unknown,* and the ways users cope with this knowledge deficit. Unlike the epidemic of prescription opioid pill overdose, which was fueled by a regulated pharmaceutical supply and relatively legible modes of distribution, this second phase of the overdose crisis is characterized by an especially unstable heroin supply. Researchers and users alike know little about the processes of production, adulteration, dilution, and distribution. Dramatic shifts in potency and adulteration are hard to appraise without adequate chemical analysis or high-risk user consumption. In the context of an especially volatile supply, what users learn (at great risk) about the effects of heroin on one day may not be a guide to the heroin on another day. This volatility is a known risk factor for accidental overdose (Darke et al., 1999), and is likely to be a contributing cause of today's crisis. While some users are more confident about their ability to appraise the drug prior to consumption, their techniques of detection have yet to be validated (Ciccarone, 2017). All of these unknowns raise the stakes for public health researchers, harm reduction workers, and many users. In these ways, the heroin-fentanyl crisis parallels the early years of the AIDS epidemic in which knowledge about transmission and cause was lacking.

The RAP model has strengths and weaknesses for investigating the current situation. For sites with relatively simple sources of supply and distribution, a single RAP visit may be sufficient to gain a general picture, but more complex locations may require repeated visits. The difficulty of following-up with individual research participants in a marginalized population is also a limitation. Conversely, the anonymity and brevity of the interview encounters can generate candid responses. Potential selection bias introduced by the harm reduction setting needs careful counterbalancing to gain as wide a possible representation of the heroin-injecting population.

Although some team members had concerns going into the project that developing rapport so quickly would be difficult, this turned out not to be the case. We believe that this reflected the research team's overall experience working with heroin users, the presence of insiders on the team, and the trust of local sponsors. Moreover, researchers and users in general shared the desire to lessen user risk through improved knowledge, which also may have expedited the development of rapport. Participants were also paid a modest cash sum in recognition of their expertise and for their time (Ritter, Fry, and Swan, 2003).

While sacrificing the depth of long-term ethnography, a positive aspect of the RAP approach is its wide geographical scope, making it especially relevant to questions of national public health. RAP enabled an agile response to reports from around the country, something impossible for longer term, more embedded research. The use of the RAP findings can stand alone but also inform and generate joint qualitative-quantitative analyses. It can also contribute to improved service delivery and the development of structural-level innovations to prevent harm (Branas et al., 2018; Messac et al., 2013).[3]

NOTES

1. Williams et al. (1992) provides excellent further reading and advice for ethnographers on this topic.

2. This may be changing with the appearance of counterfeit prescription opioid pills sold on the street and through the Dark Net (see Gilbert and Dasgupta, 2017).

3. The authors would like to thank first and foremost the research participants for their willingness to share their knowledge and experience with us. We would also like to thank the many harm reduction workers who have assisted in this research across multiple sites. Thanks to Mary Howe, Fernando Montero Castrillo, Jeff Ondocsin, and Eliza Wheeler for their reflections on their experiences as part of the ethnographic field staff. Thanks also to Christopher London for helpful comments on an earlier draft of this paper. Many thanks to the editors of this volume, Miriam Boeri and Rashi Shukla, for inviting us to contribute to this volume and for encouraging feedback. Finally, we thank the funders, the National Institutes of Health and NIDA (Grants number DA037820 and UL1TR001881). Photographs by Daniel Ciccarone.

REFERENCES

Agar, M. H., and N. J. Kozel (1999). Introduction to *Substance Use & Misuse, 34*(14), 1935–49.

Bardenheier, B., et al. (1998). Tetanus surveillance, United States, 1995–1997. *MMWR CDC Surveill Summ, 47*(2), 1–13.

Beebe, J. (2001). *Rapid assessment process: An introduction.* Lanham, MD: Rowman and Littlefield.

Binswanger, I. A., et al. (2000). High prevalence of abscesses and cellulitis among community-recruited injection drug users in San Francisco. *Clin Infect Dis, 30*(3), 579–81.

Bourgois, P. (2002). Anthropology and epidemiology on drugs: The challenges of cross- methodological and theoretical dialogue. *International Journal of Drug Policy, 13*(4), 259–69.

———. (2003). *In search of respect: Selling crack in El Barrio.* Updated 2nd ed. New York: Cambridge University Press.

Bourgois, P., and J. Schonberg (2009). *Righteous dopefiend.* Berkeley: University of California Press.

Branas, C. C., et al. (2018). Citywide cluster randomized trial to restore blighted vacant land and its effects on violence, crime, and fear. *Proceedings of the National Academy of Sciences, 115*(12), 2946–51.

Ciccarone, D. (2003). With both eyes open: Notes on a disciplinary dialogue between ethnographic and epidemiological research among injection drug users. *International Journal of Drug Policy, 14*(1), 115–18.

——— (2009). Heroin in brown, black, and white: Structural factors and medical consequences in the US heroin market. *International Journal of Drug Policy, 20*(3), 277–82.

——— (2012). Henceforth harm reduction? *International Journal of Drug Policy, 23*(1), 16–17.

——— (2017). Fentanyl in the US heroin supply: A rapidly changing risk environment. *International Journal of Drug Policy, 46,* 107–11.

——— (2019). The triple wave epidemic: Supply and demand drivers of the US opioid overdose crisis. *International Journal of Drug Policy,* epub ahead of print. doi: 10.1016/j.drugpo.2019.01.010.

Ciccarone, D., and P. Bourgois (2003). Explaining the geographical variation of HIV among injection drug users in the United States. *Substance Use and Misuse, 38*(14), 2049–63.

Ciccarone, D., and M. Harris (2015). Fire in the vein: Heroin acidity and its proximal effect on users' health. *International Journal of Drug Policy, 26*(11), 1103–10.

Ciccarone, D., J. Ondocsin, and S. G. Mars (2017). Heroin uncertainties: Exploring users' perceptions of fentanyl-adulterated and -substituted "heroin." *International Journal of Drug Policy, 46,* 146–55.

Ciccarone, D., et al. (2001). Soft tissue infections among injection drug users, San Francisco, California, 1996–2000. *Journal of the American Medical Association, 285*(21), 2707–9.

Ciccarone, D., et al. (2016). Nationwide increase in hospitalizations for heroin-related soft tissue infections: Associations with structural market conditions. *Drug and Alcohol Dependence, 163,* 126–33.

Darke, S., et al. (1999). Fluctuations in heroin purity and the incidence of fatal heroin overdose. *Drug and Alcohol Dependence, 54*(2), 155–61.

Daston, L. a. G., P. (2007). *Objectivity.* New York: Zone.

Doody, O., and M. Noonan (2013). Preparing and conducting interviews to collect data. *Nurse Researcher, 20*(5), 28–32.

Drug Enforcement Administration (2017). *National Drug Threat Assessment.* October, U.S. Department of Justice, Drug Enforcement Agency. Retrieved from www.dea.gov/documents/2017/10/01/2017-national-drug-threat-assessment.

Fitch, C., et al. (2004). Rapid assessment: An international review of diffusion, practice and outcomes in the substance use field. *Social Science and Medicine, 59*(9), 1819–30.

Gilbert, M., and N. Dasgupta (2017). Silicon to syringe: Cryptomarkets and disruptive innovation in opioid supply chains. *International Journal of Drug Policy, 46,*160–67.

Hildebrand, P. E. (1979). *Summary of the Sondeo methodology used by ICTA,* Instituto de Ciencia y Tecnología, Villa Nueva, Guatemala.

——— (1981). Combining disciplines in rapid appraisal: The Sondeo approach. *Agricultural Administration, 8*(6), 423–32.

Karandinos, G., et al. (2014). The moral economy of violence in the US inner city. *Current Anthropology, 55*(1), 1–22.

Katz, J. (2017). Drug deaths in America are rising faster than ever. *New York Times,* June 5.

Koester, S. (1996). The process of drug injection: Applying ethnography to the study of HIV risk among IDUs. AIDS. In *Drugs and Prevention: Perspectives on Individual and Community Action,* ed. T. R. A. R. Hartnoll, 133–48. London: Routledge.

Krumpal, I. (2013). Determinants of social desirability bias in sensitive surveys: A literature review. *Quality and Quantity, 47*(4), 2025–47.

Lucyk, S. N., and L. S. Nelson (2017). Toxicosurveillance in the US opioid epidemic. *International Journal of Drug Policy, 46,* 168–71.

Maher, L. (2002). Don't leave us this way: Ethnography and injecting drug use in the age of AIDS. *International Journal of Drug Policy, 13*(4), 311–25.

Manderson, L. a. A., P. (1992). An Epidemic in the Field? Rapid Assessment Procedures and Health Research. *Soc Sci Med, 35*(7), 839–50.

Mars, S. G. (2012). *The politics of addiction: Medical conflict and drug dependence in England.* Houndsmill: Palgrave Macmillan.

Mars, S. G., J. Ondocsin, and D. Ciccarone (2017). Sold as heroin: Perceptions and use of an evolving drug in Baltimore, MD. *Journal of Psychoactive Drugs, 50*(2), 167–76.

——— (2018). Toots, tastes, and tester shots: User accounts of drug sampling methods for gauging heroin potency. *Harm Reduction Journal, 15*(1), 26.

Mars, S. G., et al. (2014). Every "never" I ever said came true: Pathways from pills to heroin injecting. *International Journal of Drug Policy, 25*(2), 257–66.

——— (2015). Heroin-related overdose: The unexplored influences of markets, marketing, and source- types in the United States. *Social Science and Medicine, 140,* 44–53.

——— (2016). The textures of heroin: User perspectives on "Black Tar" and powder heroin in two US cities. *Journal of Psychoactive Drugs, 48*(4), 270–78.

Messac, L., et al. (2013). The good-enough science-and- politics of anthropological collaboration with evidence-based clinical research: Four ethnographic case studies. *Social Science and Medicine, 99*, 176–86.

Murphy, E. L., et al. (2001). Risk factors for skin and soft-tissue abscesses among injection drug users: A case-control study. *Clin Infect Dis, 33*(1), 35–40.

Needle, R. H., et al. (2003). Rapid assessment of the HIV/AIDS crisis in racial and ethnic minority communities: An approach for timely community interventions. *American Journal of Public Health, 93*(6), 970–79.

Passaro, D. J., et al. (1998). Wound botulism associated with black tar heroin among injecting drug users. *JAMA, 279* (11), 859–63.

Renkin, W., and S. de Beer (2017). The Tshwane Homeless Summit as dramaturgy: A contextual, trans-disciplinary epistemology from below. *Development Southern Africa, 34*(4), 482–96.

Rhodes, T., et al. (1999). Rapid assessment, injecting drug use, the public health. *The Lancet, 354*, 65–68.

Ritter, A. J., C. L. Fry, and A. Swan (2003). The ethics of reimbursing injecting drug users for public health research interviews: What price are we prepared to pay? *International Journal of Drug Policy, 14*(1), 1–3.

Scrimshaw, S. C., and E. Hurtado (1987). Rapid assessment procedures for nutrition and primary health care: Anthropological approaches to improving programme effectiveness. *Latin American Center,* 70 p. UCLA Latin American Center Reference Series 11.

Shaner, W. W., P. F. Philipp, and W. R. Schmehly, eds. (1982). *Readings in farming systems research and development.* Westview Special Studies in Agricultural Science and Policy. Boulder, CO: Westview.

Stein, M. (1990). Medical complications of intravenous drug use. *Journal of General Internal Medicine, 5*(3), 249–57.

Strauss, A. L., and J. M. Corbin (1990). *Basics of qualitative research: Grounded theory procedures and techniques.* Newbury Park, CA: Sage.

Trotter, R. T., et al. (2001). A methodological model for rapid assessment, response, and evaluation: The RARE program in public health. *Field Methods, 13*, 137–59.

Unick, G., et al. (2014). The relationship between US heroin market dynamics and heroin-related overdose, 1992–2008. *Addiction, 109*(11), 1889–98.

Warner, M., et al. (2016). Drugs most frequently involved in drug overdose deaths: United States, 2010–2014. *Natl Vital Stat Rep, 65*(10), 1–15.

Werner, S. B., et al. (2000). Wound botulism in California, 1951–1998: Recent epidemic in heroin injectors. *Clin Infect Dis, 31*(4), 1018–24.

White, M. S. (1998). Interview with Philippe Bourgois.

Whyte, W. F. (1955). *Street corner society: The social structure of an Italian slum.* 4th ed. Chicago: University of Chicago Press.

Williams, T., et al. (1992). Personal safety in dangerous places. *Journal of Contemporary Ethnography, 21*(3), 343–74.

SEVEN

Conducting International Reflexive Ethnography

THEORETICAL AND METHODOLOGICAL STRUGGLES

Avelardo Valdez, Alice Cepeda, and Charles Kaplan

RETURNING TO EJE MILITAR, IZTAPALAPA (MEXICO CITY)

The late-model Nissan doesn't draw much attention until we tumble out of the vehicle. Comanche, the owner of the car, operates a gypsy taxi for local residents. Now the entire street is watching, wondering who these strangers are, at this hour and on a Friday night.

The *colonia* is Eje Militar, located in Iztapalapa, the most populous *delegación* in Mexico City. It's an isolated, highly urbanized *colonia*, comprised of poor close-knit family-based networks. It is a setting for extensive substance use and local criminal networks, intermixed with hard-working people of all ages who labor at menial jobs throughout the city.

Besides another USC investigator and I, two former community field workers who are part of our research team are in the car. Neftali is the most recognized of us. He recently was here for the *Dia de los Reyes,* on January 6, a party given for kids in the neighborhood. Ever since he started working in this community, he has contributed gifts and food for the event. The young men in the street quickly recognize Neftali and Abel, and subsequently my female USC colleague and me.

Just minutes after we emerge from the car, El Mapache appears, accompanied by another, younger man. Mapache was our primary gatekeeper during our study in Mexico City. He is pleased and even delighted to see us, especially me. I haven't been to the *colonia* since we sponsored a *sonidero* dance as a way of saying thank you to the community for their cooperation in our projection mapping project. A *sonidero* is a particular type of *cumbia* DJ who connects to the crowd with comments aimed at specific persons in the audience and the colonia.

Mapache says, "I thought you forgot about us. I thought you forgot about us. We're so glad to see all of you. When are we going to do another study? We are here to serve you." You can sense his sincerity and I feel he wants to give us all a big hug. We break out a couple of twelve-packs of beer, and some tequila purchased during the hour-long ride to the colonia. These are passed around to El Mapache and others from the streets who join the impromptu street gathering.

In this colonia, our research team conducted a social epidemiological study on individual-level substance-use risk behaviors, social-interaction processes, and contextual influences on crack-use patterns. We also implemented a public health education campaign using projection mapping technology to affect social change by promoting and facilitating health-seeking behaviors among drug users and changing the neighborhood's normal environment. We were there to maintain and reinforce our ties to this community, where we had implemented several of the studies we conducted before the one described in this chapter. But the journey that led us to this international study and our presence in the community that evening took fifteen years.

In this chapter, we first briefly discuss the intellectual journey toward understanding and changing the lives of active crack users from within their own worldview and normal environment. Next, we discuss the origin of the reflexive ethnographic method we used in this study. This is followed by the description of the research we conducted in Mexico City, where our challenge was to implement an intervention aimed at inciting a "behavioral nudge" (Bill and Melinda Gates Foundation, 2014) to promote crack-use harm reduction behaviors and HIV health-seeking behaviors.

REFLEXIVE ETHNOGRAPHY: THE STRUGGLE TO
UNDERSTAND AND CHANGE A COMPLEX
AND DYNAMIC SOCIAL WORLD

We were able to develop a critical theory of the Latino health paradox applied to crack cocaine drug use through a distinct ethnographic methodology.[1] This reflexive ethnographical approach required that we radically embrace the daily lives of Latino immigrants "from within" their complex and dynamic world (Cicourel, 1964; Emerson, 1983; Garfinkel, 1967; Mehan and Wood, 1975b). The reflexive ethnographic methodological problem was to learn how to organize the fieldwork to get inside this complex and dynamic social reality and to generate, in collaboration with the drug users themselves, detailed descriptive data in the form of audio recordings, transcripts, and field notes that documented the fieldwork experience. Reflexive ethnography is immersion in the world that will eventually produce participatory change in that world. It also requires that any theoretical understanding that is obtained will eventually lead to changes in oppressive and harmful practices that have been discovered in the research (Mehan and Wood, 1975a). This methodological approach turns participant observation "on its head," resulting in varying forms of observant participation that provides the basis for designing an intervention that will effectively change the normal environment of crack use in Mexico City (Pfadenhauer, 2005).

The critical feature of our methodology was a move from a methodology model based on a single ethnographer, who perhaps is helped in certain data collection and clerical tasks by research assistants and workers, to a team ethnography model that forced us to be reflexive in dealing with novel emerging problems (Erickson and Stull, 1998). Both data collection and analysis were governed by a team model. These fieldwork teams were horizontally organized into groups consisting of community field workers and academics. A deep commitment to mutual respect was fundamental in the process of generating the interview and field-notes data sources as well as their interpretations in building a critical theory.

We applied this ethnographic tradition in an extended case study design (Burawoy, 2009) that began with our focus on drug use among poor African Americans displaced to Houston by Hurricane Katrina in 2005 (Cepeda et al., 2010). Our observations of the drug use and market dynamics associated with the disaster led us to a population from Mexico and Central America rebuilding New Orleans after Hurricane Katrina. The qualitative analysis of that study revealed how social processes and contextual factors contribute to crack use among Latino day laborers in New Orleans in a post-disaster context (Valdez et al., 2010).

Findings are significant, given that the prevalence of crack use among U.S. Latinos has been previously found to be relatively low compared to other groups (Substance Abuse and Mental Health Services Administration [SAMHSA], 2008). New Orleans' flourishing drug markets in the communities where many Latino immigrant day laborers reside provided easy access to crack, and facilitated their initiation and periods of daily use. Psychosocial factors, such as feelings of isolation and constant exposure to victimization due to day laborers' marginal status, were found to contribute further to individuals' susceptibility to crack use. In sum, Latino immigrant day laborers who migrated to New Orleans post-Katrina encountered many disaster-related challenges but also experienced the difficulty of adapting to a new city with no established Latino community to provide support and resources to facilitate their adaptation. To this end, many expressed in their interviews feelings of despair, so, since crack was easily accessible, they initiated their drug use behavior. Many reported circular immigration patterns that consisted of traveling to and from their home countries and the United States. These findings prompted us to explore crack use in their country of origin and get a better understanding of the prevalence of crack use and the process of diffusion of crack from the perspective of the crack users themselves (Valdez et al., 2015).

ADOPTION AND TRANSMISSION OF CRACK USE PRACTICES IN MEXICO CITY

Based on our findings in New Orleans, we were funded to conduct a qualitative study of crack use and the transmission of HIV and other infectious diseases in Mexico City. This city was chosen because, during the previous decade, Mexico's urban areas represented the largest communities of Mexicans going to the United States. One of our first tasks as a research team was to conduct extensive ethnographic drug fieldwork training with staff.

Our field team recruited key informants in these communities, such as established neighborhood leaders, drug sellers, political party leaders, heads of criminal networks, merchants, and others who represented key constituents. These persons were told that we were a university-based group from the United States and were involved in a health study. During frequent visits to these neighborhoods by the field team we established a rapport and trust with these leaders. This familiarity allowed us access to persons and networks of peers in the community who were current users of smoked crack. Our fieldwork team began recruiting through a snowball sampling process identifying crack users, locations where they hung out, and times that they were more likely to be on the streets.

This study found that, compared to the United States, patterns of crack use for many users in Mexico City tended to be more self-regulated and less problematic—characteristics of the stable crack user and old head type (Valdez et al., 2015). Most current crack users in this study were able to consume without major disruption to daily social functioning because they used in the context of social networks of family relations and friends, some form of work or vocation, and access to safe nonpublic places to use the drug. This study's unique social context may explain the observed pattern of controlled and moderate use, which is different than earlier descriptions of crack use in U.S. and Western or European societies (e.g., Hoffman et al., 2000; Sterk, Dolan, and Hatch, 1999; Werb et al., 2010). In Mexico City, crack use is accepted as long as it does not disrupt the established social and economic order. However, there were users who resembled the patterns of chronic uncontrolled crack use that were found in the United States. We decided, therefore, that any interventions for these communities should target all types of crack users.

WALL PROJECTIONS: *TIRANDO ESQUINA*
DISTURBING THE NORMAL ENVIRONMENT
OF CRACK PRACTICES

> I had never seen projections like this before.
> I learned that I shouldn't loan my pipe because
> I can acquire an infection.

During our ethnographic work and personal interactions with users and members of these communities in Mexico City, we learned that any intervention effort had to be designed to disrupt everyday life and connect in a special way with the target population. Given our extensive knowledge and personal interactions with the population of adult crack users, we had to ensure the intervention responded to real lives, conditions, and needs. The program Tirando Esquina: Interviniendo Muros de Salud (TE:IMS) was developed as the first of its kind aimed at inciting a "behavioral nudge" to promote crack use harm reduction behaviors and HIV health-seeking behaviors. In thinking of how to disrupt everyday life, TE:IMS used an innovative approach of projection mapping technology, where health messages were created using 3-D illusions, animation, and visual text graphics and sound projected onto buildings. Projection mapping has been defined as an avant-garde form of expression and technology that connects with audiences on the street in a new way by using any structure or object in the location as a canvas onto which to project the desired content (Kim, 2015; Krautsack, 2011; Mine et al., 2012). The projection mapping was used to promote a public health education campaign combined with the distribution of related products (HIV/AIDS education material and crack kits) to promote and facilitate key health-seeking behaviors (Cepeda et al., 2017; Frankeberger et al., 2019).

Selecting the Site

Given the innovative nature of TE:IMS and the aim of providing a behavioral nudge, we knew that the development and successful implementation of TE:IMS was centered on the research team's ability to work closely with the crack-using population and general residents in the community. Based on our previous research, the team selected one of the most highly marginalized communities in Mexico City. We knew that members of that community had limited access to health services. As one of our field notes describes:

> Eje Militar is located in the Delegación Iztaplapa. Nested along a canyon, it is one of the poorest and most densely populated areas in Mexico City. It is not hard to notice the community's isolation and marginalization in stark contrast to some of the most central colonias of Mexico City. As we drive into the area we observe rows of small homes with window burglar bars and parking spaces enclosed in cage-structures to protect cars from theft. We hear that there are only two roads that lead into the community, again highlighting the isolation and marginalization of the neighborhood. The streets are narrow and residents gather along sidewalks, at religious altars (to the Santa Muerte or San Judas Tadeo) or corner stores.

At first glance, there appeared to be no distinguishable community cohesion and/or arrangement of residents into groups. However, as we became more familiar with the area, we discovered the community was characterized by a pattern of social organization with orderly relationships (Suttles, 1968). We learned that individuals are members of subgroups, each with its own purpose that gives individuals a place in the community. Four main leaders were identified, each with their own centralized network (Mapache, Luis, Gallo, and Papito). We learned that a sense of belonging, loyalty, respect, and fear were important mechanisms through which these orderly relationships were created and maintained by these individuals. It was through such networks that our team established trust and rapport with the other community-wide residents from this poor urban colonia.

We also found that the overall organization of the neighborhood was formed through institutional arrangements focused on religion, commercial exchanges, and recreation. As found in other low-income communities, religion is one of the most important forms by which residents express their adherence to group concerns. Interestingly, this does not necessarily mean that individuals are "religious" or "moral." Commercial exchanges refer to intimate and financial transactions that are completed and rooted in trust and friendship. Therefore, those engaging in commercial exchanges are not welcoming of strangers. Lastly, recreational institutions, as activities or spaces in which a group or groups socialize, play an important role in maintaining cohesion. This was certainty the case in this community.

Thus, Colonia Eje Militar, one of the largest and most densely populated areas of Mexico City organized by these social relationships and institutional arrangements, became the basis for the implementation of TE:IMS. Since we were familiar with this area from our previous study, it was not difficult to reestablish relations with the diverse leadership in this community through repeated visits and interaction with its leaders.

The Creative Phase of the Intervention

What emerged during the development and creative phase of the intervention was an iterative process whereby repeated interactions, communications, and ideas were exchanged between the investigative team, community leaders, gatekeeper and key informant leaders, government institutions, educational and cultural organizations, local artists, and other members, including merchants and police. The aim was to generate an intervention that reflected the street-based subculture of crack users within this highly urbanized but marginalized context.

For instance, the presence of religious altars are a very prominent staple in these communities. We knew from the previous study and from our fieldwork in preparing for the implementation of TE:IMS that altars to La Santa Muerte and San Judas Tadeo were a point of congregation, veneration, and belonging. As such, the projection mapping health messages had to reflect this and other cultural beliefs. The following field note details an encounter the team had with Mapache, one of the study's gatekeepers and a daily user of crack:

> When we get to Mapache we find him and three other young men from his clique cleaning the nearby altar for St. Jude. It has a 4 foot tall image of the

saint and a crucifix of Christ on the lower right hand side of the statue. They are taking turns sweeping, cleaning and washing the glass that encases St. Jude. Mapache proceeds to tell us about the new water fall system that had been installed in the altar, a sort of waterfall effect. He proceeds to tell us that it stopped working the week prior because a "crack head" had stolen the copper tubing (a popular behavior where people steal and sell copper in the neighborhood). "When I find out who did this, he will have to answer to me."

This was just one of many encounters we had with crack users in the community, who are the primary caretakers of the altars. During these encounters we learned the importance that St. Jude and Santa Muerte had for the target population and many of the community members as intermediaries to God they prayed to, revered, and venerated. So, it was important that the creation of the projection mapping messages reflect both of these images.

Similarly, local artists participated in the creation of the projections. This included a local dance group that heard about our intervention and wanted to participate. They developed a modern (interpretative) dance, depicting movements that expressed the importance of living a healthy life. Similarly, a local rap artist wrote and performed a song for TE:IMS based on the risks, trials, and tribulations of crack use and the aim of assisting with reducing harmful health behaviors. Overall, the content and creative process required that public health evidenced-based knowledge, concepts, and facts be translated into messages, images, and audio that reflected the lifestyle, experiences, and cultural jargon reflective of the target community. This would not have been possible if indigenous members of the community such as graphic designers, graffiti artists, architects, artists, animators, photographers, actors, sound engineers, and musicians had not been involved.

Not only was the buy-in of the community residents important, but the involvement of governmental and institutional representatives was key as well. For instance, while it is known that there is not much police presence in this community, we had to contact and get to know the police in the area, as illustrated in the field notes:

> We went to leave a letter introducing TE:IMS to the police chief in the targeted Izatapalapa sector. It is located next to the Constitución de Apatzingán station on line 2 of the metrobus. We got a little turned around and approached two policemen who were outside a bank branch. They pointed us towards the direction of where they could find "the boss." One block from the police station there was an altar and life-size image of La Santa Muerte with more than a dozen different size figurines of her. Outside of the glass covered altar, there were at least three dozen fresh flowers.

Similarly, gaining access and permission for the projection sites was imperative. This typically required several visits and discussions with owners of homes, including the director of the school that was the largest projection structure for TE:IMS. The primary projection site was at the Escuela Paula Alegria located in La Primer Secciòn. It is a three-story structure painted half in green and half in white and yellow. The school is bordered by an open courtyard that leads to several convenience stores and a large court (for basketball and soccer) and a row of residential homes. To ensure a high impact and increase the visibility of the public health messages we had to ensure access to this school. This required the team to visit and attempt to set up meetings with school administrators. We were finally successful in meeting with the director, who assured us, "If it's on one of the outside walls and in the evening, I don't have any problems in you projecting the images on the school. I can also provide you with a power cord for electricity." Although there seemed to be some trepidation about having crack and HIV messages projected onto the school, we learned that some community members and parents had mentioned the importance of TE:IMS to the director.

Nine projection mapping messages (Table 7.1) were created and projected. Projection messages included universal HIV prevention for the general population and more selective messages for the crack-using population. What follows is a brief description of selected projections.

Figure 7.1 shows one of the first structures selected in Iztapalapa. The content in figure 7.2 was developed using architectural mapping, animation, and an audio message accompanied by visible text. *¿Quién se puede contagiar?* (Who can Become Infected?) emphasized HIV transmission risk through sexual practices, including having multiple partners and having sex without a condom. Figure 7.3 depicts the *Las mil caras del VIH* (Faces of HIV), which emphasized the universal impact of HIV, not limited to certain groups. The projection utilized architectural mapping, dashes of video, and audio messages.

Additional projections (not shown here) include one entitled *No te fumes el destino de tus hijos* (Your Children's Future Up in Smoke). This projection, focused on the consequences of crack use on children, utilized abstract mapping and visual animation accompanied by the sound of rain and thunder. These images were projected on a second selected structure, since no other buildings were available. Another projection, *Fumar crack te tira los dientes* (Tooth Loss and Crack Use), used abstract mapping, motion graphics, and animation timed to the beat of hip-hop audio. The content focused on the physical consequences, most visible in loss of teeth, of long-term, chronic crack use.

TABLE 7.1. Content of Projection Messages

Projection	Translation	Message
¿Qué es el VIH?	What Is HIV?	Presented HIV/AIDS health education information regarding the biology of the virus, routes of transmission, and prevention strategies.
Las mil caras del VIH	HIV Has a Thousand Faces	Depicted that everyone can be at risk for contracting HIV. This message aimed to dispel stereotypes that only certain groups, such as MSM, can get HIV.
¿Quién se puede contagiar?	Who Can Become Infected?	Discussed HIV transmission routes, particularly in regard to high-risk sexual activity and substance use. Prevention messages, such as using a condom and not sharing drug paraphernalia, were presented.
Videojuego del sistema inmune	Immune System Videogame	Described the biology of HIV, including the impact of HIV on the body's immune system. Available treatment for HIV was presented as a means to have a long and healthy life.
Cortometraje camino de piedra	Paths of Crack (short film)	Portrays the social consequences of crack use through a short story depicting a young adult experimenting with crack for the first time and the paths he takes thereafter.
No te fumes el destino de tus hijos	Your Children's Future Up in Smoke	Discussed the impact of crack use on the family and children. Stories were presented depicting how crack use can cause problems with family relationships.
Usar kit seguro	Using the Crack Kit	Presented the importance of the safer crack kit and described how to use each item safely and effectively.
Fumar tu casa	Smoke Away Your Home	Depicted the impact of crack addiction on one's life, including its influence on the family, neighbors, and the home. Crack can become all encompassing, leading to a total lack of control impacting all areas of life.
Fumar crack te tira los dientes	Tooth Loss and Crack Use	Presented the physical consequences of chronic crack use. Damage to oral health, including tooth loss, was provided as an example of crack's effects.

FIGURE 7.1. Site of projection mapping. Photo credit: Eduardo Zafra Mora, SEISYAC,

FIGURE 7.2. Segments of *¿Quién se puede contagiar?* Projection depicting HIV transmission routes. Photo credit: Eduardo Zafra Mora, SEISYAC.

FIGURE 7.3. Segments of *Las mil caras del VIH*. Projection depicting the message that anyone can be affected by HIV. Photo credit: Eduardo Zafra Mora, SEISYAC.

Implications of the Intervention

Overall, the project was a great success in establishing the feasibility of providing a nudge for HIV health-seeking behaviors and harm reduction strategies through the use of projection mapping and community members of our ethnography team who were trained to be "street *promotores*" (community health workers). In drug use research, street-recruited hard-to-reach populations differ significantly from individuals recruited from treatment programs in their accessibility, occupational instability, access to resources, and legal status (Eland-Goossensen, van de Goor, and Garretsen, 1997). In international settings, the issues are compounded by limited drug treatment and health education services, which make it hard for marginalized populations to seek or obtain services. The success of TE:IMS was grounded in the direct and intimate contact, trust, and rapport that was established by the team with the crack users and their respective families, friends, and acquaintances in the community. In keeping with the importance of community engagement, the team exited the site by sponsoring a community event that included a *sonidero*, as previously mentioned. The event attracted over three hundred multi-generational individuals that was attended by all generations of families.

Our TE:IMS team's "street presence" facilitated trust and rapport and our ability to understand the everyday lives of individuals in these communities. In addition, the participation of staff indigenous to the communities and the proper selection and training of field staff was essential for the success of this type of intervention. The staff tended to have "privileged access" to closed or restricted-risk networks. As the authors have documented in previous publications, to successfully implement this type of intervention requires staff with certain personality attributes in order to be maximally effective, including good communications skills, tact, persistence, and problem-solving abilities (Cepeda and Valdez, 2010; Valdez et al., 2016).

DISCUSSION AND CONCLUSION

This chapter has reported our experience of conducting an international reflexive ethnographic study focused on crack use among Mexican immigrant day laborers in the United States and among poor urban Mexicans. The reflexive ethnography in this instance only makes sense when considered as an extended case method that traversed nearly two decades in two distinct cities, New Orleans and Mexico City. Without this methodological background, it would have been impossible to arrive at the conclusions we have made. The extended case method was developed by anthropologist Michael Burawoy (2009). Whereas Burawoy developed his methodology over four countries and four decades, our application of the extended case methodology was more limited, covering two countries and two decades. In addition, whereas Burawoy utilized one theoretical tradition of ethnography drawn from the Manchester and Chicago schools, our own application of the extended case method utilized a different theoretical tradition of ethnography; one developed from the sociology of Georg Simmel's urban-conflict studies, the phenomenological sociology of Alfred Schutz, and the critical theoretical approach of the Frankfurt school's early member Walter Benjamin (Benjamin, 2002; Levine, 1980; Schutz, 1997; Simmel, 1902), and Robert Park (Park, 1967) from the Chicago school. Park enthusiastically brought back to Chicago from Germany the methods of observer-participation. These methods blended quite well with his own journalistic background. Insider stories and novelistic descriptions were seen as a primary source of data for ethnographic analysis.

This German tradition, which puts an emphasis on lived experience as the most valuable source of ethnographic data, greatly influenced our conception of reflexive ethnography. As depicted here, we applied it in an extended case study that included poor African-American disaster refugees, U.S. Mexican immigrants, and poor urban Mexican crack users.

Public health research, whether qualitative or quantitative, ought to translate its results quickly into interventions that lead to changes in the normal environment of communities. Our projection mapping intervention grew directly from our prior field studies and was consistent with our observer-participant principle. The intervention was designed to promote change or a nudge to reduce harm to a highly marginalized population from within their own social reality. Most interventions to promote behavioral change are predicated from psychological theories where individual differences are at the forefront. For example, one widely used model of behavior change for drug abuse assesses the individual's readiness to change behavior (Prochaska, DiClemente, and Norcross, 1992). The intervention in that model guides the individual through the stages of change, starting from the stage of precontemplation through the stages of contemplation, decision to act, and maintenance. In contrast, the intervention used in our study grew out of our ethnographic partnership with communities, not fundamentally with individuals. We learned that what needed changing was the community, and then we provided an image and the objective means that would make change possible from the community's own perspective and from within its own cultural framework.

Knowledge obtained in this manner was used to design an intervention that would act much like an ethnomethodological breaching experiment, by disturbing the normal environment. This was accomplished as described through projecting messages on existing walls while at the same time distributing crack kits en masse, which allowed individual users to change their practices of using crack. Together, the projective mapping and crack kits provided a "disruptive innovation" to diffuse knowledge and evidence-based harm reduction practices to the community (Rotheram-Borus, Swendeman, and Chorpita, 2012). This research was based on a scientific ethic that change in harmful practices within the context of the community is the strongest justification for conducting research in the first place. This was what motivated us to turn our discoveries about the normative organization of crack use into a vehicle for change in community praxis and the creation of a differential consciousness about the meaning of crack in the community (Mehan and Wood, 1975a; Sandoval, 2000).

Most of our current knowledge of crack is based on ethnographic research and quantitative studies of varying populations in one place during one period of time. The few longitudinal studies of the same individuals often already show surprising results that challenge the knowledge we have. For example, Dan Waldorf, Craig Reinarman, and Sheila Murphy's (1991) longitudinal study of mainly middle-class San Francisco cocaine users, including a subsample of crack users, provides us with an understanding of how cocaine and crack use is controlled and integrated into the daily lives of users. These kinds of findings not only support what we have found in our extended case study, but also have more recently been recognized by Carl Hart (2013), who has argued that integrated, controlled use is more the norm than the exception of crack use. Much of the literature, because of its obvious methodological limitations, has painted a false picture of crack use, characterizing it as a drug with exceedingly high addiction liability, impossible to control. However, as has been stated by Reinarman, Cohen, and Kaal (2004), this picture has more to do with moral panic and scientific and bureaucratic self-interest than with the reality of crack. This chapter fills an important gap in the literature that could not have been accomplished without the application of the extended case method and reflexive ethnography. As the opening paragraph shows, we were engaged with our study participants in a struggle, not only to scientifically understand the full scope of the world of crack use, but also how to change this world to make it healthier and better.

Once we were able to take an extended view of crack use among Mexican immigrant workers, an extreme and special population, not only were misconceptions about crack use corrected, but more general theoretical misconceptions about the health of the Mexican-American populations also fell by the wayside. Our research clearly discounts the established view that Mexicans immigrate to the United States in a healthier condition than the first and second generations of Mexican Americans. As they are assimilated into the general American population, they are exposed to the same health risks not experienced in Mexico. They choose to migrate because they see themselves as ready and able to work hard in pursuit of the "American dream." While this view might have had some credence decades ago, when migration patterns involved a rather direct line from rural Mexico to the fields, factories, and construction sites of America, in today's era of globalization, circular migration, and deportation, the picture is much more complex. Large Mexican cities have become staging points for rural migrants, as well as homes for deportees who have been uprooted from their rural backgrounds and are more adapted now to urban conditions. They also are traditionally established migration opportunities for the young rural population who have little economic prospects in the Mexican countryside.

Our studies join those other critical studies cited at the beginning of this chapter to suggest that, at least for the very specific behavior of crack use, the old paradox is invalid. Our New Orleans study discovered for the first time that crack use was frequent among immigrant day workers engaged in the rebuilding of New Orleans after Katrina. This involved aggressive marketing practices by established African-American supply networks that remained after the devastation of Hurricane Katrina. Taken alone, this would have confirmed rather than refuted the thesis of the Latino paradox. But as we struggled together with these workers to understand the narratives elicited in our conversational interviews and fieldwork, we also discovered that many were seasoned crack users *before* they ever immigrated to the United States to take advantage of the rising demand for cheap manual laborers in the wake of the relocation of the indigenous New Orleans working-class population. They brought to New Orleans, not only their established crack use patterns, but also their polysubstance use and the mechanisms of self-management of this use learned in Mexican cities. In short, these immigrants were not naive to the health risks of their host country, but rather had already established strategies of resilience in the face of severe living conditions and increased availability of crack from aggressive crack-dealing networks.

Our reflexive ethnography struggled through with our study participants to go beyond simply eliciting narratives and recording field notes. We truly wanted to dig deeper in order to make sense of the dynamic world of these two populations and the methodological struggles we encountered as qualitative researchers in the social world of crack users.[2]

NOTES

1. The Latino paradox argues that despite risk factors such as poverty, low education levels, and lack of health insurance, recent immigrants have more favorable health and mortality outcomes than their U.S.-born counterparts (Alegría, Álvarez, and DiMarzio, 2017; Brazil, 2015; Markides and Coreil, 1986; Morales et al., 2002; Patel et al., 2004; Scribner, 1996).

2. We would like to acknowledge our funding sources, including the National Institute on Drug Abuse (R21 DA031376, R01 DA021852, R01 DA021852S1), the Bill and Melinda Gates Foundation, Grand Challenges Explorations grant OPP1118561

and the Fundación Gonzalo Rio Arronte, I.A.P. We would also like to recognize our international collaborators, including the Instituto nacional de psiquiatría Ramón de la Fuente Muñiz and the Centro para la prevención y atención integral del VIH/SIDA clínica especializada Condesa. Special recognition goes to our collaborating investigators including Guillermina Natera-Rey, Victor Hugo Carapia, and Eduardo Zafra Mora. In addition, we want to acknowledge all the work and effort provided by our street promotores and field team members: Carlos Alberto Zamudio Angles, Pamela Chavez, Mario Dominguez Garcia, and Jobsan A. Rarmirez, and our research assistant Jessica Frankeberg. Finally, this work would not have been possible without the trust and assistance by gatekeepers, the users themselves, and residents in these communities.

REFERENCES

Alegría, M., K. Álvarez, and K. DiMarzio (2017). Immigration and mental health. *Current Epidemiology Reports, 4*(2), 145–55. Retrieved from doi:10.1007/a40471–017–0111–2.

Benjamin, W. (2002). *The arcades project.* Cambridge, MA: Belknap Press of Harvard University Press.

Bill and Melinda Gates Foundation. (2014). *Inciting healthy behaviors: Nudge, disrupt, leapfrog, reach (Round 13).* Retrieved from https://gcgh.grandchallenges.org/challenge/inciting-healthy-behaviors-nudge-disrupt-leapfrog-reach-round-13.

Brazil, N. (2015). Spatial variation in the hispanic paradox: Mortality rates in new and established hispanic US destinations. *Population, Space and Place, 23*(1). Retrieved from DOI:10.1102/psp.1968.

Burawoy, M. (2009). *The extended case method: Four countries, four decades, four great transformations, and one theoretical tradition.* Berkeley: University of California Press.

Cepeda, A., and A. Valdez (2010). Ethnographic strategies in the tracking and retention of street-recruited community-based samples of substance using hidden populations in longitudinal studies. *Substance Use and Misuse, 45*(5), 700–716.

Cepeda, A., et al. (2010). Patterns of substance use among hurricane Katrina evacuees in Houston, Texas. *Disasters, 34*(2), 426–46.

Cepeda, A., et al. (2017). HIV and STI knowledge, testing, and risk among adult crack users in Mexico city: Baseline findings from a feasibility study. *AIDS care, 29*(3), 350–54. Retrieved from doi:10.1080/09540121.2016.1255707.

Cicourel, A.V. (1964). *Method and measurement in sociology.* Oxford: Free Press of Glencoe.

Eland-Goossensen, A., L.A.M. van de Goor, and H.F.L. Garretsen (1997). Heroin addicts in the community and in treatment compared for severity of problems and need for help. *Substance Use and Misuse, 32*(10), 1313–30. Retrieved from doi:10.3109/10826089709039380.

Emerson, R. M., ed. (1983). *Contemporary field research*. Boston: Little, Brown.

Erickson, K. C., and D. D. Stull (1998). *Doing team ethnography: Warnings and advice*. Vol. 42. Thousand Oaks, CA: Sage.

Frankeberger, J., et al. (2019). Safer crack kits and smoking practices: Effectiveness of a pilot harm reduction intervention among active crack users in Mexico City. *Substance Use and Misuse*. Published online, January 17, 2019. Retrieved from doi .org/10.1080/10826084.2018.1528460.

Garfinkel, H. (1967). *Studies in ethnomethodology*. Englewood Cliffs, NJ: Prentice-Hall.

Hart, C. (2013). *High price: A neuroscientist's journey of self-discovery that challenges everything you know about drugs and society*. New York: Harper Collins.

Hoffman, J. A., et al. (2000). Frequency and intensity of crack use as predictors of women's involvement in HIV-related sexual risk behaviors. *Drug and Alcohol Dependence, 58*(3), 227–36.

Kim, D. (2015). Projection mapping contents development of architectural heritage. *Advanced Science and Technology Letters, 113*, 90–95.

Krautsack, D. (2011). 3D projection mapping and its impact on media and architecture in contemporary and future urban spaces. *Journal of the New Media Caucus, 7*(1). Retrieved from http://median.newmediacaucus.org/summer-2011-v-07-n-01-under-fire-3d-animation-pedagogy-3d-projection-mapping-and-its-impact-on-media-architecture-in-contemporary-and-future-urban-spaces.

Levine, D. N. (1980). *Simmel and Parsons: Two approaches to the study of society*. New York: Arno Press.

Markides, K. S., and J. Coreil (1986). The health of Hispanics in the southwestern United States: An epidemiologic paradox. *Public Health Reports, 101*(3), 253.

Mehan, H., and H. Wood (1975a). The morality of ethnomethodology. *Theory and Society, 2*(4), 509–30.

——— (1975b). *The reality of ethnomethodology*. New York: John Wiley.

Mine, M. R., et al. (2012). Projection-based augmented reality in disney theme parks. *Computer, 45*(7), 32–40. Retrieved from doi: 10.1109/MC.2012.154.

Morales, L. S., et al. (2002). Socioeconomic, cultural, and behavioral factors affecting Hispanic health outcomes. *Journal of Health Hare for the Poor and Underserved, 13*(4), 477. Retrieved from doi:10.1353/hpu.2010.0630.

Park, R. E. (1967). The city: Suggestions for investigation of human behavior in the urban environment. In *The city: Suggestions for investigation of human behavior in the urban environment*, ed. R. E. Park & E. W. Burgess, 1–45. Chicago: University of Chicago Press.

Patel, K. V., et al. (2004). Evaluation of mortality data for older Mexican Americans: Implications for the hispanic paradox. *American Journal of Epidemiology, 159*(7), 707–15. Retrieved from doi:10.1093/aje/kwh089.

Pfadenhauer, M. (2005). Ethnography of scenes: Towards a sociological life-world analysis of (post-traditional) community-building. *Forum Qualitative Sozialforschung / Forum: Qualitative Social Research, 6*(3), Art. 43, September.

Prochaska, J. O., C. C. DiClemente, and J. C. Norcross (1992). In search of how people change: Applications to addictive behaviors. *American Psychologist, 47*(9), 1102–14. Retrieved from doi:10.1037/10248–026.

Reinarman, C., P. D. Cohen, and H. L. Kaal (2004). The limited relevance of drug policy: Cannabis in Amsterdam and in San Francisco. *American Journal of Public Health, 94*(5), 836–42.

Rotheram-Borus, M. J., D. Swendeman, and B. F. Chorpita (2012). Disruptive innovations for designing and diffusing evidence-based interventions. *American Psychologist, 463*(6), 463–76. Retrieved from doi:10.1037/a0028180.

Sandoval, C. (2000). *Methodology of the oppressed.* Minneapolis: University of Minnesota Press.

Schutz, A. (1997). *Phenomenology of the social world.* Evanston, IL: Northwestern University Press.

Scribner, R. (1996). Paradox as paradigm: The health outcomes of Mexican Americans. *American Journal of Public Health, 86*(3), 303–5. Retrieved from doi:10.2105/ajph.86.3.303.

Simmel, G. (1902). Number of members as determining the sociological form of groups, I and II. *American Journal of Sociology, 8(2),* 158–94.

Sterk, C. E., K. Dolan, and S. Hatch (1999). Epidemiological indicators and ethnographic realities of female cocaine use. *Substance Use and Misuse, 34*(14), 2057–72. Retrieved from doi:10.3109/10826089909039438.

Substance Abuse and Mental Health Services Administration (SAMSHA) (2008). Results from the 2007 National Survey on Drug use and Health: National Findings. 2008, Office of Applied Studies, NSDUH Series H-34, DHHS Publication SMA 08-4343, Rockville, MD.

Suttles, G. D. (1968). *The social order of the slum: Ethnicity and territory in the inner city.* Vol. 196. Chicago: University of Chicago Press.

Valdez, A., et al. (2010). Fumando la piedra: Emerging patterns of crack use among Latino immigrant day laborers in New Orleans. *Journal of Immigrant and Community Health, 12*(5), 737–42.

Valdez, A., et al. (2015). Emerging patterns of crack use in Mexico City. *International Journal of Drug Policy, 26*(8), 739–45. Retrieved from doi: 10.1016/j.drugpo.2015.04.010.

Valdez, A., et al. (2016). Un jalón, un volteón, y otra vez: High-risk crack smoking paraphernalia in Mexico City. *Journal of Psychoactive Drugs, 48*(4), 295–302.

Waldorf, D., C. Reinarman, and S. Murphy (1991). *Cocaine changes: The experience of using and quitting.* Philadelpha: Temple University Press.

Werb, D., et al. (2010). Modelling crack cocaine use trends over 10 years in a Canadian setting. *Drug and Alcohol Review, 29*(3), 271–77. Retrieved from doi: 10.1111/j.1465-3362.2009.00145.x.

PART THREE

Navigating the Unusual

EIGHT

Hidden

ACCESSING NARRATIVES OF PARENTAL DRUG
DEALING AND MISUSE

Ana Lilia Campos-Manzo

AS A *CRIMINOLOGIST,* I EXPLORE how fathers and mothers experience parenthood while under correctional supervision. Separately, as a *sociologist of childhood,* I explore how children and adolescents (hereafter *youth*) experience adult authority and peer culture across institutional settings. The Institutional Review Board (IRB) classifies both prisoners and minors as vulnerable populations, respectively with the threatened ability or without the right to weigh the risks and benefits of participating in research.

Prisoners, involuntarily confined or detained in a penal institution, live under the legal custody of the state in coercive conditions that threaten their ability to engage in voluntary and informed consent (King and Wincup, 2008; Reiter, 2014). Minors, in contrast, are under the legal guardianship of adults and do not have the legal right to engage in voluntary and informed consent (Christensen and James, 2008; Corsaro, 2017). Accordingly, doing research with these populations involves a heavier ethical burden on both the IRB and the researcher, adding safeguards throughout the research process that limit access. One must then ask, "Why would a scholar focus her research on two vulnerable populations?" Ideally, to create platforms for marginalized voices to be heard.

This chapter explores the ethical issues of access in doing research with vulnerable populations. To illustrate the richness, complexity, and value of "hidden" narratives, I will share how youth experience parental-drug misuse (n = 10) and how male drug dealers and misusers experience fatherhood (n = 45).[1] Then, I will reflect on my IRB-review and data-collection experiences for both projects to explore the ethics of accessing vulnerable populations.

Narratives about parental-drug dealing and misuse can be accessed through studies with parents or their children. From the two studies I conducted, youth from the Northeast (2013/2015) and fathers from the Midwest (2010) share their lived experiences.

Youth's Narratives, the Residential Instability of Parental-Drug Misuse

It was not a secret. "The [youth center] is drug-free,[2] but people aren't drug-free on these streets . . . too many crack-heads pulling grocery carts. It's not looking pretty, not cute," said Carmela, twelve, an African-American girl.[3] Girls and boys openly discussed the presence of drug misusers on the streets of a Northeastern city we call D-Greenville.[4] This city had high rates of police officers (336), of violent (1,105) and property (4,226) crimes, and of drug-related deaths (342) per every 100,000 people; compared to the state rates of police officers (202), of violent (77) and property (2,202) crimes, and of drug-related deaths (36) (Federal Bureau of Investigation [FBI], 2015; U.S. Census, 2016).

These streets, however, were filled with youth living life, going to and from schools, friends' homes, stores, youth centers, family members' homes, first jobs, and other places in the neighborhood.[5] Some were driven from place to place, while others carefully navigated the streets. Zoe, fourteen, an African-American girl, explained, "There's the corner store I like, but drugs be in that area. So, my mom is never sure, 'Alright, you can go, but make s-u-r-e you walk safe.' I go quick, 'cuz I don't wanna get caught up." Similarly, Alfredo, sixteen, a Puerto Rican boy, and his younger brother, rode their bikes, but had to check in with their mother over the phone every time they traveled from point A to point B. After getting to the youth center for his interview, Alfredo called his mother, "Sí, mamá. Ya llegamos. Le llamaré cuando nos vayamos."

Walking into the youth center, one is met by an endless stream of children's voices echoing throughout the building. The modern building is extremely child-friendly, with wide steps connecting the first and second floors and glass walls to ensure minors are visible to adults. Youth were organized by age groups in different activities, such as exploring watercolors, robotics, basketball, and enjoying a snack in the lunchroom. Groups transitioned from room to room and adolescents assisted adult staff or were hang-ing out in the teen room. The teen program extended into the evening, including sports, activism, movies, college prep, and other activities. As part of the same organization, three other sites serve nearby neighborhoods.

In this youth-advocacy environment, the staff welcomed that the purpose of my research project was not to study drugs but rather to explore how youth navigated peer culture and adult authority across their socio-spatial environ-ments (Campos-Holland, Dinsmore, and Kelekay, 2016). Methodologically, youth used Google Maps to give the interviewer a virtual tour of their socio-spatial environments across streets, neighborhoods, cities, and suburbs. As they did, the virtual images elicited youth's narratives of drug use. Of the 152 youth interviewed, 64 discussed drug use, primarily as a socially distant com mentary about the drug misusers on the streets.

Parental-drug misuse, in contrast, was something deeply painful for ten affected youth. After much rapport building through multiple opportunities for interviews, youth who engaged in most or all interviews openly discussed their experiences with parents who used drugs. Vanessa, sixteen, a Puerto Rican–Dominican girl, illustrated her feelings: "My mom can't tell me what to do . . . She lost that a long time ago. *How come?* I was born when my mom was real young. She was hanging out with the wrong crowd . . . started doing drugs . . . So, my grandma became my mom. *Is she still struggling with drugs?* Not that I've seen, but she quit a long time ago and started again. Now, she says she's clean, but I'm not sure."[6] Experiences with parental-drug misuse emerged organically for one boy and nine girls who were: thirteen to seven-teen years of age; of Puerto Rican, Mexican, Filipino, Jamaican, Dominican, African-American, and multiracial/ethnic descent; and mostly under cus-tody of mothers and grandmothers, followed by a father and a brother.[7]

Residential instability dominated their experiences, with youth moving across places or caretakers. George, seventeen, an African-American–Puerto Rican boy, took the interviewer on a tour of his seven childhood homes; including his current home, a large Victorian house behind a long driveway defined by cherry-blossom trees. He stated: "This is where we live. *What a beautiful home.* Yes, I like it because it's one of the few shelters that takes sons. *How long have you lived here?* It's hard to say, 'cuz we've lived here several times . . . when I was little, my dad hit my mom . . . they took us in. [The next time], my dad left without leaving enough for rent . . . got evicted and ended up here again . . . *Where does your dad go?* He is addicted . . . He tried to get help, but it hasn't worked."

In contrast, Allie, seventeen, a Puerto Rican girl, moved across caretakers. She had lived in two cities and a suburb while moving between her grandmother (city A), her father and stepmother (city B), and, post father's divorce, with her stepmother and baby sister (suburb): "*Where did you like it the most? In [the suburb] . . . we got along. How come you moved back to your grandma's?* [My stepmom] couldn't take care of me anymore. She missed rent payments and had to move back to her mom's. *How did you feel about it?* Hell of mad . . . [but] they love me . . . *What about your mom?* She is out and about, can't count on her. *How has that affected you?* No drugs, I do n-o-t want to end up like her." Whether it was moving as a family or across caretakers, residential instability dominated youth's narratives of parental-drug misuse.

Fathers' Narratives, Parenting While Drug Dealing and Misusing

The interviews with fathers (n = 45) occurred in two community-based correctional facilities in a Midwest state,[8] including the Work Release Center (WRC) receiving inmates from federal and state prisons and a Residential Correctional Facility (RCF) housing individuals with court-ordered drug treatment, both under the same judicial district and one mile apart in a predominantly-white city (U.S. Census, 2010).

The WRC is housed in a four-story cement building near downtown. One step into the entrance, you face the control room from where a correctional officer (CO) determines who exits and enters, including COs in uniform, administrators in professional attires wearing badges, semi-incarcerated clients in worn-down clothes exiting to work,[9] searching for jobs, or leaving on an earned family furlough, and parolees coming in for mandatory meetings with parole officers (POs). Behind the control room, clients line up to use the only payphone accessible, eat at the cold cafeteria, or use a small lobby with a 1980s TV. The next three floors include the 1970s-style offices for the administrators and POs, and the male and female dormitories.

In contrast, the RCF is housed in a mustard-yellow decaying one-story building located in the neighborhood with the highest rate of unoccupied housing in the city (U.S. Census, 2010). A step into the main entrance is a short and narrow hallway leading up to a glass window where a CO determines who exists and enters. Allowed in, one immediately encounters the cafeteria, with CO offices to the left, dormitories to the right, and every wall covered by wood paneling from the 1960s. The facility's architecture has a home feel that is completely erased by COs emphasis on clients' "inmate status" in their semi-incarceration.

While women and men were interviewed, this chapter focuses on the fathers who experienced drug dealing, drug misuse, or both. Fathers interviewed were twenty-one to sixty-six years old and of Mexican-American, African-American, Caucasian, and multiracial/ethnic descent. Together, they were fathers to seventy-one daughters and fifty-seven sons of six months to forty years of age. While at the WRC and RCF, participants defined fatherhood as being present and involved, providing, and protecting. Drug dealing and misuse, however, had threatened their ability to achieve this ideal fatherhood.

Achieving presence and involvement was difficult for both drug dealers and misusers. Drug dealers initially took on a two-sphere approach, placing geographical and social distance between fathering at home and drug dealing in the streets. Ex–drug dealer Joseph, twenty-eight, an African-American father, illustrated: "I was doing daycare during the day [three infant daughters] and selling at night.[10] When [their moms] went to work, I had 'em drop off. [Whistle], very intense. One gets to crying, and they all be crying. 'Damn! I gotta change this pamper, [then this other] pamper. I gotta make you a bottle, [then another] bottle.' I'm sitting, my hands all full [with three infants]. Man! When the moms came from work, I left. For a while, I was working [a low-wage conventional job] and selling there, but I got fired. So, I started back on the streets ... but my kids and my business, separate." The two-sphere approach, however, was threatened by men's desire for an increase in profits, which demanded high investment of time and energy in the streets.

In contrast, misusing fathers' presence and involvement occurred in sync with their recovery-relapse cycle. Ex–drug dealer and recovering-misuser Derek, thirty-eight, an African-American father, engaged in his first recovery attempt after the birth of his first son, "It was great. He started walking at nine months. I took him everywhere ... He [was] my little sack of potatoes ... I would throw him over my shoulder and bounced when I walked. So ... he was just laughing all the way down the block." Recovering-misuser Ray, thirty-eight, a Mexican-American father, was similarly part of his three children's lives until his relapse, "There were times when I'd go out on binges ... leave Friday and wouldn't come back until Sunday night ... I wasn't helping 'em with their homework." Relapse snuck into fathers' everyday lives. Recovering-misuser Tommy, fifty-four, a Caucasian father, explained, "After I got my children back [from my sister], I was fine for a few years, 'til I started getting high here and there, [then] got out of control."

Furthermore, participants identified *providing* as an element of fatherhood, including drug dealers and misusers in recovery submerging themselves into legal low-wage and/or illicit-drug labor. Operating in a context of economic deprivation, drug dealing provided temporary financial relief. Ex–drug dealer Jason, twenty-seven, an African-American father, recalled his teen parenting approach: "Your girl could get on WIC to get bread, juices, cheeses, milk ... but where the clothes come from?![11] And if you wearing Jordan outfits, how you gonna let your son wear clothes [without brand]? It made you go get that money ... selling drugs was nothing." However, illicit-drug money could not be tied to a conventional source. Consequently, purchases, including the houses where the children lived, were subject to seizure. Ex-drug dealer Mason, forty-one, an African-American father, illustrated, "Them [the FBI] came, 'We're gonna put you in prison ... by the way, we want this, this, and that.' [Such] ... waste of time ... all that hustling ... It's a fake fantasy."

Lastly, participants identified *protecting* as a priority of fatherhood. However, drug dealers faced competitors, consumers, thieves, and law enforcement in the illicit-drug market. To protect themselves and their children, fathers "fronted" a tough image and used the two-sphere approach. Ex-drug dealer Elijah, thirty-eight, an African-American father, took daily caution, "The only way you could really keep 'em safe is to not let nobody know that you got children ... I lived in [city A] and I worked in [city B] ... never sold outside of [city A]."[12] The two-sphere approach was much more difficult for misusing fathers. Unable to protect their children from their own misuse, some fathers left home. Ex–drug dealer and recovering-misuser Mike, thirty-two, an African-American father, stated, "I moved [out of town] and didn't communicate back ... just disappeared. The drugs progressed ... worse and worse ... wasn't in any good shape to be in their lives ... I could have exposed them."

ACCESSING HIDDEN NARRATIVES

The few excerpts from minors and incarcerated fathers' narratives provide evidence of the critical importance of overcoming challenges in doing research with vulnerable populations. It is a scholarly priority, however, to do so in an ethical manner. The IRB emerged in response to Nazi medical war crimes (1939–45) and the study of untreated syphilis in Alabama (1930s to

1972),[13] mandating researchers to obtain participants' voluntary and informed consent, to respect their liberty to withdraw early, and to minimize risks (National Institutes of Health [NIH] Office of Extramural Research, 2018). Ultimately, the researcher-participant relationship must be based on respect, honesty, and trust. Although the IRB-review process aims to prepare researchers to achieve such relationship, real-life demands that researchers adjust in the field.

Accessing Incarcerated Parents' and Children's Narratives

For my first attempt to accessing narratives of parental-drug dealing and misuse, my starting point was incarcerated parents. This involved an intense IRB-review process at a Research-1 university (R1),[14] and a difficult fieldwork experience at a correctional setting.

Requesting IRB Approval at a Large University. The IRB-review process for the parenthood project lasted a year and a half. I was requesting access to incarcerated parents (adult women and men at WRC and RCF), their children (ten to seventeen years old), and the children's caretakers (adults). With two vulnerable population in the sample, prisoners and minors, the review involved the full IRB board, a prisoner advocate, and a child advocate. As the months passed by, colleagues encouraged me to pursue a different project. Instead, I carefully acquired access to multiple research settings and developed a suitable informed-consent process with the assistance of the "toughest" IRB in the Midwest.[15]

Gaining access to the correctional research sites involved a local connection, awareness of professional hierarchies, and respect for partner organizations. First, a colleague connected me to the sites' directors, who familiarized me with their programming, populations, and spaces, and to whom I presented my research proposal. With local interest, I was sent to meet the Department of Corrections' (DOC) research director in the state capital, who encouraged me to return with IRB approval. Second, the DOC's approval for access was professionally hierarchical, including the state DOC director, judicial district director, and WRC and RCF directors. Lastly, these correctional staff encouraged me to gain supplemental access through partner organizations serving the same populations, including the local Department of Human Services (DHS) office, three police departments and three jails, and a local youth center. Ideally, this supplemental access would inform their partners about the study and facilitate my connection to children, their caretakers, and incarcerated parents with shifting correctional status. Ultimately, I submitted eleven signed letters to the IRBs from those who agreed to provide me direct access and supplemental access.

To ensure I had a noncoercive, informed consent process, the IRB requested that I emphasize my independent scholar identity, prohibited correctional staff's involvement in recruitment, and required voluntary consent—all to prioritize participants' personhood and minimize the impact of their correctional status. Overall, the informed-consent process included two consent forms for adult incarcerated parents and caretakers, a parental-consent form for children's legal guardians, and two assent forms for pre-adolescents (ten to twelve years old) and adolescents (thirteen to seventeen years old).

The consent form for incarcerated parents highlighted the importance of potential psychological, emotional, and legal risks. I would be asking participants to reflect on their parenthood in relation to delinquency/crime and correctional supervision, all potentially psychological and emotional risks. Regarding the legal risk, "it was possible that federal government regulatory agencies, university auditing departments, and the university IRB" would review my documentation and data.[16] Accordingly, prospective participants were encouraged to not share incriminating information, and the interview was limited to delinquency/crimes for which participants had already been convicted. Also, their consent form included "special information for prisoners," which read, "Your participation will not affect the length of your sentence, your parole, or any other aspect of your incarceration . . . [declining to participate] or [early withdraw] will not be held against you . . . [if correctional sentence completion] . . . you may continue [participation]." Lastly, interviews at correctional settings could be terminated earlier than expected if the researcher concludes that "it would not be safe for [the participant] to continue" or if correctional staff "end or postpone" the interview "for any reason."

The caretakers' informed consent form was simpler. The risks included "psychological and emotional distress" in recalling "family problems" and "family member's imprisonment." Since the recruitment would be initiated with the incarcerated parent, "special information for family of prisoners" included: "your participation will not affect . . . the length of your family member's sentence," same sentiment as above. The IRB consent assumed caretakers were primarily family members, but the narratives show they were mothers and relatives, as well as nonfamily members.

Access to minor children, in contrast, involved a complicated consent-and-assent process. Incarcerated parents signed a form called "Parental Consent to Access Child's Legal Guardian." If the child was receiving DHS services, incarcerated parents signed a form that read, "I consent for the researcher to verify the legal guardianship of my child with [DHS]." If the child was not receiving DHS services, the incarcerated parent filled out a "Consent to Access Adult Family Member" for the researcher to "verify" with this family member "that the person identified is [in fact] the current legal guardian." Once the legal guardian was verified, this person would receive a letter and a "Legal Guardian Consent Form."

To reduce potential harm, eligible minors only included youth "aware of their parents' [correctional status]" who were "ten years or older." If eligible and their legal guardian consented, the child would be invited to participate. For the assent process, forms were linguistically customized for pre-adolescents, narrowed to one page, and for adolescents, the same form that legal guardians signed. Both had "special information for children of prisoners" that read, "your participation will not affect ... the length of your parents' sentence ... ," to ensure assent was non-coercive. This procedure was designed for minor children (ten to seventeen years old). The narratives above, however, involved children of incarcerated parents ranging from infants to middle-age adults.

Realities of a Correctional-Research Setting. While carefully developed, the IRB-approved research design proved not to cover all challenges met in the field. Doing research at a correctional setting involved intense power dynamics, politics of stigmatizations, and a willingness to change paths.

POWER DYNAMICS AND PROTECTING PARTICIPANTS. On the field, both at the RCF and WRC, staff gave me the list of all prisoners, referred to as "clients" since both facilities were rooted in a rehabilitation tradition. Beginning recruitment at the WRC, I wanted to meet and invite all eligible clients. I asked the correctional officer (CO) at the control room to call the first person on the list. The CO got on the phone, pressed a bottom, and stated, "[Client's name], report to the control room," which was repeated three times loudly through a speaker that reached the whole building. The client then came to the control room and was directed to the room across the hall that had been designated for my interviews. I then met the client, discussed the purpose of my visit, described the study and eligibility, and asked whether they were interested. The fourth person I met arrived almost out of breath: "Did you want to see me? *Yes, my name is Ana . . . a researcher with the [university] . . . studying parenthood . . . I want to invite you to participate . . .* [Before any more details], oh my god Miss. I was freaking out! *What do you mean?* Them over there [COs], they use the speaker to call us when we're in trouble. Yesterday they called me to give me a violation. *What happened?* I went to see my daughter when I was supposed to be at work. To them, that is enough to send me back to prison." In response, I asked the COs for an alternative process. They narrowed down the call to the individuals' room, audible only to prospective participant and roommates.

Also, the timing of recruitment and interviews needed to be in sync with participants' schedules. The WRC and RCF both required clients to spend at least eight hours a day searching for jobs, going from business to business to ask about openings and for job applications, concluding at each business with a request for a signature to confirm their solicitation. Those who succeeded in the job market had one to two conventional jobs, working eight to sixteen hours a day. Employment success without correctional violations was rewarded with furloughs to visit family. In the facilities, clients also had scheduled activities, such as mandatory drug treatment or psychological sessions. Moreover, community organizations brought programming, such as Bible study accompanied by highly desired food. I aimed to recruit and collect data in ways that respected their correctional schedules.

This recruitment process, however, was interrupted by how the correctional staff viewed me. At the end of my first week at the WRC, the director approached me: "How's it going? *Great. I have met several parents. They just have very busy schedules; but no worries, there is plenty of time.* Let me know if there is anything I can do. *I am changing my schedule to adjust to theirs [from 9 a.m.–5 p.m. to 3 p.m.—10 p.m.]. That should do it.* Sounds good." I went home planning to return the next day on the new schedule. In contrast, the director returned to his office reconsidering the change. From what I now understand, he viewed me as a young and naive female researcher who would be at-risk in a predominantly male facility without the 9-to-5 administrators.

Consequently, he decided to assist in the recruitment process without consulting me. Specifically, with previous IRB approval, I left a flyer taped to the window and a stack of signup sheets next to a locked box where filled-out signup sheets were to be deposited. That evening, the director ordered COs to approach each client, mostly in clients' rooms after eight o'clock, and have them sign up. Imagine a CO asking a client to fill out a form that asked whether they had children. Parents keep their children away from correctional settings to not expose them to danger and to avoid their parenthood being used during punishment, including COs reminding prisoners of their "bad parenting" or canceling family furloughs. The power dynamics in this coerced recruitment violated the rights of prospective research participants.

Unaware, I came in at three in the afternoon the next day to find a full box with signup sheets. The CO on duty said, "You have plenty of interest. Who would you like me to call first? *How did this happen?* I don't know . . . It was like that when I came in this morning." I organized the signup sheets by parents versus nonparents and called the first mother on the stack. Deb, a tall white-woman in her fifties came into the interview room. "Hi, my name is Ana. I wanted to meet you . . ." Before I could finish my sentence, she saw the signup sheet, "Oh, you're the lady with the interviews." She sat down decisively looking me straight in the eye with a confident voice, "Oh, you don't know what happened here last night?! They woke all of us up to fill out your little sheet. It pissed me off, them asking about my children. That's not right." I thanked her for her candor and immediately went to the directors' office. He confirmed. Accordingly, I called the IRB to seek advice, for such coercion made voluntary consent impossible.

The IRB recommended that I interrupt recruitment at the WRC and postpone it for at least two months. Time away from this coercive situation and a new recruitment process in the future would hopefully allow for voluntary consent. I spoke with the director about the power dynamics between COs and clients, research participants' rights, and the IRB recommendations. He did not apologize but agreed for me to come back in two months to the afternoon shift, especially because there would be a new client population then. In the meantime, I focused on recruitment and interviews at the RCF.

That afternoon, I contacted each client with an apology, with some clearly stating that they would never be interested in participating, while others interpreted the situation as part of COs' ongoing "power tripping" and expressed interest in participating. I told them that if they were still at the WRC and still wanted to participate two months later, they would of course be welcomed. I left the WRC with zero interviews, but much more aware of the power dynamics involved in correctional research settings and its potential for creating a harmful situation for participants.

STIGMATIZATION AND POSITIONALITY. With a very similar programming, the RCF allowed me to come in during the afternoon shift and to use the psychologist's office for the interviews. I genuinely think that my researcher-participant relationships at the RCF were based on respect, honesty, and trust. Several COs, however, warned me not to trust everything participants said, saying clients were "manipulators who say anything to get what they want." Such a stigmatizing description discredited participants' narratives and offended my intellect; most importantly, none of the participants asked for anything from me. I did verify their narratives with correctional records, but over time my commitment to participants' marginalized voices grew stronger.

Two months later, I returned to the WRC's afternoon shift. Roster in hand, I crossed out all who had already declined, reconnected with the few interested who were still there, and invited the new arrivals. The interview room was the same, across the hall from the control room. I could close the door to provide participants audio privacy; the window blinds however, remained opened. After a month of interviewing, I became comfortable at the WRC once again, but the power dynamics were still very present.

I was in the middle of interviewing a woman, a mother to four children, with a long history of drug misuse and incarceration. She had just completed half her sentence (for attempted murder) in state prison. Specifically, her drug dealer became her romantic partner who later sexually abused her minor daughter. Taking justice into her own hands, she tried to kill him. Recalling the experience, she was crying profusely. I held her hand, as she used her other hand to cover her face, preventing COs and other clients from witnessing her pain. I got up and closed the blinds to provide her the much-needed visual privacy. About to sit backdown, I hear, "BOOM, BOOM, BOOM," someone hitting the door with intense aggression. The female CO opened the door and stated, "You must keep the blinds open! There are rapists and killers here, and your safety is our responsibility!" I was aware of her criminal record, but also knew she would not hurt me. As a guest at a correctional setting, however, I kept the blinds open for the rest of the interviews.

While committed to participants' marginalized voices, facility emergencies made me very aware of my positionality as a free person. In the middle of an interview, "RRRRRRING, RRRRRRING, RRRRRRING," an endless and unbearable alarm took over the WRC building. My immediate reaction was to interrupt the interview, have the participant go with the rest of the clients, and seek shelter in the control room filled with COs. At the time, I told myself that my actions would ensure the safety of the recorded interviews I was carrying. I must now acknowledge, however, that I also went to the control room, instead of going with the clients, for my personal safety. I was a researcher, a free person, in correctional settings.

MAKING CHANGES TO REDUCE HARM. During the informed-consent process, participants were discouraged from sharing incriminating information. Clients, however, were subjected to correctional rules, and participants shared with me their correctional violations both known and unknown to COs. For instance, they told COs they were working when spending unauthorized time with their children; carried unauthorized cell phones to avoid the facility's landline that was answered with "this is the department of corrections" and could dissuade future employers; and hid employment to avoid COs collecting clients' paychecks to pay court fines, correctional institution rent, and other correctional debt, ultimately leaving clients without funds. If COs became familiar with these correctional violations, their community-based correctional status could be revoked and they would be sent to prison. The informed consent form, then, should include a warning about sharing correctional violations.

After the interviews with incarcerated parents, I also came to understand the fragile family circumstances under which participants practiced parenting. For instance, some participants had neglected or abused their children, or they had conflictive relationships with their children and the caretakers. Moreover, the multiple layers of access required by the IRB proved difficult, and I needed to receive more training on interviewing children about sensitive topics. Thus, I postponed the interviews with caretakers and minor children. I did, however, interview adult children of previously incarcerated parents who were themselves parents under correctional supervision, including a mother in her late fifties and her son in his early thirties who were at the WRC at the same time.

Accessing Youth's Narratives

My second chance to access narratives of parental-drug misuse emerged organically from youth who were not being interviewed about drugs. Instead, this study explored peer culture and adult authority within virtual and sociospatial environments. Having written extensively about this project's methodology (Campos-Holland, 2017; Campos-Holland, Dinsmore, and Kelekay, 2016), I will focus here on issues related to interviewing minors about sensitive topics. Specifically, I reflect on the IRB-review process and the realities of doing research with youth about their real lives.

Requesting IRB Approval at a Small Liberal Arts College. Both 2013 and 2015 data collections included sensitive topics and received IRB approval at a liberal arts college involving a three-month review process.[17] Sensitive topics are those that increase emotional risk, such as asking a participant to recall and discuss a topic that elicits negative emotions. The 2013 interviews about peers, social media, and socio-spatial environments involved very open-ended and participant-driven explorations (Campos-Holland, 2017; Campos-Holland, Dinsmore, and Kelekay, 2016). The only sensitive topic explored directly was peer conflict. While peer conflict is a normal part of social life (Corsaro, 2017), bullying involves an imbalance of power, perpetrator's negative intentions, and the repeated targeting of the victim (Campos-Holland et al., 2015; Pyzalski, 2012). Since my interview schedule initially addressed bullying, the IRB board requested that my research design include risk reduction, a harm reduction response, debriefing, and accessible resources.

As part of risk reduction, my research questions focused on peer conflict, leaving open the possibility of bullying but without asking youth directly about bullying. Since bullying was not the overall purpose of the study, it did not damage the research design. Instead, it widened the scope from bullying to all types of peer conflict. The discussion of online peer conflict, however, prompted the IRB's concern about confidentiality.

The research design included an interview about social media, and the IRB review was occurring at a time that society was being alerted about cyberbullying. Specifically, the *State of New Jersey v. Dharun Ravi* (2012) had recently made headlines. A male university student, Tyler Clementi, eighteen, committed suicide after his roommate, Ravi, recorded and disclosed video images of him without his knowledge that involved him kissing another man. Worried about the fatal consequences of cyberbullying, the IRB encouraged me to consider "significant harm" in relation to confidentiality.

What is significant harm? In my discussion with the IRB, the reference point became harm to self and harm to others. However, it was important that I used "significant harm" to maintain my ability to evaluate each situation and use my discretion to respond in a way that would not increase harm. The informed parental-consent and youth-assent then read, "We will keep your child's participation in this research study confidential.... In cases when a response indicates that there is evidence of *significant harm* to your child or others, we will act towards reducing or eliminating victimization."

While considering peer conflict and responses with evidence of significant harm, I developed a debriefing script, a resource list, and a response protocol.

The debriefing clarified that "the study was about peer conflict" and "peer conflict could include bullying." Therefore, "it was very normal that we discussed (or did not discuss) bullying during the interview." I then worked with the youth center to develop a resource list and a response protocol. If the participant, or anyone they knew, wanted help to address bullying, I provided a list of local resources. As discussed in the consent and assent forms, if I identified a case of "significant harm," my first contact would be the youth center's teen coordinator, who would elicit the local resources necessary, such as the psychologist in staff, to respond as the situation demanded.

The 2015 follow-up interviews were about politics, education, and media, and faced similar challenges during the IRB review process. Thus, I continued with the same risk reduction, debriefing, resource list, and response protocol. The difference, however, was that the interview schedule now included sensitive topics that the 2013 participants had identified as significantly relevant in their everyday lives, such as school shootings and police brutality (Campos-Manzo et al., 2018). Since these topics were participant-driven, the IRB did not request changes to the research design nor the informed consent and assent process. They did, however, request that the eligibility be changed from ten to seventeen years old to thirteen to seventeen years old. The IRB-review process did not involve any discussion about drugs or parental-drug misuse.

Doing Research with Youth about Real Life. Researchers and participating youth live in the real world, where drugs and other social problems are part of everyday life. During the interviews, youth, like adults, might open doors to hidden narratives or close them again.

ADULT GATEKEEPERS AND SENSITIVE TOPICS. Combining a sensitive topic, such as drugs, with a vulnerable population, such as minors, would have increased legal guardians' gatekeeping. The focus of my work within the sociology of childhood is not drugs. Instead, my goal is to create a platform for the voices of youth of color to be heard (Campos-Holland, 2017). Related, adults of color have come to mistrust researchers whether they are white researchers or researchers of color from white-dominated institutions (Campos-Holland, 2017; James et al., 2017). Considering this, and as a researcher of color, I could not imagine approaching a parent of color to request permission to interview his or her child of color about drugs. White society has used drugs to stigmatize and mass incarcerate both minors and adults from our communities of color. As a result, I find the social, emotional, psychological, and legal risks too high for youth of color. Accordingly, my interview schedules did not ask about drugs.

DRUGS, CHILDREN LIVING IN THE REAL WORLD. My interview approach is youth-centered, focused on minimizing interviewer's adult authority, and participant-driven, encouraging participants to discuss what is significant and relevant in their everyday lives (Campos-Holland, 2017). This created the space for youth's narratives about sensitive topics that neither I nor the IRB foresaw. Youth live in the real world and deal with real-world social problems. Unprompted, participants discussed crime, including drugs and parental-drug misuse. Interviewers then used follow-up questions sensitive to youth's emotional expressions, not pressing the interviewee to share anything that they were not comfortable sharing. For example, in 2013, George mentioned that his father suffered from drug misuse, but it was not until his fifth interview, in 2015, that he shared his experience in-depth. He clarified then, "I really don't mind it . . . I'm in a group for children who have parents in prison. We do panels in schools, churches, and [youth centers] to bring awareness . . . you don't want kids to be suffering by themselves."

Youth were encouraged to drive the discussion and choose "if and when" to open up about sensitive topics. I met Courtney, thirteen, a Mexican–Puerto Rican girl, on a Thursday, invited her to participate on a Friday, and she brought her signed parental informed consent form on a Monday. She then assented to participate in all three interviews. In a room at her youth center with audio privacy, I engaged her in the first interview about peers, the second interview about social media, and three hours later in the last interview about socio-spatial environments. By that time, we had built extensive rapport. Beginning the virtual tour on Google Maps, she took me to her current house and immediately began discussing her experience with parental-drug misuse. As her eyes began to water, I reminded her that she did not need to discuss anything she was not ready for. She responded, "Talking about this doesn't hurt me . . . I don't want kids like me to feel alone . . . I'ma tell you." While the research design, the IRB, and I placed obstacles to discussing drugs, youth opened the door to hidden narratives about parental-drug misuse.

RESPONDING TO SIGNIFICANT HARM. The consent and assent forms warned that the researcher would react to "evidence of significant harm" to reduce and eliminate "victimization." Out of 152 interviews, I ran into only two cases that needed this consideration. Maria, sixteen, a Puerto Rican girl, was giving the interviewer a virtual tour of her school grounds. As she described the stairs near the cafeteria, she talked about the spaces with limited adult surveillance where adolescent couples engage in public displays of affection. This discussion prompted her to recall her victimization: "I was sexually assaulted at fifteen years old [began to cry]. *Like I said, we can stop whenever you want.* No, its fine. I'm really used to sharing. I did a project about it in school . . . I denied it to myself at first. I didn't want to believe that some kid had just forced his tongue down my throat and groped me in the boob against my will." This interview was conducted by one of my trained interviewers, who quickly shared the content with me. I reviewed the situation, separately talked with the interviewer and the interviewee, to determine if the participant was currently being harmed and whether she had received help for past victimization. The victimization occurred the year before and was a one time occurrence. Her mother knew and had involved psychological assistance. After consulting with the IRB, I decided not to make the family relive this traumatic experience. Instead, we focused on writing to create a platform for her voice to be heard.

In contrast, Leafasia, sixteen, an African-American girl, was giving the interviewer a virtual tour of her social media, including her Ask.fm account. This platform is anonymous and involves people asking each other questions. In 2013, Leafasia was not very active on Ask.fm, but had answered fifty-nine questions "because it's fun," she explained. Most questions were not invasive, such as: *"Favorite number?* 7; *How much would it take to buy your love?* Love is earned; *Are you scared of the dark?* Yesssssss." Her answer to one question caught my attention: *"I heard you burn yourself, iz dat truu?* Sadly yes, I burn and cut myself. One day I'll stop, but today is not the day." In consultation with the IRB, especially concerned with "today is not the day," I decided to activate the harm reduction response protocol. Specifically, I talked to the teen coordinator who engaged the youth center's social worker to talk with the family. After their conversation, I was updated: the parents already knew, had been addressing the issue with psychological assistance, and were keeping a close eye on the matter. In 2015, Leafasia expressed interest in participating again. I said, *"Remember that interviewing is your choice.* Yes, I know. I like interviewing because it makes me reflect about my life."

CONCLUSION

Researchers working to access vulnerable populations have come to either resent or embrace the IRB. A directive from *The Nuremberg Code* (1947) states, "The experiment must yield generalizable knowledge that could not be obtained in any other way" (National Institutes of Health [NIH] Office of Extramural Research, 2018, para. 3). Using this as a baseline, some researchers have argued that their qualitative work, including ethnography, does not require IRB's full review. When a researcher approaches an IRB for an expedited review on this basis, it is assumed that the project will not produce social scientific knowledge and therefore is expedited. Methodologically, it is correct to argue that qualitative research is not generalizable, since random sampling is not employed and generalizability is not its purpose. However, reliance on this argument could lead to ethical shortcomings.

In contrast, I must confess that I have come to embrace the IRB as a partner in the research process. My IRB experiences have been a learning process, and I feel secure during data collection knowing that my research designs were carefully reviewed by multiple researchers and advocates. During both projects, the IRB committees made important suggestions, all aiming to protect these vulnerable populations. Unrealistic suggestions, such as the avoidance of unprompted discussions about sensitive topics, were negotiated without changing the project's purpose. Overall, is it possible that the IRB has kept me from fully capturing narratives about parental drug misuse? Yes, but gatekeepers other than the IRB have included incarcerated parents, legal guardians, youth-serving organization, youth, and myself.

When doing research with vulnerable populations, the IRB review and data collection processes can present serious ethical dilemmas and challenges that threaten access to hidden narratives. Why then, would I dare to focus my research agenda on the lives of two vulnerable populations? My answer is that every human being deserves dignity and respect. Part of that is understanding their lives holistically. To achieve that understanding, one must listen to their voices. Any challenge then becomes a pebble on the path to creating platforms for marginalized voices to be heard. I consider it my scholarly imperative to overcome obstacles to access while adhering to the highest ethical standards.[18]

NOTES

1. For both projects, IRB approval and informed (parental) consent (and youth assent) were acquired prior to interviews. I did not apply for the "Certificate of Confidentiality" (CoC) prior to these studies: https://humansubjects.nih.gov/coc/index.

2. Youth interviews took place at four youth centers not associated with the Juvenile Justice System.

3. Participants' legal names, in both studies, have been replaced with pseudonyms to maintain confidentiality.

4. To protect the youth centers and participating youth, I replaced the name of the city with a pseudonym.

5. The population under nineteen years of age was 30.6 percent in D-Greenville and 25.6 percent in the state (U.S. Census, 2016).

6. Italics are used through this chapter to indicate the author (researcher) is talking, usually asking a question but sometimes responding to one.

7. The gender distribution of the 152 sample was 48.02 percent girls and 51.98 percent boys; yet, the youth who discussed parental-drug misuse were 90 percent girls. The average age for the overall sample was 11.94 (10–17 range), but the average age of the youth discussing parental drug misuse was 15.2 (13–17 range). The sample is all youth of color; therefore, only youth of color discussed parental-drug misuse.

8. The state will remain confidential to protect participants and correctional staff.

9. The WRC and RCF programs are both originally rooted in rehabilitation and the staff refer to the semi-incarcerated individuals as "clients." Financially, these individuals surrendered their paycheck to the WRC/RCF to pay for housing, food, services, court fines, and child support; thus, they identified as "court-ordered consumers" in relation to the word client. In the power dynamic between clients and COs, however, COs focused on punishment as retribution, constantly reminding clients of their "inmate" status in their semi-incarceration, stripping the word "client" from its rehabilitative roots.

10. He fathered three daughters, who were only weeks apart, with three different women.

11. WIC is the Women, Infants, and Children nutrition program.

12. Cities and states remain confidential to protect the anonymity of participants.

13. The Tuskegee Study of Syphilis was conducted by the U.S. Public Health Service to observe the progression of untreated syphilis in African-American men who were not told they were not being treated.

14. Universities in the United States are identified by the Carnegie Classifications of Higher Education based on their level of research activity with R1 being the highest level.

15. The IRB at my university was known as the "toughest" in the region due to its focus on medical research, leaving little room for nonmedical research and much less for qualitative research.

16. Words and terms in quotes are taken directly from consent forms or IRB instructions.

17. By this time, I was working at a different institution.

18. This research was funded by: Woodrow Wilson Foundation's Career Enhancement Fellowship; Connecticut College's Center for the Critical Study of

Race and Ethnicity, R.F. Johnson Faculty Development Fund, Judith Tindal Opatrny '72 Junior Faculty Fund, Margaret Sheridan '67 Research Initiative Fund, Research Matters Faculty Grant, and the Susan Eckert Lynch '62 Faculty Research Fund; National Institute of Drug Abuse and American Sociological Association's Minority Fellowship Program; Augustana College's Dissertation Fellowship; and University of Iowa's Dean Fellowship.

REFERENCES

Campos-Holland, A. (2017). Sharpening theory and methodology to explore racialized youth peer cultures. *Sociological Studies of Children and Youth, 22,* 223–47.

Campos-Holland, A., B. Dinsmore, and J. Kelekay (2016). *Virtual tours: Enhancing qualitative methodology to holistically capture youth peer cultures. Studies in Media and Communications, 11,* 225–60.

Campos-Holland, A., et al. (2015). Keep calm: Youth navigating adult authority across networked publics. *Sociological Studies of Children and Youth, 19,* 163–211.

Campos-Manzo, A.-L., et al. (2018). Unjustified: Youth of color navigating police presence across socio-spatial environments. *Race and Justice, 8*(1), 1–23.

Christensen, P., and A. James (2008). *Research with children: Perspectives and practices.* New York: Routledge.

Corsaro, W. A. (2017). *The sociology of childhood.* Thousand Oaks, CA: Sage.

Federal Bureau of Investigation (FBI). (2015). *Uniform crime report.* Retrieved from https://ucr.fbi.gov.

James, D. C., et al. (2017). "You have to approach us right": A qualitative framework analysis for recruiting African Americans into health research. *Health Education and Behavior, 44*(5), 781–90.

King, R., and E. Wincup (2008). *Doing research on crime and justice.* New York: Oxford University Press.

National Institutes of Health (NIH) Office of Extramural Research. (2018). *Protecting human research participants.* Retrieved from https://phrp.nihtraining.com.

Pyzalski, J. (2012). From cyberbullying to electronic aggression: Typology of the phenomenon. *Emotional and Behavioral Difficulties, 17*(3–4), 305–17.

Reiter, K. (2014). Making windows in walls: Strategies for prison research. *Qualitative Inquiry, 20*(4), 417–28.

U.S. Census (2010). *American fact finder.* Retrieved from https://factfinder.census .gov.

——— (2016). *American fact finder.* Retrieved from https://factfinder.census.gov.

NINE

Navigating Stigma

RESEARCHING OPIOID AND INJECTION DRUG USE AMONG YOUNG IMMIGRANTS FROM THE FORMER SOVIET UNION IN NEW YORK CITY

Honoria Guarino and Anastasia Teper

[In the Soviet Union] we knew of drug users and prostitutes and that was the lowest of the low and we had never come in contact with any of them. We saw drunks everywhere but a drug user— never ... I understood that everything depended on how you raise your children ... If a child is coming from an intellectual family, is well educated and well-read, then there is no way that he or she will even be tempted to use.

LUDMILA,[1]
a Russian-born mother of a twenty-five-year-old son who misuses prescription opioids

When I was growing up ... I knew that heroin is bad and it ruins people's lives. And I had this cousin I kept hearing about ... he was much older than me. And growing up, I kept hearing that he steals everything from his family because he's a heroin addict and he goes to jail all the time. And I never even got to see him because nobody would let him in the house. So he wasn't allowed to visit on holidays, of course. I just knew that he stole his grandmother's pension and all the jewelry in the house, just sold everything, got into jail, got some—just a bad lifestyle—and because he was a drug addict for heroin. So growing up I was thinking, why is that? Like how can a person steal from their own family? What is it that drives you? What is this about, this substance that can completely change a person and you would do something you would never imagine you would? So instead of being scared of it, I just got really curious about it. And I thought even when I was a child, like maybe if the opportunity presents itself to me, then I will just give it a try. I wasn't thinking I'm going to get addicted to it and become a bad person, but I want to try it just to see what it is about this drug.

LARISA,
twenty-year-old heroin injector, born in Ukraine

HOW SHOULD AN ETHNOGRAPHER APPROACH the study of behaviors and practices that are locally understood, by the community in which the social actors are embedded, as deeply shameful, stigmatizing, and requiring concealment? As people engaged in the use of illicit drugs, the young adult immigrants from the former Soviet Union (FSU), who are the focus of the research study described here, face multiple layers of stigma from both mainstream U.S. culture and their Russian-speaking immigrant community in New York City (NYC). These youths' engagement in stigmatizing and illegal behavior presents a number of practical challenges for researchers, not the least of which concerns how to locate and connect with people based on behaviors, and by extension a social identity, they are routinely driven to hide. Beyond this, the members of NYC's FSU community we spoke with during this research consistently described their immigrant community as "insular," unwelcoming to outsiders, and loathe to reveal what they consider the shameful problem of a young person's drug use to anyone outside their immediate families. In this chapter, we engage some of the pragmatic challenges encountered, as well as some larger ethical questions we grappled with, while conducting research with this "hidden" group of young immigrants.

STUDY OVERVIEW AND BACKGROUND

Summary of the Research Study

This study's primary objectives were to examine the influence of sociohistorical context on patterns of opioid use (including the nonmedical use of prescription opioids and heroin use) and human immunodeficiency virus / hepatitis C virus (HIV/HCV) risk among young adult immigrants from the FSU living in NYC, and to explore the impact of immigration- and acculturation-related processes on these behaviors and vulnerabilities. There was extremely little systematic research or surveillance data on substance use or HIV/HCV infection among FSU immigrants in the United States, although anecdotal evidence from drug treatment providers and scattered local media reports suggested that rates of opioid use and injection drug use might be disproportionately high among young people in this community. Given the lack of existing data, the study was explicitly framed as exploratory, aimed to help establish an evidence base to inform future research and develop culturally sensitive interventions to reduce risk for HIV/HCV infection, opioid-related overdose, and related harms among young FSU immigrants.

The ethnographic components of this study consisted of: (1) in-depth, semistructured interviews with twenty-six young adult FSU immigrants (ages eighteen to twenty-nine) living in NYC who were current opioid users and/or in treatment for Opioid Use Disorder (OUD); (2) interviews or focus groups with twenty drug treatment or harm reduction service providers who had extensive experience working with the Russian-speaking community; and (3) interviews with twelve FSU immigrant mothers of opioid-using youth. The twenty-six young adults who completed qualitative interviews comprised a purposive subsample selected to represent key subgroups within a larger sample of eighty youth who had been recruited to complete structured assessments. All procedures were approved by the Institutional Review Board (IRB) of National Development and Research Institutes, our home institution, and participants provided written informed consent.

The Genesis of the Study and Our Respective Roles in the Research

In 2008, several years before the current project, I (first author) conducted a small pilot study of opioid use in NYC's Russian-speaking community. My interest in this topic emerged from observations I had made, as well as conversations I had had with service providers and fellow researchers, while conducting research with other groups of people in NYC who use opioids (e.g., methadone maintenance treatment clients). I became intrigued by evidence suggesting potentially high rates of heroin injection among Russian-speaking immigrants in Brooklyn, along with what several community members characterized to me as a distinctive culture of opioid use and drug injection in Russia and other countries of the former Soviet Union and the Russian-speaking immigrant diaspora alike. During the course of these early explorations, a mutual colleague introduced me to Anastasia (second author), given our shared interest in drug use in NYC's Russian-speaking community.

Anastasia came to this work through her personal background as a native of Russia who immigrated to NYC with her family in early adolescence and settled in a Russian-speaking neighborhood in southern Brooklyn. After a period of heroin use in adolescence, Anastasia became a committed harm reductionist and advocate for people who use drugs and who openly identify as former heroin users. Our fortuitous meeting propelled me to realize a long-standing plan to obtain funding for a larger study of young FSU immigrants' opioid use and HIV/HCV risk. Anastasia's commitment to and enthusiasm for this project was instrumental in my decision to pursue it, as

I did not believe the research, particularly participant recruitment, would be feasible without her involvement.

Collecting and analyzing data for this study was a collaborative effort that leveraged our respective strengths and expertise—my training and experience in qualitative methods and Anastasia's local knowledge of the FSU community and fluency in Russian. Anastasia was responsible for recruiting and administering structured assessments to the primary sample of eighty FSU young adults, while I conducted the subsequent qualitative interviews with a subset of these youth (in English, all were fully bilingual in English and Russian). I also conducted individual interviews with drug treatment and related service providers, while Anastasia and I cofacilitated the focus groups. Anastasia interviewed, in Russian, the mothers of young people who had experienced problems with opioid use and translated these interviews into English.

Sociohistorical and Epidemiological Background of the Research

As rates of nonmedical prescription opioid and heroin use have spiked across the United States, so too have rates of opioid overdose, drug injection, and HCV infection, with young people under age thirty a key population at risk (Suryaprasad et al., 2014). At the same time, there has been an expanding injection-driven HIV/HCV epidemic in Russia, as well as a number of Eastern European and Central Asian countries of the former Soviet Union, that emerged from the political and socioeconomic upheaval following the Soviet Union's dissolution in 1991 and continues unabated today, one of the last areas of the globe where rates of new HIV infections continue to rise (Beyrer et al., 2017). This has occurred in the context of long-standing institutionalized stigma and discrimination toward drug users in Russia, policies that, because of Russia's cultural and political dominance in the region, have had a major influence on the Eastern European and Central Asian countries of the former Soviet region. Examples of the Russian state's retrograde and repressive policies and practices toward drug users include widespread police harassment and abuse, prohibition of effective, evidence-based opioid substitution treatment with methadone or buprenorphine, and abstinence-based drug treatment requiring mandatory state registration as a drug user (Elovitch and Drucker, 2008). This hostile social climate exerts demonstrably negative effects on the lives, self-concepts, and health status of drug users in Russia, and inhibits their use of critical health services such as HIV treatment (Calabrese et al., 2016).

In previous work, we explored how this transnational context influences young FSU immigrants in NYC, shaping myriad aspects of their lives from their drug use patterns and vulnerability to associated health risks, to their social relations with families and peers, use of harm reduction and drug treatment services, and self-conceptualizations (Guarino et al., 2012, 2015; Gunn and Guarino, 2016). A key mechanism by which traditional Soviet and post-Soviet sociocultural norms, attitudes, and values are reproduced within the FSU immigrant community in NYC is through the words and actions of older community members. This includes study participants' parents, grandparents, and other extended family members who came of age in the Soviet era and experienced the collapse of the Soviet Union as adults, and with whom many participants were living in multigenerational households.

FSU immigrant youth who use opioids are in an especially vulnerable social position due to their drug use. They must negotiate pervasive and acute stigma from the local Russian-speaking community, which makes them wary of accessing services such as drug treatment and syringe exchange for fear of being publicly "outed" as drug users. At the same time, as first-generation immigrants, they must navigate a host of immigration- and acculturation-related challenges (e.g., establishing new friendship networks, becoming accepted by American peers), in an era when public sentiment and government policies toward immigrants in the United States are becoming increasingly hostile. Participants commonly explained their initiation of prescription opioid or heroin use in adolescence or emerging adulthood as a response to these pressures—a way of reducing social anxiety, fitting in with a new peer group, and coping with the emotional trauma of adjusting to life in a strange new country.

FIELDWORK CHALLENGES

Participants' Concealment Strategies

This chapter discusses the practical and ethical challenges associated with breaking into the reputedly "insular" FSU immigrant community in NYC,[2] a community that members consistently and emphatically characterized as "secretive" or even "hostile to outsiders." Furthermore, our research focused on behavior stigmatized by both mainstream U.S. society and the FSU immigrant community, and we sought to speak with community members about extremely sensitive, identity-threatening issues.

Given this context, we worried that we would be seen as a nosy outsider (in Honoria's case) and a disaffected community member (in Anastasia's case), intruding into people's business to wittingly or unwittingly expose the community's dirty laundry, and that no one would be willing to speak with us or participate in the study. Even if we were able to persuade some to take part in the research, how could we convince them to trust us enough to be open about their drug use and other deeply personal behaviors (such as sexual behavior, including, for some, sex work)? Reflecting these concerns, we expected to face significant challenges recruiting young adults—and especially, parents—to participate.

Despite these concerns, we did not specifically anticipate the diverse and often creative strategies participants employed to safeguard their privacy and conceal their real identities. These strategies were primarily encountered by Anastasia, who recruited and conducted the initial assessments with young adults. Concealment strategies included: using an assumed name while negotiating the time and location of the initial meeting and during that meeting; watching Anastasia approach the agreed-upon location of the first meeting from a position down the block or across the street; and posting a friend or partner as a lookout to watch Anastasia approach this location (typically a coffee shop or fast-food restaurant). One purpose of this observation from afar, some later confided, was to assure themselves that Anastasia was not an undercover cop attempting to lure them into a sting operation (although how these surreptitious observations would accomplish this detection was never entirely clear to us). In another common strategy of self-protection, participants arrived at initial meetings in pairs, as was common with couples, or accompanied by small groups of peers. Their wariness reflects the double-layered stigma these drug users faced, from both mainstream society and their local immigrant community. It may also reflect a distrust of government and officialdom that older participants (i.e., mothers and FSU-born service providers) described as characteristic of the Russian-speaking immigrant community, conditioned by the community's historical memory of the Soviet and post-Soviet state.

Other aspects of these youths' social position contributed to making them more "hidden" and hard-to-reach than other groups of drug users who have commonly been the subjects of research. Historically, both public health and ethnographic research on drug use has been based on the study of long-term, often street-involved drug users, many of them members of racial/ethnic minority groups, whose disadvantaged social position renders them publicly visible and, as a result, fairly accessible to researchers. In contrast, the young adults we aimed to reach were generally raised in well-educated, middle-class households, and, in many cases, had stable living situations with their parents from whom they received financial support. Because most had current or recent engagement with the "straight world" through connections to college or employment, as well as personal career aspirations and family pressure to attain conventional economic and professional markers of success, they had a vested interest in maintaining a respectable identity by concealing their drug use. Their tendency to avoid close engagements with services for drug users (e.g., drug treatment, syringe exchange programs [SEPs]), also contributed to their lack of visibility relative to other groups of drug users; becoming involved in a study of opioid users presented a potentially identity-threatening risk for them, as revealed in the following fieldwork anecdote.

During Anastasia's interaction with one of the first female participants, Tanya, a woman in her early twenties, asked Anastasia to meet with her at the apartment she lived in with her parents. Tanya was concealing her ongoing heroin injection from her parents, as became evident when they returned home while Anastasia was still in the apartment. Fortunately, Anastasia's presence did not inadvertently reveal Tanya's ongoing drug use, as Tanya had already prepared a cover story that would explain Anastasia's presence and their need for privacy. Tanya introduced Anastasia to her parents as a tutor from school who was helping her with her homework, a ruse that Anastasia did not dispel.

Different Research Traditions in Tension

Another challenge of a different nature runs under the surface of this account, one that framed the boundaries and limits of the kinds of research we were able to conduct: namely, the strictures and dictates of the grant from the federal agency that funded the research. Unlike traditional ethnography, characterized by the long-term immersion of a lone ethnographer in the daily life of a community, the more ethnographic components of this research were conducted within the context of a multicomponent, mixed-methods study that integrated qualitative and quantitative forms of data collection and analysis. This epistemological and institutional context fundamentally influenced the design of the study and informed all aspects of the research.

Federal funding mechanisms for drug-related research do not generally allow for extended field engagements typical of classic ethnography. Moreover, qualitative and ethnographic forms of knowledge have historically occupied a devalued, marginal position within the positivistic paradigm that dominates public health research and the funding streams that support it. Nonetheless, as the anthropologists J. Bryan Page and Merrill Singer outline in the introduction to their edited volume of drug ethnography (2010), ethnographic methods, such as structured observations of drug use/injection behavior in naturally occurring settings, in-depth interviewing and focus groups, have played a significant role in the development of public health research on drug use. Ethnography has been particularly influential in elucidating the dynamics of injection drug use as a socially patterned behavior that presents specific risks for HIV and HCV transmission, as well as the design and implementation of community-based prevention interventions for key populations at risk. Yet conducting ethnography within the confines of our grant required significant methodological adaptations or compromises. Because public health research prioritizes the production of generalizable knowledge obtained from representative samples of a population of interest, ethnographic methods are most commonly employed as a limited component or phase of a larger mixed-methods research study. This was true of the present study, where qualitative interviews and focus groups were positioned as secondary to the collection of quantifiable data from structured assessments.

Where to Meet with Participants: A Practical Challenge

The social context of these immigrants' lives created a logistic challenge for our research—namely, how to identify suitable sites for conducting interviews with participants, including both the structured assessments with the larger sample and the follow-up qualitative interviews with the subsample. In selecting appropriate locations, we weighed competing imperatives. Locations had to afford sufficient privacy and anonymity to avoid inadvertently outing participants as drug users, which could occur if we interviewed them in public settings in their own neighborhoods. Yet, in keeping with our ethnographic orientation, we wanted to meet with participants on their home turf, in an environment that was familiar and comfortable to them. This was important both to facilitate open dialogue and to provide an opportunity to observe the local contexts of participants' lives.

Using Peer Networks to Drive Recruitment

Because the target population was a narrowly defined subgroup of FSU immigrants—opioid users between the ages of eighteen and twenty-nine—a group neither of us had direct personal connections to at the study's outset, one of our initial fieldwork strategies consisted of reaching out to a range of individuals we knew who may be in a position to interact with young, opioid-using FSU immigrants. Most of these contacts came from Anastasia's direct service or advocacy work or my previous research, particularly the pilot study. After we had recruited a small number of young adults in this rather rounda-bout way, we encouraged all of these initial participants to refer their opioid-using peers to the study, explaining our criteria for inclusion: immigrants from any country of the FSU between eighteen and twenty-nine years old, who were either currently using opioids or in treatment for OUD. By opioid use we meant the nonmedical use of prescription opioids or heroin by any route of administration, including oral ingestion of pills, sniffing or smoking crushed pills or heroin, or injection. Asking individuals who did not meet these criteria to recruit their peers helped mitigate any disappointment or frustration they may have felt, especially since individuals were compensated twenty dollars per eligible referral. Per the study design, the final sample was stratified by OUD treatment status, and included forty current opioid users who were not engaged in OUD treatment and forty who were currently par-ticipating in any modality of OUD treatment. Of those currently in OUD treatment, nineteen (48 percent) reported using illicit opioids in the past thirty days.

Peer-based chain-referral with incentives for referring eligible individuals proved to be our single most effective and efficient means of recruitment. This strategy drove the vast majority of participant recruitment, allowing us to recruit the primary sample of youth months ahead of schedule. Peer-based recruitment was an effective strategy because it leveraged youths' preexisting social networks of trusted peers, which were also the primary contexts in which they used opioids. FSU young adults typically used opioids in small groups of similarly-aged, Russian-speaking peers, including close friends from their immigrant neighborhoods, extended family members such as cousins and, in some cases, romantic partners. Peer-based chain-referral allowed us to gain access to people we otherwise would have had few, if any, means of reaching, given their lack of connections to drug-related services and, hence, public visibility.

Accommodating to Participants' Concealment Strategies

Early in the course of fieldwork, we learned that some young adults were reluctant to provide their full names to the study on the record. This occurred in spite of Anastasia's assurances of confidentiality and explanations of the confidentiality protections in place, including a Federal Certificate of Confidentiality which allows researchers to resist court-ordered disclosure of participants' names and other identifying information. From participants' perspectives, creating an official record of their participation may have felt uncomfortably similar to the mandatory state registration as a drug user required for receiving drug treatment in Russia. Ironically, the procedures most likely to spark participants' fears of disclosure related to the standard protections for human research subjects established by federal regulations to safeguard confidentiality. Because these protections were developed in the context of biomedical research, they can be ill-suited for lower-risk ethnographic research. For example, our research institution's IRB, which is responsible for ensuring compliance with federal ethical standards and regulations governing human subjects research, required participants to read and sign an informed consent form prior to participating in an interview. (We had not requested a waiver of documentation of informed consent.)

In deference to participants' concerns, in a few instances, we allowed participants to sign consent forms with only first names and the first initial of their last names. In most cases, participants signed consent forms with their full names, but, in accordance with standard practice, we did not attempt to verify their names and identities (e.g., with photo identification). We also emphasized that, apart from the signed consent form, we would make no other record of their last names; their research data would be identified by a code number only and stored separately from signed consent forms. If requested, we also directly referred to participants by an alternative research name that was typically a street name the participant used when engaging in drug-related activities or an ad hoc invention for the purpose of this study. Participants' frequent use of assumed names did create some logistic complications and humorous scenarios, as when a participant forgot the name originally given to us, or failed to inform the person who referred them to the study of their research name.

*Reconciling Standards of Different Research Traditions: The
Problem of Eligibility Verification*

There was very little information available on the drug use patterns of FSU immigrants in the United States when this exploratory research began. This study was designed to provide a preliminary evidence base to inform future research, suggest research questions or hypotheses that could be investigated in follow-up studies, and identify salient unmet needs related to HCV, HIV, overdose prevention, and OUD treatment.

Despite the flexibility allowed for in exploratory research, we faced the challenge of reconciling competing standards of different research traditions. Strict eligibility criteria for participation in the research and objective eligibility verification techniques (e.g., requiring participants to present photo identification to verify their age or confirming recent opioid use with on-site urine testing) are not understood to be necessary, appropriate, or desirable in ethnographic studies. In fact, from an ethnographic perspective, asking prospective participants to comply with such procedures immediately upon meeting them would be a serious impediment to establishing rapport. Therefore, we resolved early on to screen young adults for eligibility verbally, on the basis of self-report only, and in an informal style.

This decision presented a conundrum: how could we be confident that prospective participants were not misrepresenting aspects of their identity or drug use to gain entry into the study and receive the cash incentives provided for participation, while simultaneously remaining true to the spirit of ethnography and not alienating prospective participants? This is an ever-present challenge in research that relies on self-reported information for screening and data-collection purposes. In a traditional ethnographic study, these concerns would have been mitigated or obviated by the ethnographer's immersion in a fieldwork setting, as long-term engagement in a community provides ample opportunities to cross-check data obtained from one informant with other community members with whom the informant is closely connected. In so doing, the ethnographer is able to develop personal relationships with trusted informants over an extended period of time which helps ensure the validity of the information obtained from them, and financial compensation is not typically provided for participation, thereby reducing a potential incentive to dissemble. However, in our adapted form of ethnography, these concerns about validity had to be addressed. For our findings to be credible within the research paradigm that holds sway in public health, we needed some way of assuring stakeholders (including funders, consumers of published study findings, and, most importantly, members of the FSU community themselves) that we were in fact studying the population and phenomenon we claimed to be studying and about which we intended to formulate evidence-based claims.

We addressed this conundrum by using a screening interview that incorporated subtle rhetorical strategies that could be adapted on the ground, in response to unfolding interactions. Since the vast majority of the young adult target population had immigrated to the United States in childhood, virtually all were fully bilingual in English and Russian, using English in public interactions and Russian at home with families and peers. Therefore, Anastasia, who was also fluent in both languages, made a point of conversing with prospective participants in Russian, or code-switching between Russian and English, during initial interactions with them. This served a dual purpose of building rapport and verifying participants' FSU identity. Again, we were willing to adapt the original research plan to realities we encountered on the ground. For example, peer-based recruitment led us to five young adults who were not first-generation FSU immigrants, as they were born in the United States to FSU-born parents. Yet, because these individuals were embedded in drug-using networks with FSU immigrant peers, resided in Russian-speaking neighborhoods, were fluent in Russian, and considered themselves to be "Russian," we included them in the sample.

With regard to age verification, for individuals on the lower end of the study's age range, it was easier than expected to judge their age by appearance. When in doubt, Anastasia used a simple interview strategy in which she asked a prospective participant to state his or her age at the start of the screening interview; then, after a brief series of intervening questions, she asked for their date of birth. The difficulty of quickly calculating a birth year that correctly corresponds to a fake age made this a useful strategy for verifying young adults' age; at the same time, the use of an indirect rhetorical technique allowed Anastasia to avoid having to directly confront an individual with an apparent lie or dispute their stated age. Prospective participants' opioid use was verified by asking them to provide details about their personal opioid use histories, including the specific types, forms, and amounts of opioids they used at various points in time and the mechanics involved in their primary route(s) of opioid administration (e.g., preparing a shot of heroin for injection, or smoking crushed pills.)

Negotiating Interview Locations

Although we were not able to find an ideal and completely satisfactory solution to the interview location challenge, we cobbled together a workable strategy that was acceptable to participants and met the essential needs of the research. In the early stages of recruitment, Anastasia scoped out and made trial visits to potential venues. She also openly addressed the question of interview location with participants, providing suggestions and inviting participants to select a location where they would feel most comfortable. Rather to our surprise, most participants wanted to meet at a fast-food establishment (e.g., Dunkin' Donuts or McDonald's), located on a busy thoroughfare close to, but not directly in, their residential neighborhood. Although these locations presented occasional inconveniences (e.g., insufficient seating at the time of a scheduled interview, interruptions caused by loud background noise or disruptive patrons), their central location and business provided a certain feeling of anonymity to the encounters.

The research plan was designed with this challenge in mind. The structured assessments preceded the in-depth interviews, so that the lower-threshold, less intrusive form of data collection (consisting of closed questions and psychosocial scales) would provide an opportunity for Anastasia to build rapport with participants before the more sensitive and personal in-depth interview. Also, we asked participants to complete most sections of the structured assessment on paper, as opposed to verbally, to minimize the risk of sensitive information being overheard by others. For audio-recorded, in-depth interviews where privacy and a quiet, comfortable location were essential, we asked participants if they would travel to our Manhattan office, a trip all those approached were willing to make. Their willingness to be accommodating was no doubt facilitated by the rapport and goodwill Anastasia had already established in her initial meetings and follow-up contacts with them.

CONCLUSION: RECOMMENDATIONS FOR ETHNOGRAPHERS WORKING WITH "HIDDEN" POPULATIONS

Forge Alliances with Well-Regarded, Trusted Community Insiders

Forging alliances with well-placed members of the community one aims to study can be the key to the success of an ethnographic study. Ideally, these individuals should occupy a social role that makes them well known in the community, with large, wide-ranging networks of social relations. Such individuals may be in a position to introduce you to potential participants. Equally, if not more importantly, these insiders can help establish your legitimacy and trustworthiness, whether directly, by facilitating personal introductions and vouching for you, or indirectly, simply by virtue of their association with you. Thus, your credibility and reputation in the community may be boosted if you are observed in the company of trusted insiders. Even if these contacts are not members of the specific subgroup that is the focus of your research, they may know people who are, or know people connected to members of that subgroup. The overarching principle here is to use whatever connections and contacts you can muster—through colleagues, for example, or other researchers who have worked in the community before you, including colleagues in different fields. Individuals especially well suited to assist an ethnographer in this capacity tend to be highly visible community members; they may occupy semipublic/semiofficial roles within the community or be connected to institutions important in the daily life of community members. Examples of FSU community members who provided valuable assistance with recruitment for this study included a peer outreach worker at a mobile SEP that regularly operated in a Russian-speaking neighborhood in Brooklyn, drug dealers, club promoters, long-time older heroin injectors, and staff members at drug treatment programs that served significant numbers of Russian-speaking clients.

This strategy of forging alliances with selected insiders represents a time-honored ethnographic tactic for gaining entry into a community that would otherwise be inaccessible to an outsider-researcher, that of soliciting the cooperation of one or more "key informants" to facilitate an ethnographer's entry into the field and acceptance within a community of strangers (Agar, 1996). If a novice ethnographer does not have preexisting personal connections in the community gained through preliminary research or the work of a mentor or colleague, establishing an affiliation with a trusted local institution may be an available means of forging such connections, especially for ethnographers working in urban settings. Volunteering for community-based service or advocacy organizations, for example, can provide a locally acceptable role that affords an ethnographer an opportunity to familiarize herself with the community (or at least some segment of it), interact with community members, and observe the surrounding physical environment and public social interactions—that is, to conduct participant-observation.

An extension of the key informant strategy well suited for team-based ethnography is to collaborate more formally with community insiders by including them as members of your research team. In recent years, a variant of this strategy has been formalized as the Community-Based Participatory Research approach in which members of a community of interest play active, well-defined roles, and may hold formal positions, throughout all stages of a project from conceptualization through dissemination. This approach can be especially useful in insuring that research aims are consistent with the community's needs and desires and that the product of the research contributes to advancing social justice for community members, as they define it.

Capitalize on Your Outsider Status and Other Roles

If you are not a member of the community you are studying, leverage the less obvious advantages that your outsider status may confer. Being an outsider carries advantages, particularly for the study of groups and behaviors heavily stigmatized within participants' own communities. From this perspective, it was helpful that both of us were outside these youths' quotidian lives: I was an outsider to the FSU immigrant community, and Anastasia's contacts among drug users or former drug users in the city's Russian-speaking community were now significantly older than our participants. Because we were not integrated into participants' daily lives, we could function as relatively safe confidantes with whom they could openly discuss their drug use, a topic they were unable to broach with many, if any, nonpeers without fear of emotional upset, social ostracism, discrimination, or other undesirable consequences. Further, we were knowledgeable and nonjudgmental about drug use, yet were not drug treatment providers, so had no vested interest in encouraging participants to disavow or discontinue their opioid use.

Other aspects of your identity as an ethnographer may give you privileged access to certain subgroups or situations—allow yourself the flexibility to seize these unexpected opportunities. This openness to emergent knowledge and flexibility to allow new insights to continually inform the refinement of one's data-collection strategy is a core strength of ethnographic research. For example, as women, Anastasia and I found that we were able to talk with female drug users about gender dynamics in FSU culture and the FSU drug scene, and even sensitive, painful experiences like stripping, sex work, and sexual victimization. Although not part of the initial conceptualization of the study's objectives, these topics emerged as salient in early interviews with female participants and we made the decision to probe these topics further, given their importance in these women's lives and their relevance to the larger topic of HIV risk and transmission.

Another example is our experience of recruiting parents of opioid-using youth. Through the pilot study, I had learned that relations with parents and other family members play a central role in shaping the lived experiences of young FSU immigrants who used opioids. While family dynamics are a foundational element in the life course development of all youth, including those who use drugs, the family sphere seemed to be especially prominent for FSU immigrants. The majority of the young adults in the study lived with their families (as is normative in FSU culture), and parents played a significant role in young people's drug use trajectories—providing financial support, pressure to stop using drugs, assistance with locating and paying for drug treatment, and practical and financial assistance with legal problems. Because we were convinced that parents' perspectives would provide critical context for this research, the research plan included in-depth interviews with twelve parents of opioid-using FSU youth. To avoid infringing on the privacy of the study's young adult participants, these would *not* be parents of any young adults who had participated in the study. Ideally, we would have interviewed both mothers and fathers, as interviews with youth suggested that mothers and fathers might have significantly different perspectives on their children's drug use. However, while mothers were generally quite willing to speak with Anastasia, and a number of them spoke eloquently and at length about the pain they felt as a result of their children's drug use, we were unable to recruit any fathers, rendering their perspectives inaccessible to us. Our failure in this regard is likely rooted in traditional Russian/FSU patriarchal gender roles which dictate that the management of the family domain is the responsibility of women, a view especially strong among older generations who came of age in the Soviet era. Thus, very few fathers participated in the parents' support group that was our main recruitment source for parents. Our own identities as women likely contributed to this as well, although we were generally effective at connecting with younger FSU men and some older men with whom we interacted in a more overtly professional capacity (e.g., treatment providers).

Be Flexible

An important rule of thumb that extends our third recommendation is to be flexible, adapt to the situation on the ground, and seize unexpected opportunities as they present themselves if your instinct tells you they may lead you to a something that will be relevant. A simple example of the unexpected benefits of flexibility involves an interaction with an obviously ineligible prospective participant. Although our peer-based recruitment strategy led to few ineligible referrals, Anastasia did on one occasion meet with a prospective participant who had misrepresented his age when prescreened on the phone prior to their face-to-face meeting. When Anastasia gently confronted him about the fact that he appeared to be in his forties not his twenties, the man readily admitted to having lied about his age. Yet, even after learning he was ineligible, he was still eager to share his experience with Anastasia. During their ensuing conversation, the man revealed that he was a drug dealer in the Russian-speaking community. Upon learning this information, Anastasia solicited his assistance in referring some of his younger clients to her, knowing that, as a dealer, he would have a dense network of connections to local heroin users. This anecdote shows the value of flexibility. Though one look at the man revealed to Anastasia that he would not be eligible to formally participate, she nonetheless took the time to listen to his story, a gesture of goodwill that also proved beneficial to the research. Moreover, the fact that she had taken time out of her day to listen to him impressed the man enough that he willingly referred his clients to the study and vouched for the study's legitimacy, increasing the likelihood that they would follow up with the referral.

Offer Something of Value to Members of the Community You Are Researching

Consider the specialized knowledge (or resources such as connections with staff members at drug-related service organizations) you may possess that study participants may not have, but might find useful. Anastasia made a point of providing practical, individualized harm reduction education to young adults after the assessments had been completed, focusing on knowledge gaps that had become apparent during their interactions and making clear that she was happy to answer any related questions they had. At the time this study was conducted, many participants were unaware of the HCV transmission risk associated with sharing nonsyringe injection paraphernalia (e.g., cookers for mixing a drug solution, cotton filters, etc.), or were unfamiliar with the overdose reversal medication naloxone (which had recently become available to lay people without a prescription following the adoption of new Standing Order legislation in New York State). Your position as a professional researcher or academic can be advantageous, as participants are likely to trust you as a source of specialized information in your domain of study and value your expertise. This was especially true in this study, given the high value placed on education and professional status in Russian culture.

Less tangible, emotional benefits were equally important for building rapport. Our experience conducting in-depth interviews with young adults and mothers convinced us of the value of being an empathetic, nonjudgmental listener. This may actually be the most valuable thing you have to offer—do not underestimate the value of an empathetic ear. Given a situation that feels safe and nonthreatening, most people welcome the opportunity to narrate their lives. A research interview can provide a rare opportunity for individuals, especially those who are engaging in behavior that is widely stigmatized, to talk about their most personal experiences with an interested listener who does not offer advice or encourage any specific course of action.[3]

NOTES

1. All participant names used in this chapter are pseudonyms.
2. Words and phrases in double quotation marks, unless otherwise attributed, were used by one or more participants in interviews.
3. This research was supported by a grant from the National Institute on Drug Abuse (NIDA), within the National Institutes of Health (NIH); Grant R03DA033899, Principal Investigator H. Guarino). The content is solely the responsibility of the authors and does not necessarily represent the official views of NIDA or NIH. The authors also wish to express their appreciation to the study participants who generously shared their time, insights, and experiences.

REFERENCES

Agar, M. H. (1996). *The professional stranger: An informal introduction to ethnography.* 2nd ed. New York: Academic Press.

Beyrer, C., et al. (2017). The expanding epidemic of HIV-1 in the Russian Federation. *PLoS Medicine, 14*(11). Retrived from p. e1002462. DOI: 10.1371/journal .pmed.1002462.

Calabrese, S. K., et al. (2016). Internalized HIV and drug stigmas: Interacting forces threatening health status and health service utilization among people with HIV who inject drugs in St. Petersburg, Russia. *AIDS and Behavior, 20*(1), 85–97.

Elovich, R., and E. Drucker (2008). On drug treatment and social control: Russian narcology's great leap backwards. *Harm Reduction Journal, 5*(23). Retrieved from DOI: 10.1186/1477-7517-5-23.

Guarino, H., et al. (2012). The social production of substance abuse and HIV/HCV risk: An exploratory study of opioid-using immigrants from the former Soviet Union living in New York City. *Substance Abuse Prevention, Treatment, and Policy, 7*(2). Retrieved from DOI: 10.1186/1747-597X-7-2.

Guarino, H., et al. (2015). Opioid use trajectories, injection drug use, and hepatitis C virus risk among young adult immigrants from the former Soviet Union living in New York City. *Journal of Addictive Diseases, 34*(2-3), 162-77.

Gunn, A., and H. Guarino (2016). "Not human, dead already": Perceptions and experiences of drug-related stigma among opioid-using young adults from the former Soviet Union living in New York City. *International Journal of Drug Policy, 38,* 63 72.

Page, J. B., and M. Singer (2010). *Comprehending drug use: Ethnographic research at the social margins.* New Brunswick, NJ: Rutgers University Press.

Suryaprasad, A. G., et al. (2014). Emerging epidemic of hepatitis C virus infections among young nonurban persons who inject drugs in the United States, 2006-2012. *Clinical Infectious Diseases, 59*(10), 1411-19.

PART FOUR

The Emotional Impact of Doing Ethnography

———

TEN

Dangerous Liaisons

REFLECTIONS ON A SERIAL ETHNOGRAPHY

Robert Gay

AS ALL ETHNOGRAPHERS KNOW, FIELD research calls for a tremendous investment of time and energy in order to establish and maintain personal relationships. Unlike the fifteen-minute survey, or the hour-long, in-depth interview, it can take literally months to get to a point at which you think you might just be getting somewhere with at least one or two members of the group you have chosen to study. Such are the challenges of fieldwork! Ultimately, however, even ethnographers pack up and leave, returning to the rarified atmosphere of academia where, if they are lucky, their hard work will be rewarded with perhaps a job at a prestigious university, critically acclaimed publications, and tenure.

But what of the individuals they leave behind? What of those who make ethnographies a possibility in the first place? In most instances, ethnographies are one and done, stand-alone case studies that capture a year or so of intensive research, followed by much shorter and more infrequent visits to the field. And, when you think about it, there are good reasons for this. Unlike a survey that can be administered again and again to provide a longitudinal view, no one in their right mind would replicate or extend an ethnography. Or would they? In this chapter I look back at the largely unforeseen circumstances that led to what is now more than thirty years of continuous fieldwork in a slum neighborhood, or favela, in Rio de Janeiro, Brazil, that produced three different ethnographic projects that were only possible because of evolving, uninterrupted and, ultimately, complicated relationships that were nurtured over many years.[1]

1986

It was never my intention to do research on drugs. In fact, it was the last thing on my mind when I arrived in Rio, in January 1986, to study the role of so-called "new social movements" in the transition to democracy. Brazil had been ruled by the military since 1964. In recent years, however, there had been an "opening" that was forced in part by civic groups that opposed not only the regime but also the traditional way of doing politics. In the past, Brazilian politics was characterized by clientelism, a system whereby votes are exchanged for favors (Gay, 1999). The civic groups that emerged in the late 1970s and early 1980s, however, were looking to replace clientelism with a more emancipatory form of political action based on the idea of universal rights (Escobar and Alvarez, 1992). My job was to see if they had succeeded.

My initial strategy was to choose one favela that engaged in clientelist politics, Vila Brasil, and another that didn't, Vidigal, in order to compare the two. Once this choice was made, based on extensive analysis of back copies of local newspapers and conversations with representatives from a wide variety of civic and religious groups, I spent the next eight months shuttling back and forth between the two favelas talking to community leaders and their friends and acquaintances, and in general "hanging out." Then, at the suggestion of my thesis advisor, I was encouraged to conduct a survey of both places to see if the differences I had observed had any effect on voting behavior (Gay, 1994).

To do this, I calculated that I had to draw a 25 percent sample of all of the houses in both Vila Brasil and Vidigal a week before the elections in November, despite the fact that there were no maps or registers. So, instead of preselecting a sample, I walked my way through the two communities, down each and every road and alleyway, picking out every fourth house as I went. Except that in Vidigal (see fig. 10.1), the research assistants I had hired to help me would say, "No, not that one," because the house in question had been appropriated by the local drug gang.

It's not that I was unaware that there was a drug gang operating in the favela, or in other favelas of the region, it's just that I didn't want them interfering with what I considered to be very important research work. Furthermore, the leaders of Vidigal assured me, as I was about to leave in December, that the gang posed no threat to their authority. Well, if the gang posed no threat to their authority then, it did by the time I returned three years later, in November 1989, to conduct another preelectoral survey. On

FIGURE 10.1. Vidigal in 1986. Photo credit: Robert Gay.

this occasion, the gang had just returned from an unsuccessful military operation in a favela across town, and, as a consequence, everyone in Vidigal was expecting a retaliatory strike. As I knocked on people's doors and asked them who they were voting for and why, I was struck by how reluctant they were to talk and by the number of people who cited public security, or rather the lack of it, as their primary concern.

The other significant thing that happened during my visit was that I got to climb the huge rock outcrop behind the favela that entailed an hour-long hike up the spine of the hill (see fig. 10.2). Our guide that day was a young

FIGURE 10.2. Lucia and Eduardo overlooking the city. Photo credit: Robert Gay.

man of sixteen named Eduardo.[2] Except that when we were about halfway up, he reached into the bag he was carrying and produced an enormous joint of marijuana. Then, a couple of hundred yards further on, out came a plastic bag of cocaine. And then finally, once we reached the top, out came a gun that my stoned and distracted companions took turns firing into the air. Eduardo, it turned out, was a member of the local drug gang. More importantly, however, he was the boyfriend of my friend Lucia.

I had gotten to know Lucia back in 1986. She was one of a group of teenagers that I taught English to, every Tuesday and Thursday afternoon. In addition, she was also one of the eight research assistants that I hired to help with my survey, a condition that was imposed on me by the neighborhood association. Now, however, her life appeared to be taking a different turn, a fact that was not lost on her family, to whom I had become close.

1996

In the years that followed my visit in 1989, I only returned to Rio a couple of times. And that was, in part, because I was looking to replicate my research on favela politics in another part of the country and, in part, because I now had a young family, which made spending time in the field a lot more difficult. In 1996, however, I made arrangements to spend a whole month in Rio visiting my original research sites with an eye to writing a ten-year retrospective.

In Vila Brasil, some things had changed but, then again, others hadn't, which was the focus of the journal article I published on my return (Gay, 1998). In Vidigal, on the other hand, things had taken a decided turn for the worse. Whereas initially, the drug gang was willing to coexist with the neighborhood association, now it was looking to take over. According to my friends, the gang had begun interfering in local elections by backing the opposition slate of candidates. And, when that didn't work, it tried to infiltrate the neighborhood association by getting individuals on its payroll to volunteer.

And then finally, the drug gang started making direct threats. Three months prior to my visit, the violence between rival gangs in Rio reached such a point that the police decided to crack down. In Vidigal, this meant that there was a patrol car stationed permanently at the entrance of the favela, which made it difficult for the drug gang to do business. Incensed by the situation, the drug gang's leader called the president of the neighborhood association on his cell phone and told him to get everyone on the directorate to sign a petition demanding that the police should leave—and that if he didn't, he would be executed along with the rest of the members of his family. The president, after thinking about it, refused to comply with the order and moved his family to a favela in another part of the city.[3]

The question for my purposes was, how was I going to write about what was happening in Vidigal, and in hundreds of other favelas in Rio? My friends from the neighborhood association wouldn't talk about it, at least not on the record. In fact, they'd only talk to me at all if it was inside their own homes and behind closed doors. And even then, they were extremely cautious and guarded in terms of what they were willing to say.

Such was the level of fear, mutual mistrust, and suspicion that I realized I had to approach the issue in a different way. And that's where Lucia came in. It turned out that Lucia had spent the past five years romantically involved with a series of drug gang leaders operating out of a favela in the western part of the state. Now, however, she was back home in Vidigal with her family and a daughter who she had, for all intents and purposes, abandoned. More importantly, at least for me, she was open and willing to talk about her experiences because, as she said, most of her friends from that life were now dead. So, from her point of view, it was her opportunity to tell their story.

The project itself required multiple trips to Rio between June 1999 and March 2001. As a recently divorced father with joint custody of two teenage girls, it was no longer an option to spend a month away from home, let alone a semester or a year! So, I'd go down for a week at a time and hang out at Lucia's house, waiting patiently for a chance to conduct an interview. Initially, out of concern for my personal safety, my plan was to have her take a bus downtown to the hotel where I was staying. I soon realized, however, that she was far too busy looking after the house, and a gaggle of young children, to have time to slip away. In fact, I considered it a good day if I managed to persuade her to set aside an hour of her precious time.[4]

As for concerns for my safety, I really needn't have worried. I don't know who knew I was there, or what I was doing, but nobody seemed to care. In fact, on one rather unnerving occasion, Lucia introduced me to a neighbor, who was also the wife of the then current drug gang leader. "This is my friend Robert," she said, as we went through her neighbor's front door. "He's writing a book about me." To which the leader's wife said, "Well make sure you get it right. Make sure you tell him the truth!" To be honest, the only people I was really scared of were the police, who were stationed at the entrance to the favela. To them, a white, middle-class male going in and out of a favela had, in all probability, something to do with drugs. Having said that, however, they never gave me any trouble. But it did make me a little nervous when, at the end of my week-long visits, I'd walk past them, minicassettes concealed in my pocket, on the way to the bus stop at the bottom of the hill.[5]

In terms of the interviews, we started out by talking about Lucia's involvement with the drug gang in chronological order. This meant how she first got in and then her somewhat harrowing experiences with a succession of violence-prone lovers. As interesting and revealing as these conversations turned out to be, however, I got the sense that she was holding back. So, on one of my visits I told her that if this was going to work she was going to have to open up and tell me "everything." And then, as we started talking about her experiences at school and at work, she started backfilling details that she'd omitted from our earlier interviews. So, for example, I only learned right at the end that it was her brother Pato who got her involved in the first place, because he was a member of the drug gang in Vidigal, and she'd run messages for him.

When I showed up to start the interviews, in June 1999, Lucia's brother was still in prison. Arrested for possessing an illegal firearm, he'd been sentenced to two years in a medium-security prison in the Gerincinó complex on the outskirts of Rio. Lucia and other members of her family visited him whenever they could, which was not that often given the two-hour-plus bus ride from Vidigal and the invasive searches and byzantine procedures that they had to endure prior to being allowed in. It was while she was visiting her brother, however, that Lucia met and eventually fell in love with Bruno, who was sitting on a white plastic chair outside the front door when I first came in.

Bruno had just been released that week from prison, having served eight years for drug trafficking. Quite honestly, I didn't know what to make of him. Lucia hadn't said anything to me about him, and yet here he was living with her and her family. Of course, looking back, he must have felt the same way about me. I mean, who knows what he thought I was doing, especially when I'd disappear into the bedroom for an hour each day with someone he considered to be his wife. In any case, at some point in the proceedings, Lucia told me to go talk to him about his experiences. And so that's what I did.

Our conversation that day, on an open rooftop, lasted around forty minutes and covered Bruno's eight-year career as a corporal in the Brazilian navy, his involvement with trafficking drugs from the border with Bolivia, and his eventual arrest and incarceration. Fascinated by this new source of information, I pushed him on subsequent days to tell me more, but he wouldn't. I can only guess that, despite the fact that Lucia had vouched for me, he was having second thoughts about who I was, where this information would end up, and if, by talking to me, he was getting himself into trouble. So I dropped it, and carried on until I had finished my project with Lucia (Gay, 2005).

2007

In the years following my last interviews with Lucia, in 2001, I returned to Rio at least once a year, not with any particular project in mind, but just to keep tabs on the situation. By then, Bruno and Lucia had had two children together. And they had constructed their own apartment within what was now a fairly extensive family compound.[6] My other friends in Vidigal kept asking me how I thought they could afford it, clearly suspecting that Bruno had not, in fact, quit the business. Personally, I have to admit that I felt uncomfortable confronting him about it, and that it was only later on that Lucia told to me that he had driven a consignment of drugs on a one-time basis from São Paulo to Rio.

FIGURE 10.3. Vidigal in 2007. Photo credit: Robert Gay.

Then, in August 2004, Bruno was arrested again, driving what turned out to be a stolen car from Rio to Paraguay, where it was to be sold. Bruno swore to me after he got out that he didn't know the car's papers were false. Whether that was true or not, it finally convinced him not to take any more risks, which meant finding a regular job. He started talking about opening up his own painting and decorating business in the favela.

The other thing that happened during this time was that we got to become friends. Bruno would confide in me about his worries for his children, living in a favela under constant threat of attack by rival gangs and the police. He'd even ask me to accompany him downtown on errands or to go visit friends, some of whom had spent time with him in prison. Then, in the summer of 2006, he turned to me one day and said, "I'm ready, I'm ready to tell my story." We agreed that I would come down to Rio as often as possible over the course of the next year or so (Gay, 2015).

My first visit was in January 2007 (see fig. 10.3), and resulted in only two days and a meager one hundred minutes of interviews, largely because Bruno's kids were out of school and he was in charge of looking after them. So, we'd set them up with a video game in their room until they got bored and came out to find us. That was ok, and not altogether unexpected given my prior experience with Lucia, and it gave me a chance to catch up with other people in the community. In February I came back again, and then again in June, August, and October, by which time we were cranking out two days and three hundred and sixty minutes of interviews each visit. In March 2008, we finished the interview process, and I got on with the somewhat laborious and painstaking task of transcribing, translating, and editing Bruno's words.[7]

Initially, I thought that the most interesting part of his testimony would be the time he spent at the naval base in Mato Grosso do Sul, where he first got involved with selling drugs. As it turned out, however, his experiences as a drug trafficker, while extremely interesting, paled in comparison with what he went through during his eight years in prison, where, unbeknownst to me, he became one of the leaders of the oldest and perhaps most notorious criminal faction in Rio, the Comando Vermelho. More specifically, because of the friendships he'd made and the conflicts he'd successfully negotiated, he was placed in charge of a prison under the Comando Vermelho's control, meaning he had power of life and death over more than one thousand inmates.[8]

While Bruno was in charge of the prison, the Comando Vermelho split apart.[9] As a consequence, he was ordered by the faction's leaders in other prisons to kill twelve members of the group that had decided to leave, which he refused to do. This put his life and the lives of his immediate friends in extreme danger, a situation that was only resolved later on when he confronted his enemies within the Comando Vermelho and managed to clear his name. As you can imagine, while he was recounting this part of his story he became overwhelmed with feelings of anxiety at the thought of what he'd been through, to the extent that I had to stop the interview. When I asked him whether he wanted to take a break, he said, "No, no, we must go on, because I need to get this off my chest." And it was at this point that I realized that our conversations were a form of catharsis for him, because by talking to me, he processed things he hadn't even told Lucia.

Needless to say, I was both fascinated and disturbed by what Bruno was telling me, even to the point of questioning whether the project should go ahead.[10] Unlike Lucia, who was involved with a relatively small drug gang in a distant part of the state, Bruno was a former leader of a notorious criminal faction, and he would be recognized by anyone who served time with him and by the authorities. Despite my misgivings, however, Bruno, insisted that it was not a problem, because if anything was going to happen to him, it would have happened by now. After all, he argued, he'd been out of prison for eight years, and during that time Vidigal had changed hands from the Commando Vermelho, which historically had controlled it, to the Amigos dos Amigos, which was the faction that split from the Comando Vermelho when Bruno was in charge.[11]

The other consequence of our conversations was that it completely changed my assessment of our relationship in the past. Because I'd known Bruno for seven years before we embarked on this project. During that time, things had happened, and people had come and gone, that made little or no sense to me. But now they did. I was, like, "So that's who you are!" For example, there was the time when we were walking down the hill together, and a young man suddenly appeared from an alleyway and pulled Bruno aside. I knew that the young man was the leader of the drug gang in the favela, because Bruno told me afterward. What I couldn't work out, at the time, was why he wanted to talk to Bruno of all people. Now I know, but I'm still not sure if I should be upset or relieved that I didn't know whom my friend was for all those years!

Ultimately, because of my concerns, Bruno and Lucia agreed that we should not pursue the publication of the manuscript in Portuguese because, as Lucia said, "We've had enough trouble in our lives." This was a significant decision, however, because Brazil was, and still is, where the market for this kind of narrative lies. It's just that I, personally, did not feel comfortable exposing them to any unforeseen and unnecessary risk. I did tell Bruno, however, as I told Lucia, that any profits from the book would be his, but not to expect too much because academic books don't tend to sell.[12]

When all was said and done, research on *Bruno* cost me approximately seven thousand dollars out of my own pocket. I received some financial support from my college but nowhere near enough to cover my travel and hotel expenses.[13] On top of that, there were the two trips that Bruno and I made after the interviews were completed. The first of these trips was to Ilha Grande, an island to the southwest of the city of Rio de Janeiro where he'd spent the first two and a half years of his prison sentence in 1991. The prison on Ilha Grande, built in the 1940s, was known among the inmate population as the "Devil's Cauldron"; more importantly, it was the birthplace of the Comando Vermelho in the mid-1970s.

The second trip we made together was to Ladário, in Mato Grosso de Sul, where Bruno had been stationed as a corporal in the Brazilian navy, and where he first got involved in the business of trafficking drugs. Both trips were extremely emotional for Bruno, especially since he got to visit old haunts and, as unlikely as it seems, to meet old acquaintances, some of whom, in the case of Ilha Grande, were guards he knew from his time in prison. Both trips also dispelled any lingering doubts I had over the veracity of his story, since he was able to take me to places we had talked about in our conversations.

The other important outcome of the two trips was that we became much closer as friends. I'd never spent time with Bruno outside of the favela of Vidigal, apart from a couple of trips downtown. Now we were far away, on our own, sharing boat journeys, long drives, hotel rooms, beers, and meals together. And with that closeness came a sense of increased obligation and responsibility, on my part. It was no surprise, at least to me, that *Bruno* (Gay, 2015) received excellent reviews but sold few copies. I know for a fact that Bruno was disappointed, however, and that his disappointment translated into more frequent and aggressive requests for money.[14] And so my dilemma was, how should I compensate him? Or Lucia? Or the other members of her family who had welcomed me with open arms over the course of all these years? I used to think that we were all friends, and that friendship was its own compensation. But now that I've had time to think about it, our friendship, and I still believe it is a friendship, is extremely lopsided, in the sense that it has provided the foundation for my entire career.

So, in the spring of 2017, I called Bruno and told him that I was going to give him a lump sum of money, as a gesture of support and thanks. And then, a month later, I committed to help pay for his and Lucia's two sons' private school tuition, as they desperately sought to provide them with a better future. At the time, it was money I simply did not have. But then again, how can you cry poverty when you are a tenured, full professor at an elite New England liberal arts college? How can you explain to someone the difficulties of paying tens of thousands of dollars a year for your daughter's tuition when your friends live in a house they built from scratch with their own bare hands? The answer is you can't. And while I have to admit that I didn't like it, and that it has already changed our relationship, in reality, it was no more than they deserved.

CONCLUDING COMMENTS

Looking back on my career, I have been extremely fortunate in being able to complete three separate ethnographic projects based on fieldwork in a single community. My ability to establish and nurture a network of personal relations over the years has meant that I have been in prime position to conduct research on the notoriously difficult subject of drug-related violence in Rio de Janeiro's favelas. While others have had to abandon communities in which they have conducted fieldwork in the past,[15] I on the other hand have been able to maintain a fairly constant presence. This somewhat unorthodox approach to fieldwork is not without its complications, however, as contacts become friends, who then become quasi kin, with all the associated obligations and responsibilities.

The most difficult aspect of my relationships has been the largely unspoken expectation of compensation. Although I have tried my best to deny it, the difference between my status, and that of my friends, has always complicated the situation. And, if I am being honest, it is something I should have recognized and addressed earlier on. Like many of us, however, I always believed that my research was serving some greater public good. I now realize that as something of a conceit. Sadly, for everyone, Bruno passed away during the time of writing this chapter. I can only say that I am glad that I came through for him before the end.[16]

NOTES

1. For an insightful analysis and perspective on field research and relationships, see Burawoy (2003).

2. All names used are pseudonyms.

3. The neighborhood association struggled on for a couple of years until it was finally forced out in 1998. From then on, the president was handpicked by the drug gang.

4. Lucia was particularly concerned about the stress and anxiety she had caused her family, and wanted to make up for the time she had lost.

5. The police in Rio are notoriously corrupt and violent. During the 1990s, they were responsible for, on average, a thousand civilian deaths per year. See Human Rights Watch (2009).

6. When I first met them, Lucia's mother and her five children slept head-to-toe in two single beds, the father on the living room couch.

7. I paid a friend of a friend of mine to do the transcribing, which was a lot easier to manage given the change in technology. For my original project and my project with Lucia, I tape recorded interviews on a minicassette. In this case, however, all interviews were recorded on my iPhone using a digital microphone. And, as long as each segment lasted less than fifteen minutes, they could be emailed and downloaded to iTunes. Translating Bruno's words proved much more of a challenge, however, since I had to imagine what someone from his social background would sound like in English.

8. The Comando Vermelho was established in the mid-1970s inside a Rio prison. In 1988 it split apart, leading to the formation of the Terceiro Comando. In 1994 it split apart again, leading to the emergence of the Amigos dos Amigos. As a consequence, the prison system in Rio is organized entirely by faction to keep members of rival gangs apart.

9. For Bruno's full story, see Gay (2015).

10. For my first project, in 1986, there was no Institutional Review Board (IRB) process. For my second project with Lucia, I received her informed consent and let her choose all the pseudonyms for the characters involved. In terms of my project with Bruno, he was the one who approach me with an eye to developing his story. I also consulted with the director of the IRB at my college and was told that oral histories do not constitute generalizable knowledge, so I did not need IRB approval.

11. Under usual circumstances, when a rival faction takes over, members of the vanquished gang are killed or driven out. Bruno, on the other hand, was allowed to stay *because* of the way he handled the dispute while he was in charge of the prison.

12. If I remember correctly, *Lucia* generated somewhere in the region of one thousand dollars, which I split (66 percent–33 percent) between Lucia and her best friend, whom I had known for an equally long time. Lucia's friend was so disgusted by what she ended up with that she abruptly ended our relationship of twenty-plus years.

13. Each trip cost approximately sixteen hundred dollars. I received two thousand dollars per year in travel support from my college.

14. At one point he said to me, "In the world of crime, no one would refuse me!" Which I interpreted as a thinly veiled threat.

15. See, for example, Goldstein (2013) and Sheriff (2001). For a similar long-term project, see Rodgers (2019).

16. I want to acknowledge Bruno, Lucia, and family, to whom I dedicate this chapter.

REFERENCES

Burawoy, M. (2003), Revisits: An outline of a theory of reflexive ethnography. *American Sociological Review, 68*(5), 645–79.

Escobar, P., and S. Alvarez (1992). *The making of social movements in Latin America: Identity, strategy and democracy.* Boulder, CO: Westview.

Gay, R. (1994). *Popular organization and democracy in Rio de Janeiro: A tale of two favelas.* Philadelphia: Temple University Press.

———— (1998). The broker and the thief: A parable (Reflections on popular politics in contemporary Brazil). *Luso Brazilian Review, 36*(1), 49–70.

———— (1999). Rethinking clientelism: Demands, discourses and practices in contemporary Brazil. *European Review of Latin American and Caribbean Studies, 65*, 7–24.

———— (2005). *Lucia: Testimonies of a Brazilian drug dealer's woman.* Philadelphia: Temple University Press.

———— (2015). *Bruno: Conversations with a Brazilian drug dealer.* Durham, NC: Duke University Press.

Goldstein, D. (2013). *Laughter out of place: Race, class, violence, and sexuality in a Rio shantytown.* Berkeley: University of California Press.

Human Rights Watch (2009). *Lethal force: Police violence and public security in Rio de Janeiro and São Paulo.* New York: Human Rights Watch.

Rodgers, D. (2019). From "broder" to "don": Methodological reflections on longitudinal gang research in Nicaragua. In *Ethnography as risky business: Field research in violent and sensitive contexts,* ed. K. Koonings, D. Kruijt, and D. Rodgers, 123–34. London: Lexington Books.

Sheriff, R. (2001). *Dreaming equality: Color, race, and racism in urban Brazil.* New Brunswick, NJ: Rutgers University Press.

———

ELEVEN

The Emotional Labor of Fieldwork with People Who Use Methamphetamine

Heith Copes

ETHNOGRAPHIC FIELDWORK INVOLVES COLLECTING people's stories. Ethnographers then use these narratives to understand the world from the perspective of the storytellers. When those being studied are people who use drugs, the stories are often exciting and intriguing (Tutenges and Sandberg, 2013). They tell sad tales of disappointment and struggle that led to use of drugs at an young age. They tell dramatic stories of near-fatal overdoses or encounters with those seeking to harm them. They tell exciting and humorous stories of the absurd behaviors and actions of others who were a little too high. They tell redemption stories of how, despite these hardships, users came out of their addictions better and stronger people. While these stories are entertaining, they are also the building blocks for theory; they are our data. As the collectors of these stories, ethnographers are tasked with organizing them and determining patterns of behaviors, thoughts, and beliefs. This is how we learn about structure, culture, and human agency.

Collecting these stories can be fun and entertaining. After all, who doesn't like to hear a good story? But hearing these stories can also cause emotional discomfort. If ethnographers become involved with their participants, these sad and tragic tales can be difficult to hear (Worley, Worley, and Wood, 2016). It is not uncommon for ethnographers to build relationships and grow concerned for those they study. Being around people's homes, eating with them, and meeting their families can lead to emotional attachments. When ethnographers get close to participants, the stories of their hardships, struggles, and setbacks can have strong emotional consequences. Despite reading numerous articles about people's experiences in the field, and many textbooks detailing ways to navigate ethnographic research, we can still find ourselves getting overly attached.

My aim with this chapter is to share my experiences of engaging in photo-ethnography with people who used methamphetamine in rural North Alabama. Specifically, I focus on the emotional labor of working with people I grew to know and care about. To do this, I thought it fitting to tell a story.[1] I begin by contextualizing the story by describing the project and our larger aims for carrying it out. I then tell how, despite interviewing people who had used drugs or engaged in crime for over fifteen years, I was still unprepared for the emotional labor of the project and its lasting impact on me.

LARGER PROJECT

In 2015, I began a photo-ethnography, with photographer Jared Ragland, of people who use methamphetamine (meth) and live in rural North Alabama. The larger aim of the project was to understand how people who use meth make sense of their lives and navigate their drug use within the context of rural poverty. The rise in the use of methamphetamine across the United States has led to increased cultural anxiety about the drug and those who use it. These perceptions are perpetuated by popular television programs and pervasive antimeth campaigns, which paint one-dimensional, demonized characters whose chronic meth use is epitomized by obsessiveness, paranoia, and monstrous physical side effects (Linnemann and Wall, 2013; Marsh, Copes, and Linnemann, 2017). While there are certainly deleterious consequences to meth use and the stereotypes of users often ring too true, existing cultural narratives fall short of more complex, contradictory, and individually considered realities. Accordingly, our study sought to act as a counternarrative and countervisual to these stigmatizing portrayals by providing a more nuanced look at those who use meth.

The ethnography consisted of formal interviews with fifty-two participants, informal observations, and photography. The data collection lasted about two years, but informal interactions extended beyond this time. We took photographs to document the lives and experiences of the participants and to aid in eliciting responses from participants. We also solicited photographs from them.

All participants were active users of meth who were living in an area in northeast Alabama notorious for meth use. To locate participants, we relied on a primary recruiter and on snowball sampling. The interviews took place at the recruiter's home, participants' homes, public parks, or other private areas. We let participants decide where they would like to meet and do the interviews. Snowball sampling extended the sample beyond the initial recruiter's social networks. After the initial interview with a participant, we asked if he or she could refer others to the study.

We obtained Institutional Review Board (IRB) approval from our university. In compliance with this approval, we obtained informed consent for all participants and let them know that the interviews were voluntary and would be kept confidential. The IRB approval included taking photographs of participants and having them send images to us. All those who agreed to photographs signed a release for themselves and for their minor children if relevant. We do not include photographs of those who did not consent to having their photographs taken. We made it clear that they could decline having their photographs taken or refuse to send us images and still be a part of the study. A total of twenty-nine people agreed to have their photographs taken and to be used in the project.

I include photographs here as a means to provide context to the story and to draw readers into the world of rural users of meth. Such use of photographs is consistent with documentary photography (Schonberg and Bourgois, 2002). It is my hope that the photographs not only give insights into the lives of those I studied but also that they will aid in connecting with and humanizing participants. I recognize that care must be taken when using these types of images in research. Decontextualized images may reinforce negative cultural stereotypes more than counter them (Becker, 2007). This is because photographs can prompt multiple meanings in the viewing process (Becker, 2007; Schwartz, 1989). As such, I cannot control how others interpret the images included here; however, I hope that readers will interpret the images within the context of the data presented and my intentions.

EMOTIONAL LABOR OF FIELDWORK

In 2015 Jared and I began our project. As is typical with ethnographic research, the first few months were difficult in terms of recruiting people and making contacts. Gaining trust or at least acceptance can be a slow process. People want to be assured that researchers aren't police. While our primary recruiter, Ana, was remarkable in helping us with initial introductions and soothing people's concerns that we might be police officers, I think what helped us to be accepted among people was our continued presence and our willingness to be honest with them. My background helped. My family is from rural Louisiana and I currently live in Alabama. While I wasn't an insider, but I wasn't completely foreign to the region and culture either. Another important factor for us was that the people we were interacting with are accustomed to having visitors come over, unannounced, and just hang out in their homes. Thus, our presence wasn't that out of the norm.

In the early stages of the project things were going well. At times Jared and I would be exhausted from the day, but that was to be expected. The drive for me took about two hours, and each visit consisted of interacting with people who were selling and using meth. Many were in desperate situations. These days were stressful, but Jared and I would process the events of the day on the drive home. I thought that our discussions were enough to cope with the events. However, as we became more embedded, things changed. We began to form closer relationships with a core group of people, and became a part of their lives. We ate with them. We met their families. We remained in contact through text messaging, even when not in the field. This latter change had a stronger impact than we anticipated; we were never more than text away from participants. Most of these contacts were mundane, but some were not. Three such messages stand out.

The first message came from Alice. When we first met Alice she was quiet and seldom interacted with us. It was not until a few weeks after meeting her that she actively contacted us. At the time, Alice was twenty-one and had recently lost custody of her daughter. She was using meth intravenously almost daily. After reuniting with her boyfriend (who was serving time in jail), she and he decided to go clean and eventually get to a point where she could regain custody of her daughter. This would not be an easy path, as neither had family nor financial resources to help them. For about two weeks they seemed to be doing well. They had found a place to live and had help from family. Alice seemed proud of her progress and would send us positive updates on how she was doing. Then late one night she sent a text with a different tone. The text was a picture of a shot glass of water and a spoon (the tools needed to shoot meth intravenously), with the caption: "Struggling." This was the first time I felt the emotional weight of the project. I was at home watching TV with my family and the text came unexpectedly. The photo and text showed that, despite their efforts, they were not going to remain drug-free (see fig. 11.1).

The second text came from Misty, who had a tumultuous relationship with her husband, JC, but she said she was in love with him. JC was a binge meth user, and when he used he was often abusive. On one of his binges he

FIGURE 11.1. The day of Alice and Ryan's relapse. Ryan is lying on a bed as Alice reaches out to him. Photo credit: Jared Ragland.

came home late at night and assaulted her, leaving bruises and scratches on her face and neck. We had heard that JC was arrested, but we didn't know for what reason. I texted Misty and asked how he was doing. She replied, "JC is probably gonna go to prison. He beat and raped me." This text hit hard. I was not prepared for such a response.

The third text came from Fred, who was in his fifties and a long-term user of meth. Fred lived in his parents' home, which he opened up to people who needed a place to stay or just to use meth. He was always generous to us and others who came to his home. When we visited he was living there with his two Chihuahuas and three other adults. We could always count on Fred being available and helping us recruit other participants. One day, a friend of Fred's texted and said that someone had burned down Fred's house. When we arrived, Fred and others were still living in the burned-out remains of the home. We noticed a change in Fred. The feelings of being betrayed by someone he invited into his home had hit him hard. Seeing him living there made us worried for his health (see fig. 11.2).

Despite JC's actions toward her, Misty still sought to have a relationship with him. One day Misty asked if we would bring her and her son, Michael, to visit JC on work release. To give Misty and JC time to talk, I walked with

FIGURE II.2. Fred sits in his home after it was set on fire. Photo credit: Jared Ragland.

Michael to a nearby bench. While I was conversing with Michael, he asked, "Why do you worry all the time?" I was taken aback. Was my anxiety really so intense that even children could sense it? Michael's question caused me to really think about why I was so anxious. What happened during this project that was different than the others to cause these emotions? Perhaps it is because many of the people reminded me of family members. I could easily see people in my extended family in similar situations. It finally dawned on me that the emotional labor of witnessing the tragedies and suffering of the people I had come to care about had taken a toll. I realized I hadn't been eating much (I lost nearly twenty-five pounds during the project), and I hadn't been sleeping well.

The weight of everything really hit me while I was visiting a trailer park, which was perhaps the worst place that we had visited. The trailers were old and dilapidated, with holes in ceilings, walls, and floors. Many of the doors wouldn't lock or even shut. Most were infested with roaches and other pests. A few had no running water or proper flooring. Many should have been condemned (see fig. 11.3). The park was home to young people squatting, parents using meth with their children present, and women selling their bodies for drugs. It was here that the sadness and suffering of these people became the most palpable to me.

FIGURE 11.3. Several of the homes had "meth monsters" drawn on the walls. This monster was drawn on the living room wall where Alice and Ryan were staying. Photo credit: Jared Ragland.

On one occasion we were in a trailer that had no furniture or running water (see fig. 11.4). It had a strong, pungent smell. People were lying on makeshift beds. A young man we were interviewing best expressed the mood of the place. He said that tomorrow he would wake up in this trailer, with no family, no opportunity for getting a job, and no hope for a future whether he was high or not, so he might as well be high. He wasn't alone in feeling this way. Many of the people we came to know lived constantly with feelings of hopelessness, abandonment, and suffering. They all had tales of people leaving them, betraying them, and treating them poorly (including family members). Few had any expectations of escape or hope for a bright future.

Being in the presence of so much suffering began to be unbearable for me. I remember standing in the trailer park one night and realizing that I couldn't be a part of the suffering anymore. It was too much. It made me question what I was doing there. Was I doing any good for these people? Was writing their stories doing more harm than good? Was I adding to their pain? One of our larger goals was to counter the stigmatized images and descriptions of those who use meth, but I began to worry that telling these stories might only enhance them. For a moment I thought I would just quit and detach

FIGURE 11.4. Personal belongings found in Fred's burned home. They all had tales of people leaving them, betraying them, and treating them poorly (including family members). Fred's home being set on fire was one of the most egregious betrayals we heard about while in the field. Photo credit: Jared Ragland.

completely from the project. I could go back home and never visit again. I already had enough interviews to analyze.

I sought advice about my feelings and what I should do from my wife and other academics. The message was clear from most of them: I had to stop. A part of me wanted to take this advice. Certainly the anxiety would go away if I didn't interact with them anymore. But, there was another part of me that thought about how everyone leaves these people. The majority of their friends and family saw them as disposable. These expectations of abandonment led many to push away the good in their lives, believing that they don't deserve it. I knew I couldn't just quit. I didn't want to give up just because things got hard, but I couldn't be a part of the suffering, either. It wasn't fair to me or to those around me.

So, instead of leaving the field and giving up on the project, I decided that I would adopt a new perspective. One of the larger takeaways from the project was that these people experienced a great deal of suffering. While I certainly could not end their pain, I could still act in ways that minimized any suffering that I caused. I sought to be more open with people. To be more giving and available for them. I tried to be aware of things the participants may need and to offer them resources. I certainly did not want to become paternalistic, but I could still provide them with the resources for getting the help they needed. Sometimes this meant providing numbers and addresses to social services. Other times it meant giving them rides to court houses, health clinics, or other government agencies. It is true that certain people sought to take advantage of this, but I decided that it wouldn't matter how they responded. What mattered for me was that I was doing the best I could to help them. As my wife's grandmother would say of those times people took advantage of her, "If they can live with it, I can live without it."

Taking this approach did seem to have an impact on the project. Participants and those around them began to open up more and encourage others to participate. But I also wanted to make these changes for others in my everyday life. I began to act this way toward other people, including family, friends, students, and strangers. In the workplace I began trying to mentor and work with more students. I was open to talking about my experiences at conferences and in the classroom. At home I began to reconnect with friends and family that I hadn't seen in a while. While these changes have made me more vulnerable, I realized that the anxiety was slowly going away. Sleep was becoming more regular. My appetite returned. I began to feel better about myself and people around me. I began to see more beauty in people. I began interacting with others more than ever before. In short, exposure to the true hardships of these drug users' lives and the necessity of a mental shift led me to be more compassionate in general.

Then the people around me began to act differently as well. About a year after the end of the project Misty sent a message: "I realized the day [my son] said, 'Momma if you die or lose me it will be only because of JC.' That opened my eyes and I thought to myself, Misty your kids see it, so now it's time you see it!!! So I got away as quickly as I could. I put myself and kids through so much dealing with drugs and JC and now I realize I was so stupid. My kids and I deserve to breathe the right way in life and now we all know what it means to truly live and breathe. Heith, thanks for all you have done."

Alice also let me know that she appreciated our friendship. Even though data collection for the project is over, she still lets me know of breakthroughs in her life. She now has a new home (see fig. 11.5), a full-time job, full visitation rights for her daughter, and has been free of meth for over eighteen months. Her boyfriend told me that her recent success was largely due to my support and encouragement .

FIGURE 11.5. Alice in her new home. Photo credit: Jared Ragland.

WITHDRAWAL FROM THE FIELD

Unfortunately, not all have acted kindly to me or have begun to repair the damage in their lives. Those who use methamphetamine for long periods can become mean, aggressive, and paranoid (Boeri, 2013; Shukla, 2016). This is true regardless of how you respond to them. The majority have continued to use meth and to engage in other self-destructive behavior. On a few occasions we were threatened by those near our participants. These threats never resulted in violence or other physical acts, but they were present. More common were rumors and accusations by those on the mountain about us. These came mostly from men. While I tried to present myself as a harmless, paternal figure, not all saw me that way. This led some men to prohibit the women in their lives to speak with us. At least two women told me that their boyfriends intimidated them into not talking to us. One young woman, Beth, seemed eager to participate. But soon after agreeing to work with us she stopped replying. Several months later I ran into her at a fast-food restaurant. When I asked what had happened she said it was because her abusive boyfriend did not like her talking to others, especially to me. Alice also stopped responding to us for a short time. She later said that it was because the man she was staying with believed that we had planned to forcibly take her and others into rehab.

Perhaps the most damaging reaction for me was an anonymous complaint to my university about me. The person alleged that I was having an affair with a participant, and that I was doing drugs—neither of which were true. I do not know who filed the complaint or what his or her motive was for doing so. While it was inevitable that I stopped visiting, this became the impetus for me to pull back from participants when I did. I was saddened about this, but stepping away was the best thing for me and my family. I had spent many hours in the field and expended a great deal of emotional energy there, at the expense of spending time and emotional energy on my immediate family. I'm not sure how much longer I would have continued visiting people if this event did not happen. I had already begun to go much less regularly and had talked to several about not seeing them any more for a while. I still am periodically drawn to go visit, but I know it is best to maintain some distance. Our communications are exclusively electronic, through text or Facebook Messenger. While not as personal as face-to-face interactions, electronic communication is a means for us to stay in contact.

CONCLUSION

When one engages in ethnographic research, one will encounter frequent ethical issues, for example how to treat participants. Is it necessary to remain detached and neutral? Is it acceptable to offer help and support to those who may need it? There are obviously no easy answers to these questions. Often the answer is determined by one's larger philosophical framework. All ethnographers seek to protect their participants from any undue harm that could result from their participation in the research. This would include trouble with the law and problems with others in their lives who may want to know more about them. The use of photographs did create issues with confidentiality. To address this, we were open and honest about the potential outlets of the photographs and how this could impact them. We respected the wishes of all who participated, including those who initially consented to photographs but then decided they did not want us to use them. We believe that by fully explaining the possible harms and benefits of a project, participants have the agency to decide if they want to participate.

Some issues were not as cut-and-dry. For instance, we often encountered people who needed help: mothers who needed clothes for their children, wives who needed transportation to visit their husbands in jail, people who needed help navigating government bureaucracies, and many who just needed food. In such situations, I often chose to help to the extent my means permitted. In doing so, I adopted a feminist approach, seeking to provide resources to help *and* empower participants when possible (Burgess-Proctor, 2015; Jansen and Davis, 1998). At times I knew I could lean toward being too paternal by providing more help than empowerment. I was wary of this and asked my research assistant to give feedback if I was being too paternalistic. It is true that my perceptions of empowerment are subjective and rooted in my own history, background, and positionality. Some who advocate feminist methodology might disagree with what I saw as acceptable and ethical. Nevertheless, I chose to actively support participants through empowerment as best as I could. This level of engagement with participants has its downsides. One downside to this style of engagement with participants is that it may lead to some people feeling obligated to continue participating. Another is that some may become emotionally dependent on the researchers. I did worry about this with some of the younger participants, who had few adults they could reach out to. However, as the positive words from Misty and Alice show, the potential positive benefits to the people we study can outweigh the negative.

As mentioned earlier, when we began this project it was our hope to serve as a counternarrative to public perceptions of those who use meth. We did not anticipate the project would have a direct impact on our own lives or on those we studied. It is not always easy to determine the impact we make on others. It is true that several of the participants said that our being there helped them in a variety of ways. The project did have a deep impact on my personal life, which I think can be seen by those with whom I interact. While it is not possible to determine the long-term impact on our participants, I can say that I have come out a better person.

NOTE

1. A version of this story was told at the November 2016, American Society of Criminology conference in New Orleans, Louisiana. The event was sponsored by a collaboration between Springer Nature Storytellers and the Story Collider. An audio recording of the story can be found at www.beforetheabstract.com and www.storycollider.org. A Danish version of the story can be found in Copes (2017).

REFERENCES

Becker, H. (2007). *Telling about society.* Chicago: University of Chicago Press.

Boeri, M. (2013). *Women on ice: Methamphetamine use among suburban women.* New Brunswick, NJ: Rutgers University Press.

Burgess-Proctor, A. (2015). Methodological and ethical issues in feminist research with abused women: Reflections on participants' vulnerability and empowerment. *Women's Studies International Forum, 48,* 124–34.

Copes, H. (2017). Hvordan jeg blev taget i at vaer dum: Mit feltarbejde på Sand Mountain, Alabama (Caught Being Stupid: My Fieldwork on Sand Mountain, Alabama). *STOF 28,* 4–12.

Jansen, G., and D.R. Davis (1998). Honoring voice and visibility: Sensitive topic research and feminist interpretive inquiry. *Affilia, 1,* 289–311.

Linnemann, T., and T. Wall (2013). This is your face on meth: The punitive spectacle of "White Trash" in the rural War on Drugs. *Theoretical Criminology, 17,* 315–34.

Marsh, W., H. Copes, and T. Linnemann (2017). Meth users' perceptions of anti-meth campaigns. *International Journal of Drug Policy, 39,* 52–61.

Schonberg, J., and P. Bourgois (2002). The politics of photographic aesthetics: Critically documenting the HIV epidemic among heroin injectors in Russia and the United States. *International Journal of Drug Policy, 13,* 387–92.

Schwartz, D. (1989). Visual ethnography: Using photography in qualitative research. *Qualitative Sociology, 12,* 119–54.

Shukla, R. (2016). *Methamphetamine: A love story.* Oakland: University of California Press.

Tutenges, S., and S. Sandberg (2013). Intoxicating stories: The characteristics, contexts, and implications of drinking stories among Danish youth. *International Journal of Drug Policy, 24,* 538–44.

Worley, R., V. Worley, and B. Wood (2016). There were ethical dilemmas all day long: Harrowing tales of ethnographic researchers in Criminology and Criminal Justice. *Criminal Justice Studies, 29,* 289–308.

———

TWELVE

Ethnography of Injustice

DEATH AT A COUNTY JAIL

Joshua Price

I AM AT A COMMUNITY MEETING for a campaign against abuse at our county jail, in Binghamton, New York. At the meeting, organizers read a vivid description of the last moments of Alvin Rios, who died while incarcerated in 2011. The jail paid out a relatively small amount to the Rios family to settle a wrongful death lawsuit.

I have been on extended leave, so I feel a bit out of step with what is going on. As the meeting ends and we file out, I turn to my friend Rozann, with whom I've done advocacy for the formerly incarcerated for more than a decade (I've used her real name with her permission). What did she think? Rozann tells me she is thinking of not attending these meetings as much in the future. Why? Rios was a friend of hers, and hearing graphic details of his death again and again at these meetings is wearing on her.

Rozann's reaction prompts the question at the core of this essay: *How do I write about a death at my county jail without putting black suffering on display?*

The inspiration for this question comes not just from Rozann but also from Saidiya Hartman. Writing of Frederick Douglass, Hartman begins her book, *Scenes of Subjection* (1997), with a refusal: "I have chosen not to reproduce [Frederick] Douglass's account of the beating of [his] Aunt Hester in order to call attention to the ease with which such scenes are usually reiterated, the casualness with which they are circulated, and the consequences of this routine display. . . . Rather than inciting indignation, too often they immure us to pain by virtue of their familiarity—and especially because they reinforce the spectacular character of black suffering" (1997, 3). As readers, we are implicitly called upon to participate in such scenes, observes Hartman. "Are we witnesses who confirm the truth of what happened in the face of the world-destroying capacities of pain, the distortions of torture, the sheer unrepresent-ability of terror, and the repression of the dominant accounts or are we voyeurs fascinated with and repelled by exhibitions of terror and sufferance?" (1997, 3). Hartman's concerns acquire new resonance against the backdrop of the rise of new social media over the last fifteen years. Scenes of graphic violence visited by white police on black bodies are now reiterated and circulated more quickly than in the past. Since 2014, the United States—the world—has viewed loop after loop of police killings of unarmed black people: Tamir Rice, Eric Garner, Philando Castile, Laquan McDonald, Alton Sterling, and others. Other vid-eos document the police unnecessarily—illegally—arresting Freddie Gray and Sandra Bland, arrests that led to their deaths.

Are we witnesses or voyeurs? The question deserves more than a simple binary. And the "we," the public, is highly differentiated: different people experience the videos differently. On the one hand, the videos put in clear and awful evidence what blacks, Latinx, and indigenous people have been saying for decades. Circulation of these terrible images has played an impor-tant social and political role and galvanized support for the Black Lives Matter movement and its aims.

But showing these videos over and over is not without its perils. In putting racialized violence on display, one risks desensitizing people to violence, "naturalizing" the violence, or, worse, titillating some viewers. More subtly, these displays give people an unearned glimpse of and even intimacy with the most vulnerable and exposing moments of a person's life.

The history of images of racial violence reflects these opposed possibilities. In many of the old photos of lynching, for example, crowds of white people stand unabashed, smirking into the camera. Postcard versions circulated at the time as souvenirs. The publicity was part of the terror, and hence part of the crime. But these same photos have also stood as unequivocal indictments of extrajudicial racial murder and white terrorism, and have exposed wide-spread white complicity. Before photography, thousands of published slave narratives expressly denounced the horrors of slavery, and helped engender social support for ending the peculiar institution. But for some white readers, the descriptions may have piqued a ghoulish fascination (see Gould, 2007, 13). Hence, Saidiya Hartman's reticence and ambivalence is a fitting entry point for the contemporary ethnographer who studies and documents racialized and gendered state violence in the form of the jail.

Let me put the problem a different way. For someone like me who has not experienced racialized state terror visited on *my* body, it is as if writing on racial terror were a moral hazard: any potential harm is borne by someone else. Thus, a corollary question: *why write at all?* Why write of premature deaths at a county jail? We all know, or should know at this late date, that every day black people and other people of color, as well as poor white people, die because of state violence. So what good does more writing do? One justification is that scholarship can promote reform. But to all appearances, any policy changes (such as body cameras) have not resulted in a decline in police brutality or police murder. Another justification for writing is to try and spark outrage, but what good will *that* do? That is, what if it is just the expression of cathartic anger, or results only in an online petition, or another bit of Facebook activism? And even if it provokes in-the-streets, in-your-face activism, what good will *that* do? Merely writing on the deaths of people of color at the hands of police or jail guards may give some authors or researchers a sense of moral accomplishment—that they are involved in a crusade, or that they are offering needed critical analyses. But some of the time, one might ask, is this anything more than self-flattery?

This line of questioning is not born of cynicism or skepticism. I do not have smug contempt for activists or critical scholars; instead, motivated by an effort at intellectual and political honesty, and as a self-described activist, I want to drill down and grapple with what am I and others really *doing*—or *not* doing. These are questions that arise from hard-won experience.

Community protests of recent deaths at our jail that insist on state accountability were the latest chapter in my collaborative effort that began in 2004 with a civil rights organization, the National Association for the Advancement of Colored People (NAACP) . For decades, the local branch of the NAACP has received letters from people in jail or from their family members on medical abuse and neglect at the county jail. In 2004, I began to collaborate with them to document the abuse systematically. The NAACP began to pass the letters along to me, a social scientist volunteering his time, and I would go up with my students to the jail to interview the letter writers. My undergraduate students and I interviewed over a hundred people over the course of several years. A handful of formerly incarcerated people joined our efforts. In our interviews, we asked about health care, racial and gender discrimination, and a variety of other issues related to the conditions of confinement and institutional, systemic mistreatment of incarcerated people. We uncovered a range of problems, from chronic illness to traumatic injuries, and neglect and failure to provide medical care from inadequate prenatal care to untreated diabetes, blood poisoning, and delays in treating burst appendices and other acute medical issues. We held biweekly meetings with NAACP staff to figure out what to do, what action to take. This was also a way to raise consciousness and promote transparency in the conditions of incarceration (see Price, 2015a).

Despite our best efforts over the course of a decade to document and publicize health care problems at our jail, in 2014, the sheriff (who runs the jail) successfully petitioned the county legislature for a $5 million expansion of the jail. We tried whatever we could to stop the expansion—letter writing, protests, and so on. Their success amid our trying to publicize the horrors at the jail was demoralizing (Price, 2015a, 145–46).

Several years down the line, I am still trying to think through whether or how I failed. I don't like to delude myself or others, I try to stay away from nostrums, and I don't like to engage in self-rationalizing behavior, in this case of political efforts that may have backfired, or simply been futile. I was left asking, what if we really had not accomplished anything? Or what if it wasn't worth the effort? I dislike the kind of despair and fatalism that leads to social acquiescence. And so I have tried to collaborate with emerging community organizations and activists to resuscitate jail visits as a community project, nested within other community-based efforts to change practices (e.g., end cash bail, end the use of solitary confinement, promote alternatives to incarceration, institute civilian oversight of the jail, and so on). Given our past experiences, I take up the community-organizing work again with some ambivalence. But for the purposes at hand, let me focus narrowly on the question of writing as a component of this multipronged, community effort to end abuse at the jail. At the outset I posed one question:

1. How can one write on state-induced racial murder without needlessly putting on display racialized violence, torture, and death?

This question suggests two corollaries:

2. What good does it do to write about these deaths at all?
3. How can the activist-scholar move beyond being stymied by the first two questions?

THE SETTING AND THE CASE

Between 2011 and the time of this writing, in 2019, as many as seven people died in the Broome County Jail in Upstate New York. They died from a variety of causes: suicide, heart attack, untreated drug withdrawal. Many died in solitary confinement. Unexpected forms of sociality sprung up under these extreme circumstances and in the wake of these deaths. People in solitary sent out letters detailing the last days of others. Many more community people have joined protests of the jail than at any time in the last several decades. Growing community outrage was palpable. As part of a community effort to investigate these deaths, I have interviewed witnesses and family members. I have also received crucial information about the circumstances and the people involved via text messages, instant messaging, and Facebook, from relatives of the incarcerated, friends, formerly incarcerated people, and other community members. Taken together, they provide a counter to the jail administration's silence and denial. This is one way incarcerated people and their families sustain themselves and struggle to live lives of dignity when assaulted by the state.

One case in particular haunts me. Salladin Barton died in solitary confinement in January 2015. He was thirty-six years old. Though charged with robbery, he had not been convicted of any crime. In fact, at the time of his death, Mr. Barton had been in jail awaiting trial for *nineteen months.* He was developmentally disabled and schizophrenic. It is not entirely clear why or how he died; according to some reports, correction officers (CO)s had brutally beaten him the day before. Toxicology tests were inconclusive. An official state report left the question unsettled.

Shortly after he died, the NAACP called me and asked me to look into the circumstances of his death. I agreed to talk to Mr. Barton's siblings and the lawyer the family had retained. Through access to medical reports and letters from people who were in jail with him, I began to put together a picture of what may have happened. With the cooperation of the NAACP and his siblings, we set up a series of community meetings to discuss what we could do about it. After researching his death for more than a year, I wrote a series of short pieces on his death for academic and nonacademic journals. An op-ed in a local newspaper and a meditative piece in the *Socialist Worker* was an additional attempt to stoke support for protest but also to push for institutional transparency on how he died (Price, 2015b, 2016). Soon, other organizations and groups started to push for answers from the jail. Nevertheless, it has been difficult to ascertain many of the crucial details.

But even if we did have more facts, this would tell us little, not only of the life he lived, but also about what his death *means:* What sense do people confer upon his passing? How has it brought a rupture in people's lives? How has it brought people together? But preoccupation with the immediate circumstances of his death may miss the underlying factors that led to his untimely death. Was he hastened to his death by the conditions of confinement? Was racism involved? Did the COs neglect their job? Or was Mr. Barton's death a predictable outcome of the cruelty and neglect embodied in the everyday practices of modern jails? Surely little distinguishes Mr. Barton's treatment from hundreds of thousands, even millions, of others: the mentally ill people are disproportionately incarcerated, and many are routinely placed in solitary for extended lengths of time. The vast majority of people in county and municipal jails throughout the country have not yet been convicted of any crime. They often languish for months because they cannot make bail. In addition to the suffering intrinsic to incarceration, they are at a higher risk for mortality. And the racial disparities in incarceration are well-known.

METHODOLOGICAL CHALLENGES

In order to learn the circumstances of Mr. Barton's death, I drew on an extraordinary trove of letters that incarcerated people wrote to Mr. Barton's lawyer both before he died and after he died. "The COs would go into Sal's cell and beat him up, numerous times. They smacked him, punched him, and sprayed Sal's face with mace." Another wrote, "They starved him on numerous occasions where they just threw his food in the garbage. And the day before he died they ran in his cell and beat him up again." Another wrote, "I could hear the CO yelling 'I'm a kill you, nigger [sic].'" Other letter writers also noted how guards deprived him of food to punish him still further. "I've seen multiple correctional officers abuse him physically and verbally, they don't give him all of his food sometimes."

One methodological question that often comes up in a case like this is whether we hold these letters to be credible. More generally, how do I know whether to believe what a person tells me in an interview? In the dominant culture, incarcerated people are often treated as incorrigible liars and inveterate hustlers. Some years ago, on reading a preliminary study I did of young people convicted of felonies, a senior administrator at a nonprofit accused me of lending my credibility to the "ramblings of drug-addled convicts" (Price, 2008, 390–92). What he took to be a mixture of my gullibility and knee-jerk sympathies for those under the thumb of the law, I thought of as reflecting a political and methodological commitment to consider the "perspectives, philosophies, and systems of logic generated by populations which are usually

In the Matter of the Death
of Salladin Barton, an inmate of
the Broome County Jail

:
:
:
:

FINAL REPORT OF THE
NEW YORK STATE COMMISSION
OF CORRECTION

To: Sheriff David Harder
    Broome County Sheriff's Office
    155 Van Winkle Dr.
    Binghamton, NY 13905

63. At 3:02 p.m., CO ▮▮ notified CO ▮▮ to call 911, and to get an AED as well as RN
    Administrator ▮▮▮ More officers arrived to include CO▮▮ CO▮▮ CO ▮▮ and CO
    ▮▮ At 3:04 p.m. Superior Ambulance was called and dispatched to Broome County Jail
    at 3:05 p.m.

64.

FINAL REPORT OF SALLADIN BARTON Page | 11

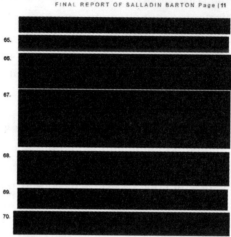

65.

66.

67.

68.

69.

70.

FIGURE 12.1. Final report of the New York State Commission of Correction: *In the Matter of the Death of Salladin Barton, an inmate of Broome County Jail.* Credit: New York State Commission on Correction.

expected to produce only unrefined data for the omniscient, powerful stranger to interpret," as John Gwaltney once put it (1993, xxx).

Developing criteria for who to believe and under what circumstances is a methodological question, but this question of belief, of knowing some people to be trustworthy, is an epistemological question (see Code, 1991, 183–84). These questions become racially and politically and ethically charged (Price, 2015a, 61–74).

To further my inquiry, I wanted to see the official account of Mr. Barton's death, but the jail refused to release any information. I filed a New York Freedom of Information Law request to get his death report from the New York State Commission on Correction (SCOC). The SCOC heavily redacted the relevant sections of the report (see fig. 12.1).

There is an irony here. I do not want to describe Salladin's death out of respect for the dead. The jail and other state agencies do not release details of that same death so that they can continue to act with impunity. I do not want my reticence, motivated by deference to his family and their memory of Mr. Barton, to collude with institutional silence and obfuscation. Indeed, a primary reason to write is that the state is suppressing that information. How to navigate between conspiracies of silence and giving in to the lurid and sensational? I leave this an open question.

Communication through social media just added layers to the dilemma. Although I previously had gotten most of my information through face-to-face interviews, now I am just as likely to learn important facts or get connected to people who have important knowledge to share through text messages and Facebook.

It is ironic that social media, often accused of being vehicles for people's narcissism and self-promotion and for serving as uncritical mills for rumor, urban myth, and disinformation, are also crucial channels for clandestine communication. Oddly, the public aspects and sub-rosa connections are intimately linked.

For example, supporters of Mr. Barton set up a Facebook page, "Justice for Salladin Barton." At first, people posted or sent private messages to the page, testifying to their experiences at the jail. The page administrators forwarded some of those messages to me. On certain occasions I followed up and contacted the person if I had their permission. This webpage served as a nodal point for other local activists. Sometimes a journalist would pick up a story first featured on the Facebook page. Yasir Barton, Salladin's brother, was crucial in publicizing previously unreported deaths at the jail (I quote him with his permission). "Hey what's going on Josh? I don't know if you been on the Facebook page ['Justice for Salladin Barton'], lately but a couple weeks ago I got a message saying that her cousin was found brain dead in jail. He died a few days later. Didn't hear anything from the media or anyone for about a week and then I spoke with the victim's sister and she confirmed it. Once we disclosed that on the page a [journalist] from Press & Sun-Bulletin [the local newspaper in Binghamton, New York] wrote an article on it." Here's an excerpt from a Facebook post about a death at our county jail that had gone unreported in the news: "Yeah I don't really remember the guy's name. He spoke very little if any English. . . . then one night he hung himself. I was up reading a book and had just put it down to go to sleep. It was around 3 to 4 A.M. and the guard came around doing his rounds and apparently found him. . . . After they called an outside ambulance and they came in and pronounced the man dead they closed him back in the cell for approximately

2–3 hours until the us marshals came to claim the man's body. At which point they wrapped him in a body bag and took him out." In response to that note, I made a series of Freedom of Information requests, and we learned that there have been four jail deaths at our little county jail in the previous two years, including deaths that had gone unreported in the media.

Through a community network, I was put in contact with a close relative of one of the deceased. Since she did not speak English, I asked my sister-in-law Marcela to translate. "I have never had any news since his death." She tells me through Marcela. "They do not send us an autopsy or any kind of report. He wasn't getting his antianxiety medication or his other pills. I spoke with him the day before he died and he told me that. The jail told me that they keep recordings of all the phone calls. Would it be possible to get the recordings of his phone calls? He didn't speak and didn't understand English. He kept getting into trouble with the guards because he couldn't understand their orders. He kept getting put into solitary confinement. Some of the other prisoners tried to help him understand the orders. They were the only ones."

As this woman sits in front of me, moist-eyed and seized by grief, I reflect on how mundane and routine it sounds to me, I feel like I've sat here, listening to this kind of story, for more than ten years. And then I feel a deep horror at myself. How can I become so jaded?

She asks me questions I don't know the answer to, such as what the jail's legal responsibility was to provide translation and interpreting. And then she asks me, "What can I do?" I tell her that I am not really in a position to give advice. But then I say she could consider suing the jail and then through the legal process known as "discovery" she might get access to information she would like to see. (On her behalf, I subsequently filed a request to see the New York State death report, but the SCOC refused to release any information.) Inwardly, I think that I'd like it if she would consider speaking to a journalist and I'd like her to make a public statement for an upcoming rally. This would energize people. But I suspect she won't, and I don't want to try and persuade her. I try to put to her evenly what I see as her options. She seems a bit dazed by it all. Later, my sister-in-law Marcela comments that she seemed mostly to want to be listened to; Marcela thought she might not have anyone who will acknowledge her story. If Marcela is right, then I should question my own impulse: I gave her a series of bureaucratic solutions. How could I so quickly reduce her fundamental, almost existential questions, to a series of queries for an official account?

This woman's anger, grief, and frustration take her directly into conflict with the state. Her grief will not be translated except as an accusation, an indictment. She wants attention to her dead, and she wants an accounting. Her questions stand as accusations.

In sum, research into jail deaths yields an ad hoc and nonsystematic collection of different forms of evidence: redacted government documents, health records, and bottomless amounts of statistics. It also yields anonymous letters, confidential messages, and notes from secret meetings.

This data can be put in the service of any number of practical, instrumental purposes, such as a lawsuit, a public campaign to end solitary confinement, to overhaul the cash-bail system, or a policy or program to divert the mentally ill from jail. The data can also be enlisted in the service of scholarship.

FRAMING: TIME AND SPACE

Here, too, I would have to arrange the elements, since the facts themselves are mere fragments, gleaned as they are from so many different kinds of sources. As Margaret Atwood has written: "When you are in the middle of a story it isn't a story at all, but only a confusion; a dark roaring, a blindness, a wreckage of shattered glass and splintered wood; like a house in a whirlwind, or else a boat crushed by the icebergs or swept over the rapids, and all aboard powerless to stop it. It's only afterwards that it becomes anything like a story at all. When you are telling it, to yourself or to someone else" (1997, 345–46). Narratives can communicate the *meaning* or *meanings* we can extract from events at the jail. On second thought—maybe leaving the fragments *as fragments* is better. The arbitrariness, the illogic, the chaos and conflict implicit in Salladin Barton's confinement, slow torture, and death defy clear causal chains. In their disorder, it is as if the very facts stand as accusations in the wake of his death, just as the questions left by the grief-stricken also stand as accusations that resist easy resolution. His life and the lives of his bereaved have been fragmented. Why impose neatness and order? When would the story begin, anyway, and when would it end?

Thus far, questions of methodology have been considered at the point of *conducting research* and gathering data. Here we have begun to take up another matter altogether—methodology at the point of *writing*. What counts as a sound argument? What kind of evidence supports a thesis for a particular kind of reader? A methodology for making an argument includes a set of assumptions and criteria for the selection of examples and evidence and "consequently carries with it not simply technical skills but deeper philosophical commitments and implications" (MacKinnon, 1991, 106; 2013, 1019; Shanley and Schuck, 1974, 638).

The methodological question at the heart of this chapter involves a paradox. Even as I claim that I do not want to put him or his death on display, I reiterate Salladin Barton's lonely death every time I evoke it (Moten, 2003, 4–5). And it is not only Barton's death I am invoking. Several people have told me that agitating for answers from the jail reminds them of the terrible death of Shirley Harris, a mother of five, found in her cell in our local jail in 1987. Ms. Harris's inexplicable death led to months of protests by African Americans (see "Pregnant Woman," 1987). New waves of jail deaths bring back those ghosts, like the return of the repressed. To outline even the basic circumstances of Salladin's death—a black person in jail, held for more than a year and a half without trial, beaten often, humiliated repeatedly, dying alone—is to point backward in time, to the deep rush of history, the long history of racial murder.

Salladin's brother Yasir Barton placed a death photo of his brother Salladin on the "Justice for Salladin" Facebook page. At first I winced at the image, and wondered at it. But then I thought of Emmett Till, lynched in Mississippi, whose body, mutilated and disfigured by his killers, was found only weeks later in the Tallahatchie River. In particular, I remember Mamie Till Mobley's decision to have an open-casket funeral for her son Emmett, to expose the awful violence the murderers visited upon his body. "I wanted the world to see what they did to my baby" (cited in Ladner, n.d.). Mamie Till Mobley's refusal to keep private grief private allowed a body that meant nothing to the criminal justice system to stand as evidence, as Claudia Rankine has put it (2015). For Rankine, the Black Lives Matter movement can be seen in the tradition of Mobley: "Black Lives Matter movement can be read as an attempt to keep mourning an open dynamic in our culture because black lives exist in a state of precariousness. Mourning then bears both the vulnerability inherent in black lives and the instability regarding a future for those lives. . . . Black Lives Matter aligns with the dead, continues the mourning and refuses the forgetting in front of all of us" (Rankine, 2015). Emmett Till's kin exposed the dead for the world to see. As has been widely reported, Diamond Reynolds, Philando Castile's girlfriend, live-streamed the death throes of Mr. Castile after police shot him. Yasir Barton is following in this grim tradition.

I honor their decision to keep mourning an open dynamic, to force us to confront what white supremacy has simultaneously wrought and disavowed. But these death images are not mine to show, not my dead.

Or are they? They are my compatriots, my contemporaries, and people whose lives—and deaths—I am implicated in, in ways so numerous that I could not fully catalog. Marking their lives is to commemorate our intertwined histories. Nevertheless, as I have been socialized as white into a racial caste and class system, I feel more implicated as captor than captive, and this serves as an inhibition, too: the fear of appropriating the dead.

The death of the racialized captive, tortured into a final silence, ultimately brings us back to slavery. "This past cannot be recovered, yet the history of the captive emerges precisely at this site of loss and rupture. In the workings of memory, there is an endless reiteration and enactment of this condition of loss and displacement" (Hartman, 1997, 99). Christina Sharpe uses the metaphor of the "wake," "as a means of understanding how slavery's violences emerge within the contemporary conditions of spatial, legal, psychic, material, and other dimensions of Black non/being as well as in Black modes of resistance" (Sharpe, 2016, 14). Reckoning with the significance of a contemporary captive life and death means reckoning with the afterlives of slavery, and how Mr. Barton lived his life against the predations of racial murder. The afterlives of slavery are reflected in the "skewed life chances, limited access to health and education, premature death, incarceration, and impoverishment" (Hartman, 2007, 6; Sharpe, 2016, 5). Salladin Barton embodied these afterlives of slavery. Writing allows for a suppressed truth to make its way through lies and silence. Shortly before his death, in a written plea to jail administrators to take him to a hospital, Barton wrote, "I had a real hard serious life, and will tell the truth, the hole [sic] truth, and nothing but the truth so help me, God, and Jesus."

PAST IS PROLOGUE

The question at the core of this essay has been how to expose the state violence at work in killing black people without parading racialized torture and morbid, gruesome portraits of abject misery. A comprehensive, critical methodology would provide criteria, not just of what to include and how, but also what to exclude. For example, the methodology would mean not indulging in any of the clichés or tropes that white researchers or journalists lazily reach for in order to tell stories of true crime, or to appeal to prurient interest in others' pain and grief. Victor Rios has referred to the "jungle book trope" of a white person visiting the denizens of the jungle (cited in Lewis-Kraus, 2016). Akin to that is the common practice of recycling the retrograde mythology that poor people are enmeshed in a culture of poverty or its variant, a culture of crime. In this kind of argument, poor people are kept in their subordinate positions, not because of economic exploitation, social marginalization, structural oppression and injustice, but by their own self-undermining mores and tendencies. To critique this kind of theory is not to absolve poor people or people of color of any responsibility for their actions or inaction, or to paint people in jail as blameless. It is rather to avoid theories that explain away economic and social oppression by implying that subordinate and marginalized people are culturally dysfunctional (also see Kelley, 1998).

Another way to avoid putting incarcerated people on display is by exemplifying a critical stance with respect to normative vocabulary in criminology. In this connection, read the late Eddie Ellis: "calling me inmate, convict, prisoner, felon, or offender indicates a lack of understanding of who I am, but more importantly what I can be. I can be and am much more than an 'ex-con,' or an 'ex-offender,' or an 'ex-felon.'" (Ellis, n.d.). Terms such as criminal, ex-con, and so on, reduce people to the crimes they may have committed. They also implicitly align themselves with state classifications. These are rhetorical tendencies to avoid.

It may be spoken-word poets who have grappled the most eloquently with the apparent lack of utility and even the sense of helplessness of writing on violent black and brown deaths by police and other state agents. Witness David James Hudson in "Another Unoriginal Poem about Police Brutality" (2014):

> Why write, then? Why
> bother? Why
> do pens and
> tongues and
> lungs feel so heavy when
> stories seem to repeat themselves?

Danez Smith echoes Hudson in the poem, "It Doesn't Feel Like A Time To Write" (2016).

> it doesn't feel like a time to write
> when all my muses are begging
> for their lives.

every word
i say translate to farewell.
poems feel so small right now

Danez Smith reflects on the contradictory communicative situation in which black people are placed: "We beg for peace but you hear fire! ... What you call country, we call the reaping."

I would be misguided, not to mention hubristic, to say that I confront the same communicative dilemma, since I am a white man. Instead, I am—a bit perilously—animating the pain of a racialized other and the potential ignominy that accrues to being incarcerated. The perils can be vividly illustrated with a public reading by poet Kenneth Goldsmith. Goldsmith, who is white, stirred controversy when, during a university conference, he read an edited version of Michael Brown's autopsy report (Goldsmith, 2015; CAConrad, 2015). The context of his reading suggests he recited the text of the autopsy *as a poem*. Activist intervention or racial exploitation? A courageous use of his platform or cultural appropriation? Edgy or death porn?

This ambiguity implies another contradiction that circulates throughout academic writing that addresses pressing social problems. Many scholars aspire to contribute to changes in prison and jail practices. This instrumental function is premised on the potentially unjustified assumption that research can stop dehumanizing treatment.

Because of our structural position as university-based researchers, producing research is an element of our careers. Even if the research is oriented to, or emerges from activism, and is undertaken in the public interest or as public service, it also usually contributes to career advancement. This is not necessarily problematic. But using socially induced unhappiness and human tragedy as the raw material for one's scholarly locomotion poses dangers—for the scholarship, for one's ethical clarity, and for the aim of stopping state violence.

CONCLUDING THOUGHTS

All of these challenges and problems have left me a bit hamstrung, what I refer to above as stymied. But this is an unsatisfactory ethical stance and rhetorical posture.

When my book on jails, prisons, and activism came out, a colleague, the wonderful Silvia Federici, arranged for a book launch in Brooklyn. Afterward, she wrote me an extended note. This note somehow shook me out of my stupefaction. It motivates me to continue—to analyze, learn lessons, and move forward. It gestures toward the future (cited with her gracious permission).

Dear Joshua,

Thank you for stimulating such a powerful discussion. The way you presented your experience in the jail allowed people to come forward and something happened that is not common in these presentations. I was very moved by it.

There is something however I encourage you to rethink. It is your idea that what you did ended in a failure. I think it is better to say that it ended with an unwanted result, but that did not condemn the whole effort that you and the students made. Otherwise, saying that may discourage others from engaging in support work for prisoners. I think that what ultimately Gilmore wanted to tell you was that when these things happen we do not throw away what we have done, but learn from the outcome so that we can do better the next time. Moreover, many good things have come from what you did. It was good that the prisoners knew there were people outside who care about what happened to them. I am sure it helped restore the sense of the value of their lives and give strength much needed in the hell hole. Also the students have taken with them a great experience which will affect their lives in many ways. It put the guards on notice that they have to pay attention, even though more people are needed and some different tactics/strategies to force them to be concerned. What should be done then is to reflect on what made it possible for the prison authorities to manipulate the mobilization for healthcare and use it to expand the jails. What has to be done to prevent that? Perhaps a larger coalition is needed. Perhaps die ins in front of the jail, perhaps going to Albany, like domestic workers have done (I was on one of those expeditions), targeting individual assemblymen.

In sum, the lesson is that this is a long struggle. Your "failure" in Broome County jail, may help others to learn what to do next, if properly reflected upon.

I say this because I believe that you have done something important and you should not regret what you have done, but, as you are doing now, share you experience with others so that we are more prepared to deal with their maneuvers.

All the best,
Silvia

This letter reached out and grabbed me, and drew me out, past bafflement, past despair. Political analysis of unwanted results, as Federici puts it, is a necessary part of the process, and can help others learn lessons. Wallowing in failure and doubt, on the other hand, can become an exercise of self-involvement. Federici's letter forestalls that possibility, urges me past defeatism and political dead-ends, and challenges me to search for new pathways. Rozann, with whom I started this essay, still attends community meetings and people have helped her launch a peer-to-peer reentry program. I continue to take students to conduct interviews at the jail with incarcerated people who request it. Like them, I too am still astonished by what I learn from people living in these extreme circumstances, and the revelatory insights they have, or that they engender in me and my students. The people we interview usually ask us to come back. This is encouraging.

Yet a week ago, as I am writing this, another person died at our jail after being denied basic medical care. There seldom seems like we can do *anything*. I try to stave off despair when I am confronted with the terror, neglect, and abuse I first discovered ten years ago. Acknowledging the messy contradictions, and the sense of a perennial return to the same damn problems, year after year, can generate a sense of futility. But it can also generate a renewed sense of mission to learn the lessons of the past and push forward. After all, the hemorrhage continues.[1]

NOTE

I would like to thank Miriam Boeri and Rashi Shukla for their incisive comments and critical feedback. I would also like to thank Yasir Barton. Errors are mine alone.

REFERENCES

Atwood, M. (1997). *Alias Grace*. New York: Anchor.

CAConrad (2015). Kenneth Goldsmith says he is an outlaw. Retrieved from the Poetry Foundation blog, www.poetryfoundation.org/harriet/2015/06/kenneth-goldsmith-says-he-is-an-outlaw.

Code, L. (1991). *What can she know? Feminist theory and the construction of knowledge*. Ithaca, NY: Cornell University Press.

Ellis, E. (n.d.). *An open letter to our friends on the question of language*. Retrieved from the Credible Messenger Justice Center website, https://cmjcenter.org/wp-content/uploads/2017/07/CNUS-AppropriateLanguage.pdf.

Goldsmith, K. (2015). Interview. Retrieved from the Campus der Kuenste website, www.campusderkuenste.ch/kennethgoldsmith/2134/?lang=en.

Gould, P. (2007). The rise, development, and circulation of the slave narrative. In *The Cambridge companion to the African American slave narrative*, ed. A. Fisch, 11–27. New York: Cambridge University Press.

Gwaltney, J. L. (1993). *Drylongso: A self-portrait of black America*. New York: New Press.

Hartman, S. (1997). *Scenes of subjection: Terror, slavery, and self-making in nineteenth-century America*. Oxford: Oxford University Press.

——— (2007). *Lose your mother: A journey along the Atlantic slave route*. New York: Farrar, Straus & Giroux.

Hudson, D. J. (2014). *Another unoriginal poem about police brutality*. Retrieved from the Artists against Police website, http://artistsagainstpoliceviolence.tumblr .com/post/106242433504/another-unoriginal-poem-about-police-brutality-by.

Kelley, R. D. G. (1998). *Yo' mama's disfunktional! Fighting the culture wars in urban America*. Boston: Beacon Press.

Ladner, J. (n.d.). Excerpts from interview with Mamie Till Mobley. *Daily Kos*. Retrieved from www.dailykos.com/stories/2009/5/14/731205/-.

Lewis-Kraus, G. (2016). The trials of Alice Goffman. *New York Times,* January 12.

MacKinnon, C. A. (1991). *Toward a feminist theory of the state*. Cambridge, MA: Harvard University Press.

——— (2013). Intersectionality as method: A note. *Signs, 38*(4), 1019–30.

Moten, F. (2003). *In the break: The aesthetics of the black radical tradition*. Minneapolis: University of Minnesota Press.

Pregnant woman found hanged in N.Y. jail cell: Angry blacks ask probe. (1987). *JET,* July, 8. Retrieved from: https://books.google.com/books?id=CbIDAAAAMBAJ.

Price, J. (2008). Participatory research as disruptive? A report on a conflict in social science paradigms at a criminal justice agency promoting alternatives to incarceration. *Contemporary Justice Review, 11*(4), 387–412.

Price, J. M. (2015a). *Prison and social death*. New Brunswick, NJ: Rutgers University Press.

——— (2015b). The ghosts of Broome County jail. *SocialistWorker,* December 9. Retrieved from https://socialistworker.org/2015/12/09/the-ghosts-of-broome-county

——— (2016). Broome jail needs transparency on deaths. *Press and Sun Bulletin,* November 10.

Rankine, C. (2015). The condition of black life is one of mourning. *New York Times,* June 22.

Sharpe, C. (2016). *In the wake: On blackness and being*. Durham, NC: Duke University Press.

Smith, D. (2016). It doesn't feel like a time to write. *Buzzfeed,* May 23. Retrieved from www.buzzfeed.com/danezsmith/poem-it-doesnt-feel-like-a-time-to-write-by-danez-smith?utm_term=.cpwj6bbdLY#.myO7yBBA2D.

Shanley, M. L., and V. Schuck (1974). In search of political woman. *Social Science Quarterly, 55*(3), 632–44.

Conclusion

LOOKING BACK, MOVING FORWARD

Rashi K. Shukla and Miriam Boeri

PURSUIT OF THE UNKNOWN

It is not the knowledge we have, but the quest for the unknown that drives us. Each study, and the projects they were founded on, represent efforts to record and comprehend complex human realities. While in some cases researchers seek to alter risky behaviors, others are primarily interested in exploring areas about which little is known. Those in pursuit of the verities and realities of hidden populations who engage in crime, deviance, and other concealed behaviors, demonstrate a willingness to venture into the unknown amid uncertainty and risk. Authenticity requires getting close to people and their behaviors, even when it is uncomfortable to do so.

Ethnography is a dynamic methodology, grounded in uncertainty. A range of diverse ethnographic methods are needed to access hidden populations in efforts to capture information about the behaviors in which they engage. The methodologies encapsulated under the ethnographic framework evolve and adapt over time. The veracities that comprise lived experiences are difficult, if not impossible, to quantify.

Though the studies presented were referred to by different terms (e.g., project, research study, extended case study, etc.) and varied on a number of dimensions, they all sought to capture the realities of people and their experiences. Each focused on acquiring insights into hidden facets of reality among populations concealed and difficult to access. Researchers must step away from the relative safety of academic and clinical settings to reach them and capture their lived realities.

Ethnography is not for those who fear gray areas or are unwilling to venture into the unknown. Rather, it is a methodological framework well suited for those in quest of discovering the undiscovered. Logistical challenges and internal and external struggles are often part of the ethnographic journey.

The behind-the-scenes trials, tribulations, and lessons unveiled through the revelations shared here rarely come to light. More often than not, such personal accounts of conflicts, decisions, and adaptations remain unspoken and unwritten. We plan. We research. We write. Seldom do we share the behind-the-scenes stories critical to ethnographic success.

The types of knowledge that can be gained by studying multifarious, concealed behaviors extend beyond findings about the observed, to findings about processes of observation, and in some cases, observers themselves. Taken together, these chapters illuminate insider information and expertise about fieldwork methods, trials, and challenges, and strategies for success. As shown here, not all situations and contingencies can be mapped out and planned for in advance. The unexpected may turn out to be not only informative but highly relevant.

FIELD NOTES FROM RASHI

We drove into the small town to meet the Police Chief. My two research assistants (RA's) and I were heading into the unknowns of rural Oklahoma to learn about the current state of the local methamphetamine problem. Though I had lived in the state for decades, I had never heard of the town. I only learned of it following the receipt of an uncompleted mail survey returned with all of the survey enclosures in tact, unanswered. The survey was sent to all law enforcement agencies in the state. It sought to assess the current state of the problem at the local level. All survey materials, including cover letters, survey document, and prepaid stamped envelope were stapled together and returned, at the expense of the police department, in a large envelope with a single page, single-spaced letter typed and personally signed by the Chief. In it, he explained his frustrations with the ongoing drug problem and the lack of assistance available to respond to the issue plaguing his community for the twenty-plus years he was Chief. The letter ended with the sentences, "I am forced to fight this battle alone. So, to me, your survey is not worth the effort" [Shukla and Bartgis, 2011, 78]. The words stung. As a novice researcher something like this had never occurred to me. It was not an experience for which graduate school or qualitative methods courses and textbooks had ever prepared me. It would take some time to process what had occurred as I sought out advice from others about if and how

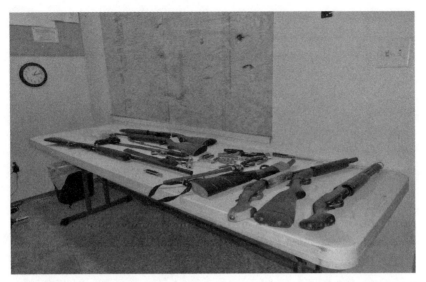

FIGURE 13.1. Confiscated weapons spread out on a table as evidence of the drug-related violence in this small, rural community. Photo credit: Rashi K. Shukla.

to respond. Eventually, I gathered the strength to reach out via phone and call to ask him about his response. The first time we talked, he spoke for over 45 minutes, educating me about the drug problem and all of the challenges he faced; he invited me to visit so that I could better understand his sentiments. In other words, to know, I had to see for myself. The reality was that this single blank survey, the field visit, and interview that followed, taught me more about research and the realities of the drug problem in small communities than all of the completed surveys combined. This single incident was an important part of all that facilitated my entrée into ethnographic fieldwork. Though I had conducted interviews with individuals with specialized knowledge during the early stages of the research, this would be the first time I found myself driving to seemingly the middle of nowhere to learn more.

The town was located just off a major highway. It was small. A single stop sign placed in the middle of Main Street in the deserted one-street downtown doubled as the community notice board. We entered the one room police department and introduced ourselves. The Chief pointed to a table in the corner of the room. "You want to understand our methamphetamine problem? There, there it is," he said. The table was covered with guns and other weapons [see fig. 13.1]. While the quantity of weapons displayed was not unusually high, it was significant considering the size of the town spatially and in terms of population.

During the interview it became apparent that the Chief felt alone in his battle to keep methamphetamine and the violence that accompanied it out of his town. Knowing that the problem was bigger than him, he talked about doing what he legally could ". . . to run it out of town. If it runs into my town, it's my job to run it out to somebody else's town around the county. We do everything within the law to run 'em out of town." When asked if he worried about methamphetamine being an issue elsewhere, he responded, "No. Just my jurisdiction. Just my town." It would be my first insight into the importance of jurisdictional boundaries, the challenges posed by tribal land, and the ties that bind those enforcing the law in small town, rural Oklahoma. The discovery that he was not trying to stop methamphetamine, but only keep it out of his town was unexpected and enlightening. All he had and all he could do was work within the confines of his geographically small jurisdiction.

Driving out of town we headed to the main road that led to the highway that led back to Oklahoma City; we were on a road in between towns on county land. As we drove past the few structures that littered the farms and grasslands, I noticed two small hand-painted signs on the side of the road. I did a double-take. "Did you see that?" I asked my research assistants. I made a U-turn to return to the place where I had seen the signs, parking the car a few feet in front them. One of my assistants jumped out of the car to take pictures. I wanted it done quickly because we had no way of knowing if someone was watching us even though no one was in sight. There, in the middle of the grass, were two small hand-constructed rectangular white signs with wooden stakes propping them upright. The first signed had the word "Shake" written in bold, black lettering. The second sign, slightly behind the first and to the left, included the following: the letter "-N-" over the word "Bake." Together, they spelled "Shake-n-bake."

Shake-and-bake was the newest process for manufacturing or cooking methamphetamine locally. And here it was, being advertised on the side of the road. The signs contained no identifying information. There was no phone number, name, or address. None of us had ever seen such a thing. While we as outsiders had no way to know who placed the signs there or where one would go to find the drug, there was no doubt that the people who needed to know, did. The importance of leaving the university setting to go into the field became clear. Because if we hadn't gone there, on that day, at that time, we, as researchers, would never have even known that such things existed. (Paraphrased from field notes, Rashi Shukla.)

These encounters confirmed the importance of ethnographic fieldwork for understanding drugs, crime, and the challenges faced by rural law enforcement. Before the survey, I had never considered the relevance of rural crime and place. Thus, a study not initially designed to be ethnographic, ended up as one that was. The thirty-three former methamphetamine users, dealers, and cooks I eventually interviewed provided insights that proved perspective-altering. The data collected through their interviews filled critical gaps in knowledge about why those immersed in a methamphetamine lifestyle did what they did and why (Shukla, 2016).

AUTHENTICITY

The search for authenticity lies at the heart of ethnography. Trustworthiness and authenticity are among the criteria used to evaluate qualitative research (Lincoln and Guba, 2000). Maintaining authenticity requires honesty and transparency. One cannot be untruthful and be authentic. Reflexivity increases the authenticity of findings (Atkinson, 2006; Malterud, 2001), resulting in data that is rich and insightful.

Authenticity, like many concepts, can have different meanings depending on how it is used. The term can relate to the validity of findings, the transparency of the writing, and the manner with which ethnographers share and reflect on their experiences and journeys when disseminating research findings. It also applies to objectivity when it comes to the interpretation of the data as well as the trustworthiness of the interpreter (Marco and Larkin, 2000). Each chapter presented throughout this book is demonstrative of the search for authenticity among people and their lives.

Genuineness was seen in the chapter by Lindegaard (chapter 1) who painstakingly explored her role and motives in her quest to understand violent acts she abhorred from the perspectives of those who committed them. The authenticity of ethnographic methods was revealed to Soltes (chapter 4), the business professor who came to appreciate the power of qualitative research for what he referred to as "deep observation" and the capturing of critical information on decision-making processes and mindsets. It was understood in the honesty with which Price (chapter 12) exposed his struggles with the meaning and consequences of his lifelong work. It was demonstrated by others as well.

Ethnography is characterized by heterogeneity. Projects that fall within the methodological framework can differ from one another in numerous ways. What it means to be in the field in terms of duration and depth can vary from study to study. So, too, can the distances that researchers travel to meet study participants and gather other forms of data. Geographically speaking, field-work can take place in a single location as well as within multiple locations subject to change over time. Ethnographic studies diverge on a number of dimensions, including, but not limited to: the problem of interest, the research purpose, samples, methods of data collection, research settings, and methods of dissemination of research outcomes. Despite such diversities, fieldwork is central to the ethnographic journey.

While ethnography sometimes involves extended periods of time in field settings (see Bourgois, 2003; Williams, 1990), the methodology has been adapted for the study of time-sensitive and emerging topics. For example, "rapid ethnography" or "rapid assessment projects" are used to collect data from multiple locations in short periods of time (Valdez, Cepeda, and Kaplan, chapter 7; Fessel, Mars, Bourgois, and Ciccaone, chapter 6), allowing for more immediate information to be gathered and compared. In line with a more traditional ethnographic approach, some maintain an extended presence over periods of time in a single setting, such as a park (Bonomo and Jacques, chapter 2) or community (Lindegaard, chapter 1; Copes, chapter 11). Others establish their presence in one or more locations over years (Soltes, chapter 4) or decades (Gay, chapter 10).

The numbers of researchers involved ranged from a single researcher operating individually to entire research teams. Teams were comprised of diverse parties including academics, professionals with specific skillsets, and community members (Fessel et al., chapter 6; Valdez et al., chapter 7). Others worked primarily alone (Lindegaard, chapter 1; Soltes, chapter 4; Gay, chapter 10; Campos-Manzo, chapter 8; Price, chapter 12). In between were those with partnerships with a few others (Copes, chapter 11; Guarino and Teper, chapter 9). Unique insights into the challenges experienced by those conducting ethnographic doctoral dissertations were noted by Smith and Anderson (chapter 3) and Bonomo and Jacques (chapter 2). In terms of researcher presence in field settings, there was disagreement about covert versus overt roles. While Singer and Page (chapter 5) argued against identity deception by researchers and discussed strategies for responding to "active concealment" when needed, Bonomo and Jacques (chapter 2) found it necessary to enter the field setting covertly to gain access. Differing perspectives on issues and practices are not uncommon among ethnographers.

The studies in this book demonstrated the range of conditions within which fieldwork occurs. Research activities occurred within institutional settings such as correctional institutions including prisons (Lindegaard, chapter 1; Soltes, chapter 4) and jails (Price, chapter 12). Fieldwork also took place on the streets and in an array of other types of settings. As demonstrated throughout, often, ethnography does not occur in just one place (Lindegaard, chapter 1; Bonomo and Jacques, chapter 2; Soltes, chapter 4; Singer and Page, chapter 5; Price, chapter 12).

THE IMPORTANCE OF RELATIONSHIPS

Ethnographic research is grounded in relationships with others. Most, if not all, ethnographic pursuits involve interacting with others in some way. Factors including the availability of institutional resources, faculty/mentor support, funding, and time may dictate how many people are involved in a project, how a problem or issue is studied, and how many participants are to be included.

Navigating relationships is an important aspect of the process. Key relationships include those with other researchers, collaborators, informal and formal assistants (e.g., community members, gatekeepers), and study participants. Relationships may be based on a single meeting with study participants and through interactions that occur over periods of months, years, and even decades.

Gay's (chapter 10) relationships with Bruno and Lucia were essential, serving as the foundation for multiple studies within a single favela in Rio de Janeiro. Soltes's (chapter 4) insider status established his legitimacy within the white-collar world. Guarino and Teper's (chapter 9) collaborative research team, consisting of an insider and an academic, proved crucial to accessing and understanding illicit drug use among immigrants living in the United States. Singer and Page (chapter 5) discussed the importance of networks and informal social relations for participant recruitment of those engaged in active concealment. Having individuals with insider access and cultural or subcultural knowledge made a difference in terms of initial access and beyond.

Emotional costs were noted by Copes (chapter 11) who after spending an extended time in rural Alabama studying people who used methamphetamine became concerned about the danger to this emotional and mental state; eventually, "being around so much suffering" became too unbearable, resulting in him reevaluating his role and adopting a new perspective. Lindegaard (chapter 1) faced a personal toll during her years of work with violent young men as she struggled with "going native with evil." Gay (chapter 10) experienced emotional costs in his journey of over three decades, wherein he eventually found himself saddled with additional responsibilities and obligations, including financial ones, to participants who had transformed into quasi kin over time.

Emotional costs were weighed by Valdez et al. (chapter 7), as they engaged in reflexive ethnography and struggled to create effective methods for developing and implementing meaningful, grounded responses to act as "behavioral nudges" for altering risky behaviors in the community. They arose during Fessel et al.'s (chapter 6) urgent fieldwork in the midst of an opioid crisis when the investigators reflected on their discomfort stemming from observations of difficult injection use practices. Based on years of engagement over long periods of time, Singer and Page (chapter 5) challenged the "Chimeraness" of those engaged in drug use and trafficking.

Bonomo and Jacques (chapter 2) confronted emotional challenges as Bonomo balanced covert fieldwork as a novice researcher graduate student, making critical decisions of what to do or not do as research came to dominate her life. Smith and Anderson (chapter 3) faced them during Smith's dissertation research on the "aggressive advocacy" of social service providers seeking permanent housing for the homeless. They impacted Campos-Manzo (chapter 8), as she researched vulnerable populations, including incarcerated adults and children of drug users; motivated by her convictions to human dignity and respect, she held steadfast to the belief that it was her "scholarly imperative" to help provide a voice to those who are marginalized. They were recognized by Guarino and Teper (chapter 9) as they sought to protect the young Russian immigrants and their families while conducting research on illicit activities within the communities in which they resided. They influenced Soltes (chapter 4) as his project progressed from one grounded in personal curiosity into a more scientific journey aiming to learn more about individuals involved in corporate misconduct, including those evading the law. They impacted Price (chapter 12) as he powerfully painted a picture of his struggles to understand and then write about racialized state violence without somehow putting victims on display. He pondered the implications of contributing to the suffering of those he observed. His story about the letter he received at the end of the chapter reveals the dilemma faced by others. He wrote that the letter "shook me out of my stupefaction," and motivated him "to continue—to analyze, learn lessons, and move forward." He described the impact, stating, "this letter reached out and grabbed me, and drew me out, past bafflement, past despair."

As the stories and tales of fieldwork experience shared in these chapters demonstrate, fieldwork can take real and significant personal tolls. Focused thinking on dark and deviant topics for long enough in an immersive and intense manner can result in troublesome thoughts and dreams and can negatively impact eating or sleeping habits. One cannot know how engagement with individuals who are part of the hidden populations we seek to learn about will impact one's own life. Nor can one know what type of impression mental and psychological immersion in stories about lived experiences that are dangerous, harmful, deviant, disturbing, gut-wrenching, or otherwise unfathomable in some way may impact oneself, mentally or psychologically. At some point, to really know the impact of engaging with the suffering of people and collecting what can be dark data, one has to be willing to get close.

LESSONS LEARNED

The research snapshots presented provide critical insights into the realities of ethnography. Important lessons and warnings were shared throughout. While not exhaustive nor mutually exclusive, the following "lessons learned" can guide future researchers seeking to engage in these types of endeavors.

Seek Engaged Mentors and Institutional Support

Personal and institutional support are important. Those new to ethnography, including doctoral students engaging in fieldwork for the first time, can benefit from the mentorship of their faculty sponsors and other forms of support. For students, the ability to engage in ethnographic research may be dependent on having available mentors with qualitative experience or, at the very least, knowledge.

The quantitative focus that exists within departments in diverse disciplines has the potential to restrict opportunities to engage in qualitative research. This is something that Smith and Anderson (chapter 3) elaborated on as they discussed the importance of "meso-organizational level" factors that may inhibit or enhance opportunities for engaging in ethnography within an academic setting.

For those pursuing graduate studies and engaged in thesis or doctoral research, access to faculty with knowledge and experience to advise on qualitative projects is essential. The lack of institutional support can be detrimental and prohibit the types of studies discussed here. Students in departments at institutions of higher learning that do not have faculty versed in qualitative research methodology may never be provided the chance to conduct qualitative research or ethnography.

To the extent that faculty mentors engage with, train, and supervise students differentially, the intensity and depth of training received during their graduate studies can vary considerably. For some, strong and engaged mentors make all the difference. Toward the end of the production process, we (the editors) struggled to understand the importance of mentorship and training as it related to the ethnographic journeys shared throughout this book. The following email from Leon Anderson describes his role in Curtis Smith's ethnographic journey and what their collaborative relationship looked like:

> As for Curtis' and my experience with his dissertation research, I was something of a hands-on mentor, reading all fieldnotes on an on-going basis. While I did not go into the field with him at any point, we did have at least weekly meetings to discuss his progress and to discuss next steps in the research. Given my greater experience with our university's IRB, I took the lead role in communicating with them when questions arose. When he turned to coding and analyzing his data, we continued to meet regularly to discuss the coding categories he was developing as well as building connections across coding categories in his analysis. In terms of the book chapter, Curtis and I were equally involved in organizing and writing the chapter.

This type of engaged and extended mentorship can be invaluable during the research process and beyond.

Understand Institutional Policies on Ethics

Institutional policies and practices vary from place to place. The types of decisions that ethics committees make may be impacted by a number of factors, including, but not limited to, having members knowledgeable about qualitative research. Rather than being viewed as adversaries, IRBs can be regarded as partners in the research process (Campos-Manzo, chapter 8). Though the decisions of IRBs and other ethics boards may place restrictions on and limit the types of research activities that are allowed, the external review and oversight they provide potentially diminish the weight of having to make decisions in the field, taking the burden off the researchers. Recommendations include becoming familiar with local IRBs by getting to know board members, and for those engaged in qualitative research to consider taking opportunities to serve on ethics boards (Singer and Page, chapter 5).

Prepare for Uncertainties

Fieldwork settings are often characterized by unknowns. With enough time in the field, the chances are that researchers will encounter unforeseen situations characterized by uncertainty. Situations and the appropriate responses are not always black and white. Gray areas exist, and responding to the unexpected in real time increases the risks that less than ideal decisions might be made. This is especially the case when volatile conditions arise unpredictably and without warning. The potential problems increase for studies conducted abroad, far away from researchers' home bases and the ethics boards that approved the study (if applicable).

Researchers, particularly those who enter and journey through field settings alone, may not always have the time or ability to seek advice or feedback in real time. Lindegaard argued that researchers may need to be prepared to make compromises during the course of research (chapter 1), though not all necessarily agree. Thinking about this in advance of entering the field allows for an opportunity to process possible scenarios and ponder the various options that could result. Lindegaard advises researchers to consider the worst types of mistakes that could be made and develop lists of expected compromises prior to entering the field. According to Smith and Anderson (chapter 3), uncertainties may occur at any stage of the research process.

Ruminating upon unexpected and potential missteps can be useful exercises for novice and more experienced ethnographers alike.

Understand How to Manage Risks

Ethnographic research with populations engaged in deviant or criminal behaviors potentially places researchers at risk. Understanding the diverse types of risks that may arise is an important first step. Outlining potential risks and developing risk management strategies begins in the research planning stage. Developing strategies for managing and responding to risks is important for those contemplating moving forward with ethnographic research.

Researchers may follow the safety guidelines outlined by others (e.g., see Singer and Page, chapter 5), develop their own strategies for maintaining safety, or both. For example, when presented with an opportunity to meet a white-collar fugitive who evaded authorities in the United States and moved to Sweden, Soltes (chapter 4) consulted with an attorney about the risks involved before flying abroad to meet him.

It is wise to think about potential legal risks to researchers and study participants early in the process. Researchers can remove identifiable information from data completely, not collect any identifiable information at all, or keep all data confidential to protect study participants. Acquiring a Federal Certificate of Confidentiality is also a practical risk reduction strategy, particularly when recording data in such a manner that participants and their illegal activities can be identified (Fessel et al., chapter 6).

Maintain Flexibility

Maintaining flexibility is critical. Flexibility can involve adapting to situations as they arise, following one's instincts, and seizing upon opportunities that present themselves (Guarino and Teper, chapter 9). When combined with reflexivity, flexibility can enhance researchers' efforts to develop culturally grounded interventions aimed at initiating change (Valdez et al., chapter 7). Rather than going into a study with predefined notions and conceptions of what types of policy outcomes are needed, as Valdez et al. (chapter 7) demonstrated, working with local community members to determine best approaches can result in interventions that are culturally grounded, increasing the chances of their effectiveness.

Flexibility allows for research strategies and approaches to shift and be revised over time as conditions and circumstances change. Decisions about how to proceed with research efforts planned at a project's inception may change as studies progress. Decisions to not disclose one's status as a researcher to study participants may result in methodological challenges and require reassessment midstudy (Bonomo and Jacques, chapter 2).

Prepare for the Dark Side

Those who study crime and deviance have to confront and face the dark side of humanity. Ethnographers risk vulnerability; they may be troubled by the people encountered, the stories shared, and the gut-wrenching behaviors witnessed. Each can leave permanent impressions on their minds and lives. Observations that shock, provoke, or may be difficult to swallow have the potential to leave significant impressions on researchers regardless of whether they occur directly (e.g., in person), or indirectly (e.g., via CCTV). Researchers may be impacted at any stage of the process. This is something that is rarely addressed.

The closer one gets to the dark side of the human experience, the more one risks becoming personally affected. While this is something researchers can think about and plan for during the development stages of projects, confronting darkness face-to-face is something for which it is difficult to prepare. Not everyone has the chutzpah to engage with such personal tragedies and suffering. Learning how to process and handle inhumanity, pain, and injustice is often overlooked in academic training. Depending on discipline, researchers may not receive any specialized training on how to manage traumatic interactions and situations. Even seasoned researchers may find themselves being impacted in ways not anticipated in advance (Copes, chapter 11, Price, chapter 12). Those considering engaging in ethnography to study stigmatized behaviors among marginalized populations must consider the personal toll it may take.

Learn to Navigate Relationships

Engaging in ongoing relationships with study participants over periods of time has its pros and cons. Such relationships can be important for gaining and maintaining access to the hidden populations (Guarino and Teper, chapter 9). While relationships may enhance one's understanding of the phenomenon being studied, they may also come with unexpected costs and consequences.

Developing relationships with subjects can increase the expectations of study participants. Even a shift in communication, such as the evolution from sporadic face-to-face interactions to regular, ongoing communications via phone or text, can increase the potential for conflicts. This is particularly true for researchers exposed to life-changing struggles study participants face and share in real time (Copes, chapter 11). Researchers should consider the types of boundaries that need to be set to avoid getting into situations where demarcations separating researcher from subject begin to disappear. The failure to set boundaries may result in study participants developing potentially unrealistic expectations (Gay, chapter 10).

Navigating relationships extend beyond the researcher and study participant. Scholars working as part of teams or collaborators risk encountering a diverse array of situations that may need to be negotiated or carefully traversed. Every stage of the process may present opportunities for conflict and dissention when more than one party is involved in research activities and data collection efforts.

Developing a leadership plan or strategy for dealing with potential disagreements and conflicts is beneficial. Individuals may disagree not only on how to handle situations that occur during the course of fieldwork, but also during later stages of the research process, including data management, coding, analysis, and dissemination. Working as part of a team led by experienced, senior team members can mitigate these types of concerns (Fessel et al., chapter 6; Valdez et al., chapter 7). Thinking through research collaborations in advance and identifying potential issues that may arise allows for strategies for success to be developed and implemented. However, just like fieldwork, planning will not prevent all issues from arising. Challenges are just part of the ethnographic journey. Learning to navigate through them is essential for success.

CONCLUDING THOUGHTS

There is no single ethnographic method or path. Textbooks alone cannot teach everything one needs to know. Researchers plan their studies and are forced to adapt, negotiate, and renegotiate along the way. Unexpected and unanticipated issues are expected to arise as researchers operate within social settings and situations filled with unknowns and uncertainties. It is a point made by Soltes when he states: "The rough-and-tumble, learning-by-doing process that characterized much of the fieldwork is largely unspoken" (chapter 4).

Ethnographers are thrust into situations and encounters that not everyone is able to face, handle, process, and sometimes, even stomach. As Smith and Anderson eloquently note, "ethnographic research is not for the lazy or the faint-of-heart" (chapter 3). It is also not for those who adhere to complete objectivity as the gold standard. As C. Wright Mills (1962, 10) denoted, "I have tried to be objective but I do not claim to be detached."

The idea behind this book was to put together a collection of essays outlining rarely told background stories and unexpected challenges faced by ethnographers studying hidden and vulnerable populations. Just as those in the field never really know if subjects will present themselves and participate, we never knew if ethnographers would be willing to share personal insights, conflicts, struggles, and lessons learned. This fascinating merging of unique ethnographic stories by scholars from diverse backgrounds and disciplines is a testament to the power of ethnography.

We are indebted to our contributors for entrusting us with their stories and collaborating on this distinct collection of chapters that highlight such diverse and extraordinary projects. We are humbled by the honesty and authenticity displayed. We hope that the stories shared inspire more ethnography.

REFERENCES

Atkinson, P. (2006). Rescuing autoethnography. *Journal of Contemporary Ethnography,* 35(4), 400–404.

Bourgois, P. (2003). *In search of respect: Selling crack in El Barrio.* 2nd ed. New York: Cambridge University Press.

Lincoln, Y. S., and E. G. Guba (2000). Paradigmatic controversies, contradictions, and emerging confluences. In *Handbook of qualitative research,* ed. N. K. Denzin and Y. S. Lincoln, 2nd ed., 163–88. Thousand Oaks, NY: Sage.

Malterud, K. (2001). Qualitative research: Standards, challenges, and guidelines. *Lancelot,* 358, 483–88.

Marco, C. A., and G. L. Larkin (2000). Research ethics: Ethical issues of data reporting and the quest for authenticity. *Academic Emergency Medicine,* 7(6), 691–94.

Mills, C. W. (1962). *The Marxists.* New York: Dell.

Shukla, R. K. (2016). *Methamphetamine: A love story*. Berkeley: University of California Press.

Shukla, R. K., and E. E. Bartgis (2011). Methamphetamine: The resurgence of manufacturing after Oklahoma House Bill 2176. *Law Enforcement Executive Forum*, *11*(4), 71–90.

Williams, T. (1990). *The cocaine kids: The inside story of a teenage drug ring*. Reading, MA: Addison-Wesley: Da Capo Press.

CONTRIBUTORS

LEON ANDERSON, PH.D., is a Professor of Sociology at Utah State University. He is the author of *Deviance: Social Constructions and Blurred Boundaries* (University of California Press, 2017) and the coauthor, with David Snow, of *Down on Their Luck: A Study of Homeless Street People* (University of California Press, 1993) and with John Lofland, David Snow, and Lyn Lofland of the fourth edition of *Analyzing Social Settings* (Thomson/Wadsworth, 2005). He is currently completing a book, *Great Northern: A Young Man's Search for America and Himself,* that recounts his experiences riding freight trains across the United States in the late 1960s.

MIRIAM BOERI, PH.D., is an Associate Professor of Sociology at Bentley University. Her research focuses on ethnographic studies of marginalized populations and the social aspects of drug use. She is author of *Hurt: Chronicles of the Drug-War Generation* (University of California Press, 2017) and *Women on Ice: Methamphetamine Use among Suburban Women* (Rutgers University Press, 2013).

ELIZABETH BONOMO, PH.D., is a Lecturer of Criminology and Criminal Justice at Northern Arizona University. She is coauthor of *Learning from the Offenders' Perspective on Crime Prevention* (Springer, 2016), with Scott Jacques.

PHILIPPE BOURGOIS, PH.D., is a Professor of Anthropology and Director of the Center for Social Medicine in the Semel Neuropsychiatric Institute and Department of Psychiatry at the University of California, Los Angeles. He is author of *In Search of Respect: Selling Crack in El Barrio* (Cambridge University Press, 1995; updated 2nd edition, 2003) and coauthor of *Righteous Dopefiend* (University of California Press, 2009) with Jeffrey Schonberg.

ANA-LILIA CAMPOS-MANZO, PH.D., is an Associate Professor of Sociology at Connecticut College. She specializes in the study of parenthood practices under correctional supervision. She is author of a "Sharpening Theory and Methodology to Explore Racialized Youth Peer Cultures," a chapter in *Researching Children and Youth: Methodological Issues, Strategies, and Innovations,* edited by I. E. Castro, M. Swauger, and B. Harger (Emerald Publishing Group, 2017).

ALICE CEPEDA, PH.D., is an Associate Professor of Social Work at the University of Southern California. Her work has focused on the social epidemiology of drug use and the related health risk behaviors that disproportionately affect urban Mexican-origin minority populations. She is coauthor of "Social Stressors, Special Vulnerabilities and Violence Victimization among Latino Immigrant Day Laborers in Post Katrina New Orleans," a chapter in *Punishing Immigrants: Policy, Politics, and Injustice*, edited by C.E. Kubrin, M.S. Zatz, and R. Martinez (New York University Press, 2012).

DANIEL CICCARONE, M.D., M.P.H., is a Professor of Family and Community Medicine, University of California San Francisco School of Medicine; Principal Investigator of "Heroin in Transition Study" (NIH/NIDA); and Board certified in Family Medicine and Addiction Medicine. His research is centered on the contextual issues of treatment and prevention of HIV/AIDS and related diseases in socially marginalized populations. His articles have been published in numerous peer-reviewed journals.

HEITH COPES, PH.D., is a Professor at the University of Alabama at Birmingham. His primary area of research involves understanding the ways that offenders make sense of their lives and crimes. He is coauthor of *Identity Thieves: Motives and Methods* (Northeastern University Press, 2012), with Lynne M. Vieraitis, and editor of *Advancing Qualitative Methods in Criminology and Criminal Justice* (Routledge, 2012).

JASON N. FESSEL is an Independent Scholar in San Francisco, California. He is interested in the history and sociology of psychiatry and public health. This is his second scholarly publication with Ciccarone, Mars, and Bourgois regarding the opioid overdose crisis.

ROBERT GAY, PH.D. is a Professor of Sociology at Connecticut College. He is an ethnographer who has spent the past thirty years doing field research in the favelas of Rio de Janeiro. He is author of *Popular Organization and Democracy in Rio de Janeiro: A Tale of Two Favelas* (Temple University Press, 1994), *Lucia: Testimonies of a Brazilian Drug Dealer's Woman* (Temple University Press, 2005), and *Bruno: Conversations with a Brazilian Drug Dealer* (Duke University Press, 2015).

HONORIA GUARINO, PH.D., is a Research Associate Professor at City University of New York (CUNY) School of Public Health and Health Policy. She specializes in mixed-methods research on drug use, HCV, HIV, and related health issues. Her articles have been published in numerous peer-reviewed journals.

SCOTT JACQUES, PH.D., is an Associate Professor of Criminal Justice and Criminology at Georgia State University. His research focuses on crimes against drug dealers, the offenders' perspective, and theorizing method. He is coauthor of *Code of the Suburb: Inside the World of Young Middle-Class Drug Dealers* (University of Chicago Press, 2015), with Richard Wright. He is author of *Grey Area: Regulating Amsterdam's Coffeeshops* (University College London Press, 2019).

CHARLES KAPLAN, PH.D., is a Research Professor at the Hamovitch Center for Science in the Human Services Department of Adult Mental Health and Wellness,

Edward R. Roybal Institute on Aging in the Suzanne Dworak-Peck School of Social Work at the University of Southern California. He is coauthor of *Lines across Europe: Nature and Extent of Cocaine Use in Barcelona, Rotterdam and Turin* (Swets & Zeitlinger, 1993), and author of "Drug Craving and Drug Use in the Daily Life of Heroin Addicts," a chapter in *The Experience of Psychopathology: Investigating Mental Disorders in Their Natural Settings,* edited by M. deVries (Cambridge University Press, 1982).

MARIE ROSENKRANTZ LINDEGAARD, PH.D., is a Senior Researcher at the Netherlands Institute for the Study of Crime and Law Enforcement (NSCR) and an Associate Professor of Sociology at the University of Copenhagen. Her research interests include interactional aspects of violence, victimization and guardianship, agency, street culture, observational methods, and urban ethnography in South Africa. She is the author of *Surviving Gangs, Violence and Racism in Cape Town: Urban Chameleons* (Routledge, 2018).

SARAH G. MARS, PH.D., is a Qualitative Project Director at the University of California, San Francisco, and Honorary Research Fellow at the London School of Hygiene and Tropical Medicine. She is author of *The Politics of Addiction: Medical Conflict and Drug Dependence in England since the 1960s* (Palgrave Macmillan, 2012).

J. BRYAN PAGE, PH.D., is a Professor in the Department of Anthropology at the University of Miami. He is coauthor with Merrill Singer of *Comprehending Drug Use: Ethnographic Research at the Social Margins* (Rutgers University Press, 2010) and *The Social Value of Drug Addicts: The Uses of the Useless* (Left Coast Press, 2014; Routledge Press, 2016).

JOSHUA PRICE, PH.D., is Professor and Chair of the Sociology Department at the State University of New York, Binghamton. His ethnographic research on race, gender, and state violence in jails and prisons serves as the basis for his two books, *Prison and Social Death (*Rutgers University Press, 2015) and *Structural Violence: Hidden Brutality in the Lives of Women* (State University of New York Press, 2012).

RASHI K. SHUKLA, PH.D. is a Professor of Criminal Justice at the University of Central Oklahoma (UCO). Her research interests include examining drug use and decision-making, rural crime and law enforcement, and drug policy. She is conducting ethnographic research on challenges faced by rural law enforcement, and is documenting the history and current state of the methamphetamine problem. Her first photo exhibition, based a collaboration with Agent Dub Turner (Ret.) and photographers Jesse Lee Miller, M.F.A., and Angela Cejda Mackey, M.F.A., *Oklahoma Meth Labs: Decades of Chaos,* was displayed from July to September 2019 at UCO. She is author of *Methamphetamine: A Love Story* (University of California Press, 2016).

MERRILL SINGER, PH.D. is an Emeritus Professor of Anthropology at the University of Connecticut. He is author of *Introduction to Syndemics: A Critical Systems Approach to Public and Community Health* (Jossey-Bass, 2009); coeditor, with S. Lerman, B. Ostrach, and M. Singer, of *Foundations of Biosocial Health: Stigma and Illness Interactions* (Lexington Books, 2017); and coauthor with J. Bryan Page of *The Social Value of Drug Addicts: The Uses of the Useless* (Left Coast Press, 2014; Routledge, 2016) and *Comprehending Drug Use: Ethnographic Research at the Social Margins* (Rutgers University Press, 2010).

CURTIS SMITH, PH.D., is at Bentley University. His research focuses on issues of poverty, social inequality, and social justice with an emphasis on homelessness and social policy research. He is currently working on a book based on issues of homelessness, and his articles have been published in numerous peer-reviewed journals.

EUGENE SOLTES, PH.D., is the Jakurski Family Associate Professor of Business Administration at Harvard Business School. His research focuses on corporate misconduct and fraud, and how organizations design cultures and compliance systems confront these challenges. He is author of *Why They Do It: Inside the Mind of the White-Collar Criminal* (Public Affairs, 2016).

ANASTASIA TEPER, M.A., is a Research Assistant III at UT Health McGovern Medical School in Houston, Texas. She works in the fields of human rights and justice, using direct social services, education, and research as vehicles for positive change.

AVELARDO VALDEZ, PH.D., is a Professor of Sociology and Social Work and Endowed Professor, Cleofas and Victor Ramirez Professor of Practice, Policy, Research and Advocacy for the Latino Population at the University of Southern California. He is author of *Mexican American Girls and Gang Violence: Beyond Risk* (Palgrave Macmillan, 2007); and coauthor, with J. Tejeda and A. Valdez, of *Puro Conjunto: Seventeen Years of Collected Writings from the Tejano Conjunto Festival* (University of Texas Press, 2001).

INDEX

Connecticut College's Center for the Critical Study of Race and Ethnicity, 181n18
Copes, Heath, 6, 14, 16, 19, 256
Corbin, A., 74
corporate misconduct. *See* white-collar crime/misconduct
"corporate violence," 106
correctional officer (COs), 166–67, 171, 172–73, 175, 181n9, 236, 237
crack use: accepted, 145; characteristics of, 145; disruption in behavior, 145, 154; and ethnographic research, 154–55; harm reduction approach to, 145; longitudinal studies of, 155; misconceptions of, 155–56; patterns of, 145; and provision of crack kits, 154; subculture of, 147
critical theoretical approach (Benjamin), 153
cultural relativism (anthropology), 125, 132–33
C. Wright Mills Award, 68
cyberbullying, 176–77

data: analysis, 56, 143, 186, 189. *See also* ethnography, data analysis in; coding of, 74; collection, 56, 60, 76, 143, 186, 189, 220; descriptive, 143; interpretation of ethnographer(s), 13; recording of, 143; saturation, 133; triangulation, 5–6, 133
Dell, Michael, 95
Department of Corrections (DOC), 169
Department of Human Services (DHS), 169, 171
DOPE (Drug Overdose Prevention and Education) Project (Bay Area, CA), 127
Douglass, Frederick, 232
Down on Their Luck (Snow and Anderson), 67, 69
drug dealers, two sphere approach, 168
Drug Enforcement Administration (DEA), 131
drug gangs, 205–18
drug overdose: death from (OD), 120, 123; phases of, 120
drug use: in Central Asia, 186; in Eastern Europe, 183, 186; and ethnographic research, 188–89; and harm reduction, 187; observations of minors, 165–66;

parental, 165–66; relapse, 167; research, 190; in Russia, 183, 186; two-sphere approach, 168
Dutch National Research Council (NWO), 47

Ellis, Eddie, 244
empiricists ("theory testing"), 97, 98
Enron, 91
epidemiology, 124–25, 126
ethnographer: as activist, 19, 232–48; advice, 257–62; and analytic focus, 68, 73, 77; and anthropology, 27; and assumptions, 27–28; and bias potential, 87; and boundaries, 47, 262; and concealment, 8, 20n3, 50–51, 115–16, 254–55; and decompression, 39, 41; differences with participants, 33–34; desensitization of, 240; emotional toll on, 15–16, 19, 32–33, 43, 60–61, 219–31, 256–57, 261; ethical dilemmas of, 37–38, 134–35, 163; and evidentiary artifacts, 90; experienced, 3–4; and faculty mentor, 66; false complaints about, 229; and field notes, 1, 57–58, 59–60, 146, 147–48, 156, 250–52; flexibility of, 17, 58–60, 61n10, 198–99, 260–61; as former drug user, 129; as graduate student, 16, 17, 20n2, 20n3, 49–64, 65–80, 256, 257–58; and honesty with participant(s), 33; and "hypothesis building," 83–84; ideals/realities of, 31–32, 108–9; and identity deception, 115–16; and immersion with participants, 27, 30, 39, 90, 127, 133, 143, 189, 193, 257; and "impression management," 36; as insider, 255; and interviews with participants, 86, 94, 110; as mentor, 17, 20n2, 49–64, 257–58; and moral dilemmas, 10, 53–54, 57–58, 88. *See also* ethnography, and moral dilemmas; narrative(s) of, 1, 39–40, 128, 129, 130, 133, 250–52; and network method, 111–15. *See also* informal social relations; novice, 3–4, 17, 46–47, 49–64; as outsider, 30, 32, 51, 197–98; and personal disclosure, 87; and personal space, 39–41, 46; perspective shift, 226–27; photo-, 219–31; preparation prior to

beginning research, 109–10; previous work experience as participants, 67–68, 71–72, 74–75; and PTSD (post-traumatic stress disorder), 19; and reciprocity, 108–9; reflection(s) of, 32–33, 46–47, 65–66, 75–76, 128, 129, 130, 133, 134–35; release of control, 32; research prior to participant contact, 86; as research "tool," 4, 27; role of, 27; and safety risks, 45, 120–31, 260; and scope of research study, 96; similar experiences as participants, 71; skepticism of, 92–93; skill of, 110; as "sponsors" of, 126; as story collectors, 219; and stress, 41, 129; as "theory builders," 97, 98; and transitional space, 39, 41; and trust, 7, 255–56

ethnographic analysis, 153–54

ethnography: analytic, 72, 73, 78; and anthropology, 10, 114, 115, 125–26, 132–33; and authenticity, 253–54; challenges of, 32, 36–38, 50, 55, 68, 85–86, 89–90, 92, 95, 190; classic, 190; communication in, 92; compromises during, 46; and corporate misconduct, 81–119; in correctional setting, 171–75; and covert work, 78, 20n2, 50–51; and culture reconstruction, 90, 92, 98n3; dangers in, 1–3, 15–16, 69, 21n13, 21n14; data analysis in, 97. See also data, analysis; and decompression process, 39, 41; defined, 4–5, 105; and discretionary decisions, 71, 74, 77; in dissertation research, 17, 49–64, 65–80, 111, 254, 256, 257–58; and documentary evidence, 91–92, 93; and drug users, 103–19, 183–201; and ecological approach, 154; and "edgework," 77; and emails, 84; and emotional toll, 3–4; and epidemiology, 124–26; and ethics, 20n6; as exploratory research, 193; and federal grants, 189–90; and feminist approach to, 230; field notes, 57–58; and fieldwork, 1–3, 4, 19, 43–44, 70; flexibility in, 4, 5, 58–60, 70, 71, 72, 73, 89; and heterogeneity, 254; and hidden populations, 105–8; and the homeless, 49–64, 65–80, 125, 126–28, 129, 256; ideals of, 28, 46, 90;

and immersion with participants, 39–40; and indigenous staff, 153; and insider perspectives, 42, 56–57; interviews in, 28–29, 86, 129, 172; as intruder, 50, 51; and law enforcement, 78n2, 148, 229; and legal records, 93; long term immersion and, 127, 137, 254; and marginalized populations, 69, 77; and "meso-organizational level" factors, 76–78, 258; methodology/methods in, 4–5, 29, 54–55, 57, 78, 237–38, 241–42, 243–44, 249–50, 254; mistakes made conducting, 28, 33–35, 46–47; and moral/ethical dilemmas, 914, 69–70, 229, 232–48. See also ethnographer, and moral dilemmas; and multiple perspectives, 41, 43–44, 46; narrative(s) of, 31–32; observations in, 28; oversharing of ethnographer in, 34, 35–36, 46. See also ethnography, safe boundaries in; and patience, 109; and phone interviews, 84; and police involvement, 69–70; rapid. See rapid assessment projects (RAP); reflection in, 72; reflexivity in. See reflexivity; and repercussions to participants, 88; as research boundary pusher, 5; safe boundaries in, 36–37, 55. See also ethnography, and oversharing of ethnographer in; safety in, 15, 116; short-term, 254; street, 65–80; and structured assessments, 190, 195; team(s), 4, 14, 16, 120–40, 141–59, 254–55; and technologies, 6, 14; traditional, 123; uncertainty in, 68; and videotaping, 42–43; voluntary risk taking. See ethnography, "edgework"

ethnomethodological breaching experiment, 154

extended case method, 153, 155

220–21; and order of questions, 130; recording of, 216n7; semi-structured, 123; truthfulness in, 212–13; with youth, 178–79

Israel, I., 20n6

"It Doesn't Feel Like a Time to Write" (Smith), 244–45

Jacques, Scott, 7, 17, 20n2, 20n3, 61n1, 254, 255, 256

Judith Tindal Opatrny '72 Junior Faculty Fund, 181n18

Kaal, H.L., 155

Kaplan, Charles, 6

Katz, Jack, 72–73, 75

key informant(s), 8–9, 20n4, 113, 115, 131, 185–86, 193, 196–97, 199, 209–10. *See also* community consultant(s) (recruitment); leaders, 144, 146, 147; recruitment of, 144; strategy, 197; terminology, 9, 20n4; and trust, 114, 144

KMPG Global, 91, 98n2

Librett, Mitch, 72

Lindegaard, Marie Rosenkrantz, 6, 8, 11, 15, 17, 253, 256, 259

Lipsky, Michael, 68, 71, 73

Lockup, 81

Lockwood, D., 69

London, Scott, 91*fig.*

Madoff, Bernard, 87

Maher, L., 69

Margaret Sheridan '67 Research Initiative Fund, 181n18

Mars, Sarah G., 6, 7, 126

McDonald, Laquan, 233

methamphetamine use, 16, 219–31, 223*fig.*, 224*fig.*, 225*fig.*, 226*fig.*, 228*fig.*, 250–53. *See also,* participants, drug users; campaigns against, 221; and rural poverty, 220; stereotypes of users, 220

Mills, C. Wright, 263

Mitchell, J. Clyde, 111, 112

Mobley, Mamie Till, 242

Montero, Fernando, 126, 128, 129

Murphy, Sheila, 155

National Association for the Advancement of Colored People (NAACP), 234–35, 236

National Development and Research Institutes, 185

National Institute on Drug Abuse (NIDA), 117, 135, 137n3, 156, 200n3, 181n18

National Institute of Health (NIH), 121, 137n3, 200n3

National Institutes of Mental Health (NIMH), 117

National Transportation Safety Board (NTSB), 97–98

Needle, R. H., 114

networks, 111–15; covert, 113, key leaders in, 144, 146, 147, 206, 209, 210, 213, 214; and linkage, 111–15; types of (morphology), 111–12, 113; violence in, 112–13

New York State Commission on Correction (SCOC), 238, 240

noninterference (anthropology), 125

The Nuremberg Code (1947), 179–80

Ondocsin, Jeff, 126

operational construct sampling, 73–74

opioid(s): counterfeit, 137n2; crisis, 120–40; overdose (OD) epidemic, 123, 126, 132; synthetic, 120, 129, 131; use, 185, 191, 198

Opioid Use Disorder (OUD), 185, 191

Page, J. Bryan, 7, 8, 16, 18, 21n13, 109–11, 115, 190, 254–55, 256

Parental Consent to Access Child's Legal Guardian form, 171

Park, Robert E., 78, 153

parole officers (PO), 166

participant(s): absenteeism of, 58–59; and access to other participants, 105, 114, 129, 144, 153; as agents, 1; age verification, 194; anonymity of, 134, 135; and attorney representation, 85, 88, 89, 91, 92; compensation of, 52–54, 137, 215, 256; and concealment strategies, 187–89, 192; and contradictions, 88; crack users, 105, 142; difficulty in detection of, 105, 136, 188; disparity in behavior, 28; as drug dealer, 167–69; drug users, 167–68,

biomedical field, 125; ethnography in, 77; mixed methods, 18–19, 189; positivist philosophies, 13; preparation prior to beginning, 259; qualitative, 4, 5, 12, 18, 49, 62, 70, 72–73, 76, 77, 78, 83, 103, 121, 122–23, 124, 126, 133, 137, 143, 144, 154, 156, 180, 181n15, 185, 186, 189, 190, 250, 253, 258, 259; quantitative, 4, 5, 17, 18, 19, 76, 83, 84, 97, 121, 122, 124–25, 126, 137, 154–55, 189, 258

Research Matters Faculty Grant, 181n18

researchers of color, 177–79

Residential Correctional Facility (RCF), 166, 169, 171, 172, 173–74, 181n9

Reynolds, Diamond, 242

Rice, Tamir, 233

Richards, Stephen, 81

Righteous Dopefiend (Bourgois and Schonberg), 67

Rios, Victor, 244

sample assessment, 185, 188, 190, 206

Sanchez-Jankowski, M., 69

San Francisco Homeless Youth Alliance, 126–27

Scenes of Subjection (Hartman), 232–33

Schonberg, Jeffrey, 12, 21n11, 67

Schutz, Alfred, 153

Scrimshaw, S.C.M., 114

selection bias, 128, 136

Sharpe, Christina, 243

Simmel, Georg, 153

Singer, Merrill, 7, 8, 16, 18, 106, 112–13, 115, 190, 254, 256

Skid Row as a Way of Life (Wallace), 67

slavery, 243

Smith, Curtis, 11, 17, 20n2, 254, 258, 259, 263

Smith, Danez, 244–45

snowball sampling, 28, 144, 220–21

Snow, David, 67, 78n2

social epidemiological study, 142

Socialist Worker, 236

social plausibility, 12, 126

Soltes, Eugene, 5, 11, 17, 98n5, 253, 255, 256, 260, 263

State of New Jersey v. Dharun Ravi (2012), 176

Stations of the Lost (Wiseman), 67

Strauss, A.L., 74

Street-level Bureaucracy: Dilemmas of the Individuals in Public Service (Lipsky), 68, 71

street level bureaucrats (SLBs), 68, 73

Sterling, Alton, 233

Susan Eckert Lynch '62 Faculty Research Fund, 181n18

Symbol Technologies, 85

Tenbrunsel, Ann, 93

Teper, Anastasia, 9, 12, 18–19, 255, 256

Terceiro Comando (Rio crime faction), 217n8

Till, Emmett, 242

Tirando Esquina: Interveniendo Muros de Salud (TE:IMS), 145, 146, 147, 148, 149. *See also* projection mapping project; projection sites of, 149, 151*fig.;* success of, 146, 149, 152; team and street presence of, 146, 149, 153

Transactional Records Access Clearinghouse (Syracuse University), 106

Trotter, Robert, 115

True, W.R., 111, 112, 113

Tuskegee Study of Syphilis, 181n13

universal rights, 206

University of Iowa's Dean Fellowship, 181n18

urban conflict studies (Simmel), 153

U.S. Department of Health and Human Services (HHS), 20n7

U.S. Public Health Service, 181n13

Valdez, Avelardo, 6, 8, 14, 18, 256, 260

The Value of Homelessness (Willse), 66

Waldorf, Dan, 155

Wallace, Samuel, 67

Wall Street Journal, 82

Westmarland, L., 69–70

Wheeler, Eliza, 126–27, 129, 134–35

white-collar crime/misconduct, 82, 83, 90, 92, 255, 256–57, 260; definition for study of, 95; scope of, 94–95, 106

Founded in 1893,
UNIVERSITY OF CALIFORNIA PRESS
publishes bold, progressive books and journals
on topics in the arts, humanities, social sciences,
and natural sciences—with a focus on social
justice issues—that inspire thought and action
among readers worldwide.

The UC PRESS FOUNDATION
raises funds to uphold the press's vital role
as an independent, nonprofit publisher, and
receives philanthropic support from a wide
range of individuals and institutions—and from
committed readers like you. To learn more, visit
ucpress.edu/supportus.